DICTIONARY OF CARIBBEAN ENGLISH USAGE

DICTIONARY OF CARIBBEAN ENGLISH USAGE

EDITED BY

JEANNETTE ALLSOPP

AND

WENDY GRIFFITH-WATSON

The University of the West Indies Press

Jamaica • Barbados • Trinidad and Tobago

The University of the West Indies Press
7A Gibraltar Hall Road, Mona
Kingston 7, Jamaica
www.uwipress.com

A catalogue record of this book is available from the
National Library of Jamaica.

ISBN: 978-976-640-872-5 (print)
978-976-640-874-9 (ePub)

Cover and book design: Robert Harris
(email: roberth@cwjamaica.com)

Set in Minion Pro 10.5/14.5

Printed in China by Regent Publishing Services Ltd.

This work is dedicated to the memory of the late Richard Allsopp, pioneering compiler of the original *Dictionary of Caribbean English Usage* on which this school edition is based, and also to the secondary schoolchildren of the Caribbean, their teachers, parents, and the wider Caribbean.

CONTENTS

THE DICTIONARY

FOREWORD

The *Dictionary of Caribbean English Usage: School Edition* was written in order to address the need to make available to secondary schoolchildren age eleven and over the rich lexical heritage of the English-speaking Caribbean, without their having to try to understand the often complex linguistic information contained in the original *Dictionary of Caribbean English Usage*. It is meant to serve as a practical and working reference tool in the Caribbean classroom and to be a source of information on life and culture in the English-speaking Caribbean.

This new edition has been updated to include some of the more recent vocabulary that has come into use, and some vocabulary that are not originally Caribbean, but belong to the wide range of international English usage. Some of these are items of food, where particular dishes are not typically Caribbean but have become absorbed into its cuisine because they were inherited from our British colonizers. Also included are abbreviations and acronyms that are typically Caribbean, representing organizations, institutions, national orders and awards, since some of these items are not always easily accessible.

The *Dictionary of Caribbean English Usage: School Edition* includes verbs, particularly in the General Vocabulary section, but is largely a list of ostensive items that embody the lifestyle and culture of the English-speaking Caribbean. However, it also incorporates a list of idiomatic phrases, some of which are verb phrases, as samples of the unique phraseology of Caribbean English. In addition, the work lists a selection of Caribbean English proverbs that are fairly well known by previous generations, but not necessarily by the current one. One of the features of this dictionary that needs to be highlighted is that the headwords are syllabically divided in order to show the students the way in which Caribbean English words are spelled and the rules of Caribbean orthography, which generally follow the morphological pattern of Internationally Accepted English or World Englishes.

The body of the *School Edition* is divided into topics or themes (unlike the original *Dictionary of Caribbean English Usage*, which is a general dictionary), for example of fauna, flora, foods, festivals, folklore, architecture, clothing, music and dance, religion, and so on. This thematic approach has been used to make the acquisition of the vocabulary of Caribbean English an easier task than if the material is treated in the same way as it is in a general dictionary. Definitions are simplified as far as possible but are still phrased in the way that a dictionary for adults use would be phrased. Although the dictionary is, in effect, a list of ostensive items that are nouns for the most part, the part of speech is still identified in every case because the work is being used as a teaching and learning tool of the structure of the language.

Etymologies are given for words that are indigenous in origin or that are foreign, such as African words, Indic words, and French, French Creole, Spanish, Dutch and Portuguese loanwords. The way in which the definitions are treated includes both descriptive and encyclopedic information. The descriptive information usually makes up the first part of the entry followed by a semicolon, while the latter part of the entry lists the encyclopedic information.

Jeannette Allsopp and Wendy Griffith-Watson

ACKNOWLEDGEMENTS

As is normally the case, no reference work can be completed without the input of other persons apart from the authors.

In the case of the *Dictionary of Caribbean English Usage: School Edition*, there are a few people who were of particular help to the authors in the compilation of the work.

I begin by acknowledging the work of Richard Allsopp, whose pioneering *Dictionary of Caribbean English Usage* was compiled with assistance from myself, as his research associate, and also from my co-author of the *School Edition*, Wendy Griffith, later Griffith-Watson, who worked with me on the part-time team to the original DCEU as a research assistant. The original *Dictionary of Caribbean English Usage* formed the base of the *School Edition*, which is a simplified version, revised to meet the needs of secondary schoolchildren from eleven to eighteen years old.

Although there was no formal team working on the *School Edition*, but just the two authors, I would like to thank the following persons who assisted for brief periods of time. First of all, I would like to acknowledge the work of my co-author, Wendy Griffith-Watson, who, although terminally ill, did the best she could in assisting in the production of the work, and particularly in the final reading and revision of the manuscript

The work of the two reviewers of the manuscript, Dr Jason Siegel and Dr Hélène Zamor, is also much appreciated.

Warm thanks are due to Dr Glenda Niles, who willingly assisted with proofreading the manuscript before submission and proofread the printed version. Her care and attention to detail are duly recognized and noted. Dr Niles also assisted with the transfer of the photographs from the computer or phone into one file, as requested by the University of the West Indies Press, while Dr Jason Siegel produced the art log of the photos submitted.

Grateful thanks are due to the persons who kindly provided many of the photographs that are in the *School Edition,* free of cost. I recognize Professor Sean Carrington of the Department of Biology of The University of the West Indies, Cave Hill campus, who kindly allowed me to use a number of his own photos of Caribbean flora in this work; Richard Farley here in Barbados, who also provided additional photos of flora as well; Robert Lalljie and Nazela Razak, in Guyana, who assisted with photos of items across the themes of the School Edition – flora and fauna, foods, architecture, and festivals; Janet and Indira of Janet and Indira's Restaurant in Stabroek Market, as well as vendors of both Bourda and Stabroek Markets in Georgetown, Guyana; and Jason Aguiton in Trinidad, who provided a few additional photos needed to replace some of the original photos that needed to be more well-defined. Additional photo credits appear at the end of the book.

Also the assistance of the tireless secretary-keyboarder to the Richard and Jeannette Allsopp Centre for Caribbean Lexicography of The University of the West Indies, Cave Hill campus, Krista St. Juste, must be warmly appreciated, as she was always willing to reproduce printed material, scan any items needed, or perform any small tasks that were requested of her, for which we are eternally grateful. Furthermore, Krista greatly assisted in the sourcing of additional photographs which she obtained from a couple of additional websites recommended by Shivaun Hearne, formerly of The University of the West Indies Press. Shivaun spared no pains in taking the work as far along as she could before leaving the UWI Press, and we are therefore deeply grateful for all her work in helping to bring the *Dictionary of Caribbean English Usage: School Edition* to fruition.

Finally, and last but certainly not least, our heartfelt thanks are extended to Robert Harris, book designer and producer who worked tirelessly and with great dedication to produce the book as it appears and to encourage and patiently correct what needed to be corrected.

INTRODUCTION

The general concept held by most people is that a dictionary is a simple list of words in alphabetical order, but dictionary makers are always faced with some difficult decisions to make. In the case of the *Dictionary of Caribbean English Usage: School Edition*, the decision had to be made as to whether to list all the items in alphabetical order or to divide them up into themes. The thematic approach was chosen, but the items in each theme are themselves alphabetically listed.

The question of syllabic division of the headwords had to be considered and the overall objective of the dictionary as a teaching tool had to be clarified. The inclusion of this division proved challenging to the formatting of the manuscript within a dictionary program, since most dictionary makers do not divide up headwords into syllables, so Microsoft Word was the program originally used.

Furthermore, the microstructure of the dictionary – namely, the actual entries – include several interesting features, which are explained in the following paragraphs, including the fact that Caribbean English uses some words that appear to be normal international English words but are used with a totally different sense in the Caribbean. A good case in point is the word **abstract**, which can be used both as a noun and an adjective in Internationally Accepted English. The word also performs the same double syntactic function in Caribbean English, but it is used as a noun in Belize to mean 'any pendant worn on a necklace', and as an adjective to mean 'odd' or 'bizarre'. Consequently, the territorial labelling that is used both in the *School Edition* and in the parent *Dictionary of Caribbean English Usage* plays an important role in relation to usage, namely, in which territory an item is used and the meaning assigned to the item.

An important aspect of Caribbean English is that in several cases, words from indigenous Amerindian languages are either adopted into Caribbean English as loans or else are the source from which certain lexical items are derived.

Words such as **anato**, a tree whose pods contain seeds which yield a red dye; **avocado**, a well-known Caribbean fruit often used as a vegetable in Caribbean cuisine; **guava** and **papaya**, fruits also known Caribbean-wide; insects such as **bachac(k) (ant)**, as well as types of timber found in Guyana, such as **mora**, **wallaba**, **simarupa**; birds, such as **powis**; fishes, such as **arapaima**; animals such as **abouya**, **labba** and **agouti**; items from everyday life, such as **matapee**, a long cylinder made of basket-work used to squeeze the juice from grated cassava in order to expel the poison, found in Belize, and so on. These items all have their source in indigenous languages, such as Aztec, Arawak, Carib, Taino and Tupi.

Furthermore, there are many items in Caribbean English that are derived from the many languages of sub-Saharan Africa brought by the enslaved Africans during the transatlantic trade. Not only are there single items, but the majority of Caribbean English idioms and proverbs stem from West African roots. Words such as **accra**, meaning a fritter made of saltfish and coming from the Yoruba *akara,* 'an oily cake made from beans ground and fried'; **dukuna**, a small pudding made of a mixture of grated sweet potatoes, cornmeal, grated coconut, raisins, spices, sugar and essence and known in some territories as **conkie**, from Akan languages, Gã-Adangme and Twi, occur with high frequency in Caribbean English. Also compound nouns like **eye-water**, for tears; **foot-bottom**, for the sole of the foot; **hand-middle**, for the palm of the hand; **hard-ears**, meaning stubbornly disobedient; **big-eye**, meaning greedy, covetous; as well as idiomatic phrases, such as **give somebody basket to carry/fetch water**, meaning to give someone a difficult or almost impossible task, or to pass on a difficult responsibility to somebody else, all have their sources in West African languages.

Another factor that had to be taken into consideration in the *School Edition* is that French Creole–speaking territories like St Lucia and Dominica, along with Trinidad and Grenada to a lesser extent, use French Creole words and phrases in their English. An example of this is the word **djablès**, sometimes written **ladjablès**, coming originally from the French word *diablesse* 'a she-devil'. The word refers to a legendary evil creature that appears on lonely roads in moonlight and assumes the form of a pretty woman in order to lure men into bushy places, whereupon she reveals her true identity as a hideous old woman whose feet are cloven hoofs. The frightening revelation usually makes the men either go mad or die.

Apart from French Creole words forming part of the English of some territories, there are a number of loanwords or words from other languages, such as French, Spanish, Dutch and Portuguese, that have become part of Caribbean English. Examples are French **flamboyant,** used throughout the Caribbean, referring to the tree that bears flame-coloured flowers between June and August; Spanish **empanadas**, used in Belize, which are large patties made of a tortilla fried and folded over with a filling of fish inside and served with onion and vinegar; Dutch **stelling**, used in Guyana to mean a large wooden jetty or wharf extending out over the muddy bank of a river, to permit people to embark on a ferry-boat or steamer; and Portuguese **bacalao**, used throughout the Caribbean to mean salted codfish.

In addition to the loanwords from European languages, there is also a large body of Indic loanwords in the English of Guyana and Trinidad, the two territories to receive the largest number of East Indian immigrants after Emancipation. They were brought in to work on the sugar estates which were abandoned by the Africans, who were now free to pursue their own occupations off the plantations. These Indic words are found in many different lexical areas, such as food, clothing, festivals, household items and so on. Examples are **achar**, which is a mixture of pieces of green mango and other fruit with peppers; ground **massala**, pepper and salt in mustard oil, used as a condiment with cooked food; **bhaji**, which is calalu or any dish made up of largely green leaves; **diya**, a lamp made up of a small clay saucer filled with oil or ghee and having a cotton wick, hundreds of which are lit to celebrate the Hindu festival of lights, known as **Divali** or **Diwali**. There is also the Muslim festival of **Hosein** or **Hosay**, celebrated in Trinidad to observe the martyrdom of Hassan and Hosein, sons of the prophet Muhammad, during late February or early March, with processions, drumming and dancing. In the area of clothing there is an **ornhi**, a head covering made of light material worn by East Indian women, which hangs down to the shoulders and is often used as a veil, particularly during religious ceremonies. Peculiar to Guyana is the **tilari**, an elaborate gold necklace, made of linked gold discs or coins and filigree work, worn by East Indian women.

The items cited above from the diverse sources of Caribbean English reflect the rich mix of cultures that combine to make up the Caribbean and contribute significantly to its languages. Also worthy of note is the fact that many ostensive items in Caribbean English have more than one name, so that the same item found across different territories would have its own name in the particular territory where it is found. It is vital that Caribbean students acquire the lexical items that label different areas of Caribbean life and culture across territories, which is one of the main aims of this dictionary. This feature is dealt with in a specific way which will be explained in the section "How to Use the School Edition".

The words cited above are usually the ones that have etymologies which give a brief history of the word and its source and which are usually enclosed in round brackets at the end of the entry. The only other feature that would be found after the etymology would be the usage note and it is usually preceded by a small square.

In addition, included as appendices at the back of the *School Edition* is a photograph of a steelband performing at Trinidad Carnival, a list of national symbols of English-speaking Caribbean territories, and a number of suggested activities which teachers can use when showing their students how to use the dictionary creatively, which should prove both instructive and fun for students. Appendices 3 and 4 show that the function of a dictionary is not just to look up a word and find its meaning, but also to learn something about the word, what it refers to, the way in which it is used and something about its history, provided that the source or etymological information can be accessed by the dictionary maker (which is not always the case). By this means, students are given valuable insights into the culture from which the languages came and into our own Caribbean culture.

FEATURES OF A DICTIONARY ENTRY

1. **Headword**: The first word in the entry which deals fully with the item being treated. Headwords are usually listed in alphabetical order within the topics this dictionary covers, namely Fauna; Flora; Food; Music, Musical Instruments and Dance; Religion; Festivals; Folklore; Architecture; Body Parts; Clothing; Children's Games; Organizational Abbreviations and Acronyms; and General Vocabulary.
2. **Headword with superscript numbers**: Two or more headwords with the same spelling, but with different meanings or different grammatical functions, for example **ab.stract**^{1} *noun*, **ab.stract**^{2} *adjective.*
3. **Headword with variant spellings**: For example, **em.pa.na.das (em.pa.na.des, em.pe.na.da)** – the variants are listed right next to the headword and are enclosed in brackets, and if there is more than one variant, it is separated from the rest by commas.
4. **Headword with related form(s)**: For example, **dub; dub-mu.sic** – the related forms are forms that are similar to the headword and they are listed right next to the headword and separated from it by a semicolon.
5. **Headword with one or more letters or words in brackets**: For example, **es.ca.veitch(ed) fish, heel and toe (dance/pol.ka)** – the bracketed letter(s) or word(s) can be omitted.
6. **Headword with explanatory phrase in square brackets** usually preceding the definition, sometimes just after it.
7. **Phrase**: Any sequence of words, one of which is the headword in whose entry it is listed.
8. **Headwords that are loanwords from other languages**: For example, French **fa.rine**, French Creole **chou.val bon.dyé**, Spanish **ha.ba.ne.ro**, Dutch **pol.der**, Portuguese **ba.ca.lao,** Indic **a.char**.
9. **Part of speech**, that is, *noun, adjective, transitive verb*, are always written in italics.

10. **Territorial labels** are always in four-letter codes enclosed in round brackets, for example (Bdos, Gren, Guyn StLu) = Barbados, Grenada, Guyana, St Lucia.
11. **Cross-reference, other name**: This is another name for the headword in another territory, which follows the headword in the entry and is preceded by the territory or territories in which it is found. The territories are written in bold followed by the other name(s) of the item in bold italics. For example, **dunk(s)** *noun (plural)* (Bdos, Guyn, StKt, StVn). **Angu, Nevs, StKt** ***pomme surette*****; Antg** ***dumbs, dumps*****; Baha, Jmca** ***juju(be)*****; Belz** ***governor plum***[2]**; CayI** ***coco-plum, Jew-plum*****; Guyn** ***dungs*****; Jmca** ***coolie-plum***[1].
12. **'See' item**: This is a headword that contains a number of names of other territories. Each of these names is listed in its alphabetical position, but the main headword under which is falls will have all the information on the item, that is, the headword written in small caps because it is the main headword. For example, **cas.sa.va-bake** *noun* (Bdos). See CASSAVA-BREAD.
13. **Definition**: The description of the headword, which normally consists of what the item is, if it is a noun, especially an item of fauna, flora or food, how it looks and what it does, what it is used for etc., is called encyclopedic information. The two parts of the entry are usually separated by a semicolon. For example, **ca.ram.bo.la-jam** *noun* (CarA). A fruit preserve made by boiling pieces of CARAMBOLA with sugar and water and letting the mixture cook slowly until it thickens; it is then cooled and stored in bottles. (All headwords are not defined this way.)
14. **Subject label**: This indicates a particular area in the topic under which the headword falls; for example, within the topic General Vocabulary there is the item **in.den.tured la.bour** *noun phrase* (CarA). [Historical]. Note that the subject label comes just after the territorial label and before the rest of the entry.
15. **Etymology** is the historical source of the headword and is found in round brackets at the end of the entry, for example, **hag**[1] **(heg, higue)** *noun* **1.** (Baha, Belz, StVn). See SOUKOUYAN. **2.** (Baha, Belz, StVn). An extremely troublesome person. (An obsolete English word. See *Oxford English Dictionary hag* sb[1], 1, 2, 3.)
16. **Usage note**: In some cases, there is some particularly interesting information about the way in which the headword is used and that note is usually preceded by a small square and comes right at the end of the entry, for example, **Main Guard** *noun phrase* (Bdos). The Central Police Station in Barbados. (From Standard English *main-guard*, 'the building in which the main guard of a garrison is lodged'.) □ In Barbados, this is the term used instead of 'Central Police Station'.

Note: Most entries do not have all the features above, but these are all the features that can be found in a dictionary entry.

Following this section is a diagrammatic sketch of the type of information that is included within an entry.

STRUCTURE OF A DICTIONARY ENTRY

Headword with syllabic dots in bold in order to be easily identified	**al.li.ga.tor** *noun* (CarA)	Part of speech/ grammatical function in italics and highlighted. Territorial label outlined.
Headword with cross-references	**dunk(s)** *noun (plural)* (Bdos, Guyn, StKt, StVn,). **Antg, Nevs, StKt** ***pomme-surette*; Antg dumbs, *dumps*; Baha, Jmca juju(be); Belz *governor-plum*[2]; CayI *coco-plum*, *Jew-plum*; Guyn *dungs*; Jmca *coolie-plum*[1]**	Cross-references or other names are preceded by the territory or territories to which they belong, followed by a semicolon after each cross-reference or set of cross-references.
Headword with variant spellings, definition, etymology or word source and usage note	**em.pa.na.das (em.pa.na. des, empe.na.da)** *noun plural* (Belz). **Belz** ***panades.*** A type of large PATTY made of a fried tortilla folded over, filled with fish, usually served with onion and vinegar. (From Spanish *empanada* from *pan* 'bread', the name of this food.) □ The plural form is used as the singular in Belize, but PANADES is the form used in speech.	Definition highlighted. Variant spellings are in bold and in round brackets right next to the headword. Etymology or word source in red. The usage note, preceded by a small square, is in blue.

Headword with related form, sense numbers and sub-sense numbers	**dub; dub-music** *noun* (CarA). **1.** A rhythm with two beats provided mainly by bass drums without an actual tune, originally derived from REGGAE, and usually recorded on the flip side of a record. **2.** **(i)** (CarA). A type of dancing in which partners keep their bodies very close to each other. **(ii)** A public dance at which only DUB-MUSIC is played.	Related form next to the headword, also in bold, and separated from it by a semicolon. Sense numbers **1.** and **2.** Are always written in bold. So are sub-sense numbers, but they are instead written in lowercase letters **(i)**, **(ii)**, **(iii)**, etc. and are always enclosed in round brackets. If the sub-sense is found within a particular territory or territories, the territorial label(s) come just after the sub-sense number.
Superscript numbers are always just placed next to the headword	**big-up**[1] *noun* (Bdos). An important person. **big-up**[2] *adjective* (Bdos). In a top position, socially highly placed. **big-up**[3] *transitive verb* (Bdos). To flatter, praise somebody highly. **ab.stract**[1] *noun* (Belz). Any pendant worn on a necklace. (Probably from designs that remind one of abstract art.) **ab.stract**[2] *adjective* (Belz). Odd, extremely unusual, strange.	In this case, the three superscripts of **big-up** represent three different grammatical functions, a noun, an adjective and a verb. Superscript numbers are also used when one word has two or more totally different meanings as in the case of **abstract**.

Headwords that produce phrases	**gu.zu(m) (gu.zung)** *noun* (Belz, Jmca). **1.** An act or wish by which some supernatural bad influence is believed to adversely affect somebody's effort. **2.** A charm prepared in order to protect somebody against evil. **3.** *PHRASES* **3.1 put/set guzu on (somebody)** *verb phrase* (Belz, Jmca). To try or intend to cause harm by ill-wishing or by some act influence by superstitious belief.	When a headword produces a phrase, the word PHRASES in capital italics is usually placed before the set of words making up the phrase which then follows it in bold with its part of speech and territory as well as the definition of the phrase. Note that the actual phrase coming after the word PHRASES usually keeps the same number as the word but then that number is followed by **.1**, **.2**, etc., e.g. **3.1**, in bold. In this case, the phrases derive from the third sense of the headword.
Headword with explanatory phrase in square brackets, usually preceding the definition	**co.lour.ed** *adjective* (CarA). [Of persons] Having a brown, light-brown or CLEAR skin, being of mixed black and white races; not East Indian and not dark-skinned; racially mixed as seen from the person's skin and hair. **buck.et-a-drop** *adverb* (Gren, Guyn, Tbgo). **1.** [Of rain or tears] In large amounts.	Sometimes the explanatory phrase follows the definition.

Subject labels	**chi.na.man** *noun* (CarA) [Cricket] A left-arm bowler's ball spun from the wrist and turning into the right-handed batsman. (Refers to Ellis 'Puss' Achong, a Chinese West Indian test cricketer who first bowled that kind of ball at Manchester, England in 1933 and dismissed an English batsman, who remarked 'Fancy being bowled by a bloody Chinaman!')	In some entries, what is called a subject label, which is usually in square brackets, occurs after the territory where the headword is found. It simply indicates the topic that the headword is covering which may not be immediately obvious to the user, especially in the case of items of historical significance or some items that are Indic.
See entries.	**dup.py-cher.ry** *noun* (Jmca). See CLAMMY-CHERRY.	Entries preceded by 'See' usually refer to a particular headword with several cross-references. This is regarded as the main headword under which all the cross references or other names occur. As each cross-reference is listed alphabetically, it is more economical to refer each of them back to the main headword. In this case, all the information, including the name **dup.py-cher.ry** would fall under CLAMMY-CHERRY.

TERRITORIAL ABBREVIATIONS

Angu	Anguilla
Antg	Antigua
Baha	Bahamas
Bdos	Barbados
Berm	Bermuda
Brbu	Barbuda
BrVI	British Virgin Islands
CarA	Caribbean Area/Region
CayI	Cayman Islands
Crcu	Carriacou
Dmca	Dominica
ECar	East Caribbean
Gren	Grenada
Guyn	Guyana
Jmca	Jamaica
Mrat	Montserrat
Neth	Netherland Antilles
Nevs	Nevis
StKt	St Kitts
StLu	St Lucia
StVn	St Vincent
Tbgo	Tobago
TkCa	Turks and Caicos
Trin	Trinidad
USVI	US Virgin Islands
ViIs	Virgin Islands (US and British)

LANGUAGES CITED IN ETYMOLOGIES

African

Akan
Ewe
Efik
Fulani
Gã-Adangme
Hausa
Ibibio
Igbo
Kikongo
Mende
Nembe
Soninke
Swahili
Twi
Wolof
Yoruba

There are two other languages, namely Ashanti and Fon, that are not cited in the *School Edition*, but are nevertheless important as sources in Caribbean English.

Indic

Bhojpuri
Hindi
Tamil

Indigenous Languages

Arawak
Akawaio
Carib
Tupi
Makusi

HOW TO USE THE SCHOOL EDITION

Although this dictionary is one that is divided into themes, the items under each theme are listed alphabetically, so if the student knows the word that they would like to find, they simply need to know into what category it falls, whether it is a fruit, a flower, a tree, a bush or a shrub, which would indicate that it falls under the theme of flora, and so on.

Given the fact that in Caribbean English, items have many different names, depending on the territory in which they are found, those items have had to be included. However, there is a simple principle whereby the item can be found easily and that is through the cross-referencing function of the dictionary. Wherever one particular name or label is given to items in several territories, that item usually is the one entered as the headword, because of the high frequency of its occurrence. The other names for the item are then listed, in bold italics, preceded by the names of the territories in which they occur, in boldface type. For example, the fruit **dunks,** usually plural, is called by that name in Barbados, Guyana, St Kitts and St Vincent, four different territories. However, it has a number of other names, such as ***byre*** in Guyana, ***coco-plum*** in the Cayman Islands, ***coolie-plum*** in Jamaica, ***dum(b)-fruit*** in St Kitts, ***governor-plum*** in Belize, ***Jew-plum*** in the Cayman Islands, ***juju(be)*** in the Bahamas and Jamaica, and ***pomme-surette*** in Anguilla, Nevis and St Kitts. All of these items will be listed under the headword **dunks**, which will have the full definition of the item. Each of the other names will also be listed wherever it falls alphabetically, but instead of repeating the definition every time, the headword with its territory or territories will be listed, there will be a fullstop after the name of the territory or territories, and that will be followed by the word 'See' and the main headword DUNKS in small capitals. An example would be the following: **Jew-plum** *noun* (CayI). See DUNKS.

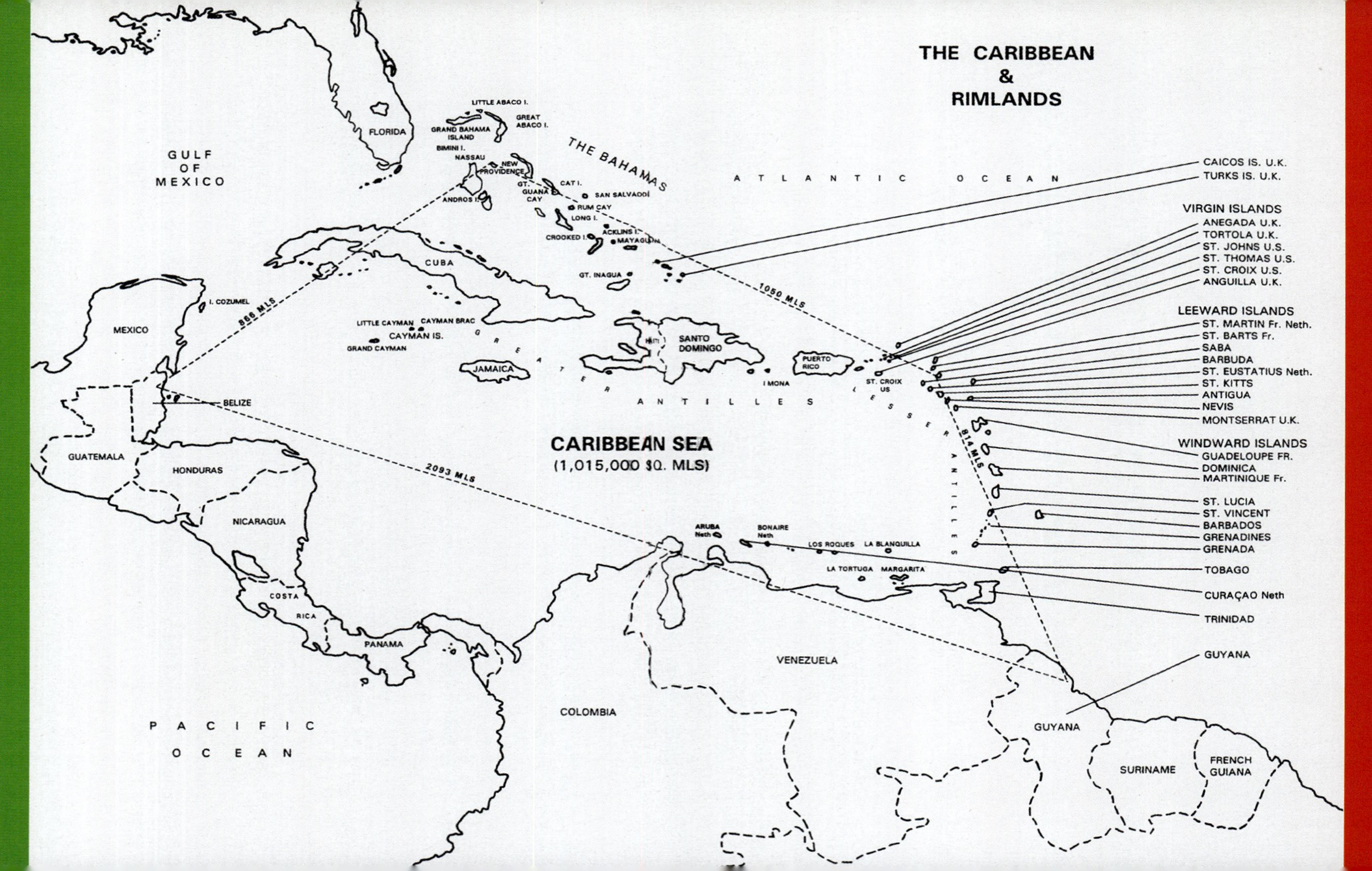
THE CARIBBEAN
&
RIMLANDS
GULF OF MEXICO
FLORIDA
LITTLE ABACO I.
GREAT ABACO I.
GRAND BAHAMA ISLAND
BIMINI I.
NASSAU
NEW PROVIDENCE
ANDROS I.
THE BAHAMAS
CAT I.
GT. GUANA CAY
SAN SALVADOR
RUM CAY
LONG I.
ACKLINS I.
CROOKED I.
MAYAGUANA
GT. INAGUA
ATLANTIC OCEAN
CUBA
MEXICO
I. COZUMEL
866 MLS
LITTLE CAYMAN
CAYMAN BRAC
CAYMAN IS.
GRAND CAYMAN
JAMAICA
HAITI
SANTO DOMINGO
I MONA
PUERTO RICO
ST. CROIX US
1050 MLS
GREATER ANTILLES
LESSER ANTILLES
814 MLS
BELIZE
GUATEMALA
HONDURAS
NICARAGUA
COSTA RICA
PANAMA
CARIBBEAN SEA
(1,015,000 SQ. MLS)
2093 MLS
ARUBA Neth
BONAIRE Neth
LOS ROQUES
LA BLANQUILLA
LA TORTUGA
MARGARITA
VENEZUELA
COLOMBIA
GUYANA
SURINAME
FRENCH GUIANA
PACIFIC OCEAN
CAICOS IS. U.K.
TURKS IS. U.K.
VIRGIN ISLANDS
ANEGADA U.K.
TORTOLA U.K.
ST. JOHNS U.S.
ST. THOMAS U.S.
ST. CROIX U.S.
ANGUILLA U.K.
LEEWARD ISLANDS
ST. MARTIN Fr. Neth.
ST. BARTS Fr.
SABA
BARBUDA
ST. EUSTATIUS Neth.
ST. KITTS
ANTIGUA
NEVIS
MONTSERRAT U.K.
WINDWARD ISLANDS
GUADELOUPE FR.
DOMINICA
MARTINIQUE Fr.
ST. LUCIA
ST. VINCENT
BARBADOS
GRENADINES
GRENADA
TOBAGO
CURAÇAO Neth
TRINIDAD
GUYANA

FAUNA

A

a.ber.deen *noun* (Tbgo). See CIGALE.

a.bou.ya *noun* (Guyn) **Guyn** ***bush-hog***. A wild pig hunted for its meat. (An Arawak name.)

ac.cou.ri *noun* (Guyn). See AGOUTI. (A Carib name.)

a(c).cou.shi-ant(s) *noun* (Guyn) **Belz, Guyn** ***umbrella-ant(s)*****; Dmca** ***tac-tac-ant(s)*****; Trin** ***bachac, parasol-ant(s)***. A tiny black or brown ant that bites off pieces of leaves which it stores underground for food, and which moves in columns, holding the pieces of green leaves over its head, giving it the alternative names of PARASOL or UMBRELLA ANT. (An Arawak name.)

a.gou.ti (a.gu.ti) *noun* (CarA) **Belz** ***Indian rabbit***. A greenish-brown rodent resembling a rabbit, hunted for its meat. (An Arawak and Carib name.)

Agouti

al.ba.core *noun* (CarA). A type of TUNA with long fins.

al.li.ga.tor *noun* (CarA). A large amphibious reptile native to America with a large head.

Alligator

am.ber.jack *noun* (CarA) **StLu** ***amber*****; Berm** ***amberfish***. An edible greenish-red fish which weighs an average of 18 lb.

a.na.con.da *noun* (Trin) **Guyn** ***water-camoodi***. A large snake of the boa family that can live on both water and land and that crushes its victims.

A.nan.cy (-spider) (nan.cy(-spi.der)) *noun* (CarA). A large, brown house-spider. (From a W. African language, Twi.)

an.cho *noun* (Trin) **Trin** ***blue-fish***. An edible fish, blue in colour, with a stout body, which usually weighs about 15 lb.

an.cho.vy *noun* (StLu, Trin) **Gren** ***anchoa*; StVn *antrovy, windward sprat*; StLu *pisiette*; Trin *za(n)chwa*.** The name given to a number of small, edible, sardine-like fishes, one of the commonest being silvery in colour.

an.gel.fish (an.gel-fish) *noun* (CarA). Any variety of a small, flat, roundish fish with brilliant colours, noticeably wing-like fins, and a fan-shaped tail.

a.ni *noun* (Jmca). See JUMBIE-BIRD[3].

an.ni ant *noun phrase* (Guyn). An inch-long, black forest ant noted for its ferocious bite.

a.no.le (a.no.li(s)) *noun (plural)* (Gren, StLu). **Dmca, StLu, Trin *zandoli*.** The common grey or green tree lizard.

ant-bear *noun* (Belz, Guyn). **Belz, Guyn, Trin *ant-eater*; Guyn *giant ant-eater*.** The largest of several species of ANT-EATER, a mammal with a long, sticky tongue and a long snout that feeds largely on ants.

Ant-bear

An.til.le.an crest.ed hum.ming.bird *noun phrase* (CarA). A small, green bird with a blackish tail and underparts, and a crest that is violet-blue, bright green, or both green and blue, found throughout the Lesser Antilles.

An.til.le.an mock.ing.bird *noun phrase* (Baha, CayI, ViIs). A small grey bird with mostly whitish wings, outer tail-feathers and white to greyish underparts, which lives mainly in towns, but also in open country. It is noted for its melodious song.

an.tro.vy *noun* (StVn). See ANCHOVY.

a.ra.pai.ma *noun* (Guyn). A large, river fish, weighing over 400 lb, found in Guyana. (A Carib name.)

Arapaima

ar.ma.dil.lo *noun* (Guyn). **Gren, Trin *tatu*.** A nocturnal, burrowing, forest animal, covered completely with a hard, horned coat, looking like armour; it has a rat-like head and a horned tail and is hunted for its flesh. (A Spanish word meaning 'little armed one'.)

ar.my-ant(s) *noun (usually plural)* (Guyn) **Guyn *ya(c)kman*; Trin *soldier-ant(s)*.** A type of forest ant, that at a certain point in its reproductive cycle, marches off in columns; one of the columns carries food and the others attack small animals, such as birds and lizards.

arse.nick.er *noun* (Baha) **Dmca, Gren, StLu *kwabyè nwè*; CarA *greater blue heron*.** A large blue heron that is more than 4 ft tall when fully grown.

Arsenicker (Greater blue heron)

Aun.tie Nan.nee *noun phrase* (BrVI). See POND-FLY.

B

ba.b(r)e dove *noun phrase* (Guyn). A brown woodland dove, about a foot long, with a greyish-white forehead, red-circled eyes and red legs.

ba.chac(k) (ant) (ba.chak. bat.chak) *noun (phrase)* (Tbgo, Trin). See ACCOUSHI-ANT(s). (From a South American Amerindian language or Spanish *bachaco* 'a large reddish or black ant'.)

ba.li.sier bird *noun phrase* (Trin). A hummingbird which nests in HELICONIA bushes and feeds on its flowers. (From French *balisier*, through French Creole, referring to plants of a particular family.)

ba.l(l)a.hoo *noun* (ECar). A slim, blue and silver bony fish, about 6 to 12 in. long, with its lower, spear-like jaw longer than the upper one.

Balahoo

bam.boo-chicken *noun* (Belz). The fully grown iguana, particularly the female, whose meat when cooked is said to taste like chicken. □ Iguanas are often found to frequent bamboo clusters, and their meat has been compared with chicken, hence the name.

ba.na.na.quit *noun* (CarA). **Antg, Bdos, USVI** ***yellow-breast*****; Baha** ***banana-bird*****; Bdos, USVI** ***sugar-bird*****; Gren** ***see-see bird*****; Jmca** ***beany bird*****; Trin** ***sikyé-bird***. A small dark-grey bird, with a yellow breast and a white streak over its eye, known for its love of ripe bananas and also sugar.

Bananaquit

ba.na.na-bor.er *noun* (CarA). A weevil whose eggs tunnel or bore into the banana tree, destroying its roots.

ban.ga ma.ry (ban.ga-ma.ry) *noun* (Guyn). An edible river fish about 8 in. long, with silvery scales.

Bangamary

bar.jack *noun* (CarA). A silvery, grey-blue and white fish, with a long body and pointed snout, having a double row of teeth in its upper jaw and a long, dark bar along its back.

Bar.ba.dos green mon.key *noun phr* (Bdos). See GREEN MONKEY.

bare-neck fowl *noun phrase* (Bdos, Nevs, StKt). **Belz, Guyn, Jmca, StVn** ***peel-neck fowl***. A type of chicken that has no feathers on its neck, and whose body feathers are turned backwards.

Bare-neck fowl

barn-owl *noun* (Trin). See JUMBIE-BIRD[1].

ba(r).ra.cu.da *noun* (CarA). **Dmca *bètjin*.** A savage, spotted, silvery-grey, deep-sea fish, which is poisonous when caught in some areas. (Probably from an Amerindian language.)

Baracuda fish

bass 1. *noun* (Guyn). Any one of several groups of edible fresh or salt water fishes with spiny fins. **2.** (USVI) See TARPON.

bat 2. *noun* (Guyn) **Bdos *leather bat, night bat*; Antg *micy-bat*; Belz, Jmca, Mrat, TkCa *rat-bat*.** A nocturnal flying animal that tends to come out at dusk.

Bats

ba.ti.manm.zèl (ba.ti.mam.selle, bat.ty-mam.selle) *noun* (Trin). See POND-FLY. (A French Creole word.)

bean.y bird *noun phrase* (Jmca). See BANANAQUIT.

bee.tle *noun* (CarA). A small insect that comes out at night, attracted mainly by light.

bell-bird *noun* (Trin). A pale-grey bird with a coffee-brown head and black bill and feet, whose song is a long, clanging sound, repeated at long intervals.

bête-rouge (bèt-wouj) *noun* (Gren, Guyn, StLu, Trin). A tiny red insect that burrows into the skin of humans who are in low bushes or grass, causing intense itching before it dies. (A French word meaning 'red animal'.)

bèt.jin (bé.chine) *noun* (Dmca). See BARRACUDA. (A French Creole word.)

big-eye *noun* (ECar). Name given to several types of small fish with big eyes.

bill-fish *noun* (CarA). **ECar *ocean-gar*.** The name given to a number of huge ocean-fishes, which weigh hundreds of pounds when they are fully grown, such as marlin, sailfish or swordfish, but are caught for eating when they are smaller.

bird-of-paradise *noun* (Tbgo, Trin). A chocolate to reddish-brown bird, with a bright yellow streak from its crown to its shoulders, and a bright green throat and beak.

black-ant *noun* (CarA). A small common ant usually found on fruit trees, particularly on mango and citrus trees, which reduces fruit output.

black-bel.ly sheep *noun phrase* (Bdos). A hornless sheep, with brown hair (not wool) and a black undercarriage, which is reared in Barbados and prized for its meat.

Black-belly sheep

black.bird *noun* (CarA). **Jmca** ***kling-kling***[1]. A name given to any bird that is black, blackish, or nearly black, especially by city-dwellers.

black jack *noun phrase* (CarA). A fairly large, edible fish that can grow up to 3 ft long and is usually dark brown in colour with a blackish tint, from which it gets its name.

black mar.gate *noun phrase* (CarA). A large, edible fish, silvery in colour but with dark markings on its body, large eyes and large scales, considered to be of good food value.

black spi.der *noun phrase* (Trin). See TARANTULA[1].

black-witch *noun* (ViIs). See JUMBIE-BIRD[3].

blue-fish *noun* (Trin). See ANCHO.

blue land crab *noun phrase* (CarA). A species of crab, lavender-blue or white in colour, with a broad, egg-shaped shell, pincers that are unequal in length and slightly hairy legs; it lives and burrows in low-lying ground.

Blue land crab

blue mar.lin *noun phrase* (Baha, Bdos, ViIs). A large, edible fish with a dark-blue to chocolate-brown back; it can weigh as much as a few hundred pounds and is of excellent food value.

blue par.rot.fish *noun phrase* (CarA). **Antg** ***macaw***[2]***(-chub)***. A fairly large, edible fish, deep blue in colour and with a large fleshy lump on its forehead which increases as the fish grows older.

blue-run.ner *noun* (CarA). A small, edible fish of that is considered to be quite nutritious.

blue sack.i(e) *noun phrase* (Guyn). A fairly large silvery-blue bird with dark-blue to violet wing feathers which likes to feed on mangoes and gives a little shriek 'ski-ski', hence the name.

Blue sackie

blue shark *noun phrase* (CarA). A large, ocean shark, blue in colour, shading off to white, which eats anything, including garbage from ships.

boa con.strict.or *noun phrase* (CarA). A large serpent, known to feed on small mammals and birds. It is easily captured and takes well to captivity.

Boaconstrictor

bo.ni.to *noun* (VIls). A large, edible fish of the TUNA variety which is considered to be of good food value. (A Spanish word meaning 'pretty'.)

bot.tle.nose dol.phin *noun* (CayI). **CarA** ***porpoise.*** The largest of all dolphins or porpoises, growing to a length of up to about 12 ft, black on top, with dark-brown sides and a white belly; the fish is found in all the large oceans of the world and is known to be able to jump long distances.

Bottlenose dolphin

bous(se) *noun* (Dmca, StLu). See OLD-WIFE.

box-fish *noun* (Baha, TkCa). See COW-FISH.

bri.go *noun* (Gren, StLu). See WILK.

brim *noun* (Bdos, Mrat, Nevs). See RED-SNAPPER.

bull frog *noun phrase* (CarA). A large greenish-chestnut coloured frog with grey and brown spots which prefers large bodies of water such as lakes and swamps, but can also be found in ponds.

Bull frog

bum.ble.bee *noun* (CarA). A large bee known for the buzzing sound that it makes.

bush-cow *noun* (Guyn). See TAPIR.

bush-hog *noun* (Guyn). See PECCARY.

bush.mas.ter *noun* (Guyn, Trin). **Trin** ***mapepire zanana***. A huge dark-coloured snake, with pinkish underside and large triangular patches on its body, said to be the largest poisonous snake in the world.

Bushmaster

but.ter-fish *noun* (CarA). The name given to several varieties of small fish, suitable for frying, which are either pink, grey or yellow, easily cleaned and prized for their tasty flesh.

but.ter.fly *noun* (CarA). A group of insects that come out either by day or by night, with bodies divided into head, thorax and abdomen, three pairs of legs and two pairs of brightly coloured wings. Some species are harmful to humans and plants, others are not.

Butterfly

C

ca.bou.ra(-fly) *noun* (Guyn). See KABOURO(-FLY).

ca.brit (Dmca, StLu, USVI). See COW-FISH.

ca.ca-bel.ly[1] *noun* (Gren, StLu, StVn). **Dmca, Gren, StLu *cacabarwee*; StLu, StVn *chub*[2]**. A name given to a number of fishes which, when caught, pass large amounts of messy waste matter usually stored in their large abdomen. Also the WRASSE or the CHUB. □ CACABARWEE is a French Creole word from *caca* 'shit' + French Creole *bawi* from French *baril* 'barrel'.

ca.ca-bel.ly[2] *noun* (Gren, StLu, StVn). **Guyn *kakabelli***. Any one of a number of fishes which, when caught, pass large amounts of messy waste matter usually stored in their large abdomen.; they are usually found in foul, shallow river or trench waters. Also the WRASSE or the CHUB[1].

ca.moo.di *noun* (Guyn). A huge non-poisonous snake that crushes its victims. There are two kinds of this snake, the MACAJUEL and the ANACONDA, which can grow over 30 ft long. (An Arawak word.)

Camoodi snake

cam.pa.ne.ro *noun* (Trin). A common, whitish, forest bird with a coffee-brown head, well known for its bell-like song. (A Spanish word meaning 'bell-ringer'.)

ca.na.ry *noun* (CarA). See YELLOW-WARBLER.

can.dle-fly *noun* (Guyn, Trin). **Baha *lamp-lighter*; Dmca, StVn *labelle*; Jmca *peeny-wally*; StKt *lamp-fly***. A small brown insect with a luminous yellowish-brown abdomen that blinks like a light every time that it raises its wings to fly.

Can.je phea.sant *noun phrase* (Guyn). A large bird about 22 in. long, from head to tail, and a brown and white body and creamy white breast. The national bird of Guyana. (Named after an area in Berbice, Guyana, *Canje* + *pheasant* because it resembles a pheasant.)

Canje pheasant

ca.rey *noun* (Grns, USVI). See HAWKSBILL TURTLE.

ca.rite *noun* (Trin). **Angu, Antg, Bdos, Gren, Guyn *Spanish mackerel***. A dark blue fish, weighing about 5 to 6 lb, with oval orange-yellow spots on its back and sides, and a silvery belly with few scales, well known for its good food value. (Venezuelan Spanish word meaning a 'sea fish with a long body and a wide mouth'.)

car.rion-crow *noun* (Guyn. Jmca). **Baha, Guyn *crow*; Belz, Jmca *John Crow*.** A black crow about 2 ft long with an almost naked grey or red head, that feeds on rotting animal carcasses.

cas.ca.du (cas.ca.du.ra) *noun* (Trin). **Guyn *hassar, toe-nail fish*.** A river fish about 6 in. long, with dark, curved, interlocking scales which are only removed after boiling, and creamy-white flesh, considered a delicacy.

Cascadu fish

ca.ter.pil.lar *noun* (CarA). The larva of a butterfly or moth.

cat.fish *noun* (CarA). **Guyn *skinfish*.** An unscaled bluish-grey to dark-brown edible fish, usually about 20 in. long, with an arched head and a short tail which feeds mostly on small fishes and invertebrates, found in shallow, coastal waters, lagoons and river estuaries in the Caribbean.

cat.tle-e.gret *noun* (Bdos, Guyn, Trin). **Angu, Bdos, Jmca *white egret*; Angu, Dmca, Gren, USVI *white gaulin*; BrVI, Jmca *cow-bird*; Guyn *crane*; Trin *tick-bird*[2].** A white or buff-coloured bird, with a yellow bill and legs and a longish neck,

Cattle-egret

usually found near cattle, sometimes on its own, and sometimes in flocks.

ca.val.li (ca.va.li, ca.val.la, ca.va.ly) *noun* (CarA). **Gren, Trin *couva(l)lie, crevalle*; Guyn *jack*, *toro*[1].** A large sea-fish, bluish-green on the back with greyish-gold sides and a yellow belly; it is one of the fiercest fish in the sea but is not considered to be of good food value.

cen.ti.pede *noun* (CarA). A carnivorous, segmented animal with a jointed reddish-brown body of about 15 to 21 segments, each with a pair of legs, usually found in warm damp places or among old wood.

chick.en-hawk *noun* (CarA). **Gren *gri-gri*[1]; StLu *malfini*.** A small hawk, about 15 to 19 in. long with a black and white banded tail and broad wings; it lives in wooded areas and lowlands, where it feeds on a variety of small animals, including chickens.

chick-man-chick *noun* (Jmca). See HOPPING-DICK.

chi.go(e) (chi(g).ga(h), chig.ger, chig.goe) *noun* (CarA). **CarA *jigger*.** A blood-sucking flea found in sandy ground, the female of which burrows under the human foot, where it lays eggs and swells up, causing great itching and irritation, which can result in loss of toes; it can also be removed with a sterile needle, or may drop out on its own.

chin.cha.ry *noun* (Angu, USVI). See RAIN-BIRD[1].

chou.val-bon-dyé *noun* (Dmca, StLu). See GOD-HORSE. (French Creole word fr French *cheval* 'horse' + *(bon) dieu* '(good) God'.)

Christ.mas bird *noun phrase* (Bdos). A small, almost entirely black, bird with bright orange patches on its wings and tail; it warbles, spreading its tail and displaying its yellow or orange bases.

chub[1] *noun* (CarA). **CarA** ***parrot-fish***. Any one of several varieties of a fish of different colours, blue, purple, etc., with prominent teeth, a slimy head, and tough, but tasty flesh. Its habitat is usually coral reefs.

chub[2] *noun* (StLu, StVn). See CACA-BELLY[1].

ci.gale *noun* (Trin). **Tbgo** ***aberdeen***, **Gren, StLu** ***rain-bird***[3]. A large, dark-coloured insect which lives in tall trees and makes a high-pitched, screeching sound at dusk.

cob.bler *noun* (BrVi, Dmca, StVn). **Dmca** ***kawang***. A broad, flat-headed, silver-coloured fish about 2 ft long and of excellent food value.

cock.le *noun* (Guyn). A small, shiny, hard-backed beetle that flies into houses at nights, during the rainy season, attracted by the lights.

cock-li.zard *noun* (Bdos). The male of the common grey-green tree lizard. It is larger than the female and has a yellow throat-fan.

cock-ma.cla.la *noun* (Belz). See MACLALA.

cock.roach *noun* (CarA). A brown beetle-like insect with fairly long antennae which gets into houses and tends to live in kitchens and cupboards. It is a house pest.

co.coa-bird *noun* (Baha, Jmca). See GREATER ANTILLEAN BULLFINCH.

Cocrico bird

C

co.cri.co *noun* (Tbgo, Trin) **Belz** ***coquericot***. A large, brownish-olive bird which usually congregates in flocks. Its song is a harsh *cocrico*, repeated several times, which gives the bird its name.

co.li.bri *noun* (Dmca, Gren, Grns). See DOCTOR-BIRD. (A Carib name.)

conch *noun* (CarA). A large, tropical sea creature, with a large, bright-pink, spiral shell, usually about 10 in. long. It is much used in Caribbean cuisine, and the shell is often blown by fishermen to attract sales or call people together.

Conch

co.ney sea-bass *noun phrase* (CarA). A small olive-coloured, brownish-red or yellow fish with a large head covered with bluish-black spots and a long mouth.

con.ger (eel) *noun (phrase)* (CarA). A large and notably aggressive type of eel, usually caught for food.

co.que.ri.co *noun* (Belz). See COCRICO.

cow-bird *noun* (BrVI, Jmca). See CATTLE-EGRET.

co.que.ri.cot *noun* (Belz). See COCRICO.

cow-fish *noun* (Baha, Gren, Mrat, StLu). **Baha, Guyn, TkCa** ***box-fish*****; ECar** ***shell-fish*****[2]; StLu** ***kabwit*****[2]**. A yellowish, triangular or squarish fish with spots and pale blue stripes; it has horns over its eyes and its entire body, except the tail, is covered by a hard shell. It can be roasted in the shell and is considered of good food value.

Cow-fish

crab *noun* (CarA). A land crustacean with a broad, flat shell under which its abdomen is folded; it has two pincers that are hairless, but its other limbs are quite hairy.

crab-dog *noun* (Guyn). **Guyn** ***crab-eating racoon***. A small, stout, greyish animal, about the size of a fox, with short legs, pointed ears and a broad face with 'spectacle' marks over its eyes and a sharp snout; it feeds on crabs and snails, hence the name, and has an unpleasant odour.

crane *noun* (Guyn). See CATTLE-EGRET.

cra.paud *noun* (CarA). A large frog or toad, that tends to stay on land, with a dry, rough skin which contains poison-sacs, used by the animal to defend itself. (A French word meaning 'toad'.)

cray.fish (craw.fish) *noun* (CarA). A small freshwater crustacean often found in rivers.

cre.valle *noun* (Gren, Trin). See CAVALLI.

crick.et *noun* (CarA). Any of several brownish grass-hopper-like insects, with long antennae; the male produces a chirping sound by rubbing its legs together.

cro.co.dile *noun* (CarA). A large, tropical amphibious reptile with a broad head, tapering snout, massive jaws and a thick skin made up of bony plates.

Crocodile

crow *noun* (Baha, Guyn). See CARRION-CROW. □ This item does not refer to the European crow, which is a much smaller bird and is of a different species.

cuck.oo-ma.ni.oc *noun* (Dmca, Gren). See RAIN-BIRD[2].

cui.rass-fish *noun* (Guyn). A relative of the CASCADU covered in similarly dark, interlocking scales resembling a coat of armour.

cut.lass(-fish) *noun* (Jmca). A long, slender, silvery-blue fish, prized as a food fish and given this name because of its shape.

D

dead-peo.ple bird *noun phrase* (Baha). See JUMBIE-BIRD[3].

death-bird *noun* (Baha). See JUMBIE-BIRD[1].

devil-fish *noun* (Guyn). A giant, bat-like fish of the RAY family with a double snout resembling horns, which give it this name; a strong fish that can leap high into the air.

dew-fish *noun* (Guyn). See JEW-FISH.

djèp *noun* (StLu). See JACK-SPANIARD.

doc.tor-bird *noun* (ECar, Guyn). **1. Bdos** ***doctor-booby***. Any of several varieties of greenish HUMMINGBIRDS. **2.** (Jmca). **Jmca** ***long-tail doctor-bird, streamer-tail***. A HUMMINGBIRD of which the male is greenish with two long black tail feathers, which the female does not have. The national bird of Jamaica.

doc.tor-fish *noun* (CarA). One of three varieties of a flat, oval-shaped fish with two lancet-type spikes on each side near its tail; it is considered to be of good food value.

Dolphin fish

dol.phin *noun* (CarA). **StLu** ***dorado***; **Bdos** ***mahi-mahi***. A large, edible sea fish with a long metallic, blue-green body which feeds mainly on smaller fishes and crustaceans.

don.key-spi.der *noun* (StKt). See TARANTULA[1].

dup.py-rid.in(g)-horse *noun phrase* (Jmca). See GOD-HORSE.

Doctor bird

E

earth.worm *noun* (CarA). Any of several worms that burrow in the ground and help to loosen the soil.

egg bird *noun phrase* (CarA). A large bird with a black crown and brownish-grey wings and tail, with a white streak running to its eye. It has a high-pitched cry.

e.lec.tric eel *noun* (Guyn). **Guyn *numb-fish*[1]**. A large, snake-like fish, with a dark, slimy body that lives in the rivers of Guyana and Brazil and delivers a shock of 500 volts, if touched.

Electric eel

F

fer-de-lance *noun* (Dmca, StLu, Trin). **Trin *mapepire (balsain)*; StLu *serpent* 2.; Belz *tomagoff*.** A poisonous, brownish snake with a triangular head

Fer-de-lance

and upturned snout that can grow to 6 ft long. (A French phrase meaning 'lance-iron', or 'lance's head', because of the triangular shape and the poisonous strike of its head.)

fid.dler *noun* (Jmca). See SIFFLEUR MONTAGNE.

fine shrimp(s) *noun phrase (plural)* (Guyn). **Guyn *white belly shrimp(s)*.** A variety of tiny, white shrimp, usually caught in large quantities and often dried in small quantities, either in the shell or unshelled.

fla.min.go *noun* (CarA). A large, rose-pink water bird with long, slender legs, a long neck and black-tipped wings.

fly.ing-fish *noun* (CarA). A tropical, Atlantic fish, usually about 9 in. long and of good food value, with well-developed pectoral fins that enable it to rise out of the water and move above it for some distance.

Flying-fish

fork-tail.ed fly-catch.er *noun phrase* (Gren, Tbgo, Trin). A fairly large bird, with two elongated tail feathers, a black crown with a yellow patch, and pale grey back and white underparts.

fri.gate-bird *noun* (CarA). **CarA *man-o-war-bird, scissors-tail.*** A large sea-bird, with a very wide wing span, sometimes up to 7 ft, a hooked beak and a forked tail. The male is entirely black with a

Frigate-bird

bright orange throat pouch and the female is white-breasted, and both are built for long flight over the sea and for seizing fish from other sea-birds.

frog *noun* (CarA). Any one of many insect-eating amphibians, with a short, tailless body, damp, smooth skin and long hind legs, especially adapted to hopping.

gar(r)[1] **(gar.fish)** *noun* (CarA). **Dmca, StLu** ***zòfi***. Any of several varieties of the needlefish family, small, slim and bony fishes with spearlike jaws. Only some of these species are edible.

gar(r)[2] **(gar.fish)** *noun* (CarA). One of some varieties of the BILL-FISH family, large, tough-skinned and with long, spear-like jaws, but of poor food value.

gau.lin *noun* (CarA). See CATTLE-EGRET.

ghost-crab *noun* (Jmca). A small, flattish white crab that lives on the seashore and looks for its food at night, hence its name.

Ghost-crab

gi.ant ant-eat.er *noun phrase* (Guyn). See ANT-BEAR.

gib.nut *noun* (Baha, Belz, Jmca). **Belz, Guyn** ***paca*****; Guyn** ***labba*****; Trin** ***lappe***. A sturdy, brownish, coarse-haired rodent with streaks or rows of white spots along its sides, valued for its meat.

Gibnut

gil.back.er *noun* (Guyn). A large, yellow and grey to bluish-grey scaleless fish of the catfish family, usually caught at the mouths of rivers and prized for its meat.

glass-eye snap.per *noun phrase* (CarA). A large fish with a deep body, large mouth and large eyes, red to silvery-pink in colour, much valued for its meat.

gloss.y cow.bird *noun phrase* (ECar). A glossy black bird with violet tints, whose song is melodious and which lives in dry, open country. It tends to deposit its eggs in other birds' nests.

Glossy cowbird

goat *noun* (CarA). A sturdy, short-haired mammal with horns and (in the male) a beard, highly valued for both its milk and its meat.

goat-fish *noun* (CarA). Any of a few varieties of MULLET, pink, yellowish or spotted, with two long feelers under its mouth, and much valued for its firm flesh.

Goat-fish

god-bird[1] *noun* (Gren, Guyn, StVn). **Gren, Guyn *house-wren***. A small brown bird with black bars on its wings and tail, which is quite noisy; it nests in crevices in walls or buildings, or in the ceilings of houses.

god-bird[2] *noun* (Baha, TkCa). Any one of three or four varieties of green-backed HUMMINGBIRD.

god-horse *noun* (CarA). **Dmca, StLu *chouval-bondyé*; Gren *guava-lobster*; Jmca *duppy-riding-horse***. The green praying-mantis or the brown, wingless stick insect.

God-horse

grass ca.na.ry *noun* (Bdos). A small yellowish-green bird with brownish underparts which lives chiefly in open fields and whose song is shrill and melodious.

grass.hop.per *noun* (CarA). A green or brown jumping insect that lives on plants.

Grasshopper

grass.quit *noun* (CarA). One of a few varieties of sparrow which is either grey, brown, or dark-green, some varieties having white or yellow patches on the neck or head.

grass-snake *noun* (CarA). Any one of a few varieties of small, harmless, non-poisonous brown or green snakes that live on the ground.

great blue he.ron *noun phrase* (CarA). See ARSENICKER.

great.er a.ni *noun phrase* (Trin). A large, black bird, with a deep blue sheen, a ridged, black bill and black feet which has a loud, harsh cry and usually lives near MANGROVE swamps.

great.er An.til.le.an bull-finch *noun phrase* (Baha, Jmca). **Baha, Jmca *cocoa-bird***. A small, black bird, with a red stripe, which makes a harsh *wichi-wichi-wichi* sound then a buzzing screech. It lives in shrubs or low trees.

great white he.ron *noun phrase* (CarA). See WHITE GAULIN.

green-back tur.tle *noun phrase* (CarA). See GREEN TURTLE.

green-chub *noun* (StLu). See CACA-BELLY.

green heron *noun phrase* (CarA). A small, dark-brown and glossy green water-bird, common throughout the Caribbean, where it nests in bushes, trees or bamboo, usually in a swamp.

Green heron

green ho.ney creep.er *noun phrase* (Trin). A small, greenish-blue forest bird which nests high in trees and is generally found in jungle areas.

green hum.ming bird *noun phrase* (CarA). See HUMMINGBIRD.

green king.fish.er *noun phrase* (Tbgo, Trin). A small green and white bird usually found near swamps and trees.

green mon.key *noun phrase* (Bdos, Gren, StKt). **Bdos *Barbados green monkey*.** A fairly large, long-tailed monkey with a brownish-grey coat, mixed with several greenish-yellow hairs, which give it a greenish appearance. It is now considered a pest in the Caribbean.

Green monkey

green-tur.tle (green sea-tur.tle) *noun* (CarA). A large sea-turtle with a smooth, oval-shaped, greenish-brown shell. It can weigh more than 400 lb, and is much prized for its meat for which it is still hunted, although it is illegal to harvest it.

Gre.nada dove *noun phrase* (Gren). A rare species of dove with no markings on its wings which makes a mournful, cooing sound. It is found on the hillsides of southern Grenada.

Grenada dove

grey snap.per *noun* (CarA). A large, edible, greenish-bronze fish with a bluish-black streak that runs from its nose across its eye, and highly valued for its flesh.

Grey snapper

G

gri-gri[1] (gree-gree) *noun* (Gren). See CHICKEN-HAWK.

gri-gri[2] *noun* (Gren). See SPARROW-HAWK.

ground-dove[1] *noun* (CarA). **Baha *tobacco-dove*; Dmca, Gren *toutwèl*.** A small greyish-brown bird with scaly neck and breast feathers; it nests on the ground and hardly flies, it feeds in pairs and makes a constant cooing sound.

ground-dove[2] *noun* (CarA). **Baha, VIls *mourning-dove*; Bdos *wood-dove*; Gren *seaside-dove*; VIls *mountain-dove*.** A hardy, pinkish-brown dove, with black spots on its wings, which has a strong coo, and nests on the ground, usually in open country.

ground-drum.mer *noun* (CarA). A fairly long, greyish-silver fish with faint dark streaks on its sides, found throughout the shallow waters of the Caribbean, but not noted for its food value.

ground-li.zard *noun* (CarA). **Gren *zagada*[1]**. A large lizard with a beak-like snout which wriggles along the ground and never climbs trees.

Ground-lizard

group.er *noun* (CarA). Any one of a number of varieties of large fish found in warm seas and usually prized for their good food value.

grunt *noun* (CarA). Any one of many varieties of medium-sized fish with a red inner mouth and characterized by the grunting sound they make when they are taken out of the water.

gua.bin(e) *noun* (Trin). **Guyn *hoori, huri*.** An edible fresh-water fish found in rivers and swamps, not easily caught because of its slippery belly.

gua.na *noun* (CarA). See IGUANA. □ The /i/ at the beginning of the word is omitted for easier pronunciation.

gua.va-lob.ster *noun* (Gren). See GOD-HORSE.

gui.nea-bird *noun* (Bdos, Guyn, Jmca). A greyish-black bird spotted with white, which lives mainly on the ground, but is sometimes seen in tall trees.

gui.nea-shark *noun* (ECar). A large dark-grey shark, with reddish or green tints on its body and covered in white spots, and a wide tailfin, but said to be harmless to man.

gul.ly-watch.man *noun* (Tbgo). See POND-FLY.

gup.py *noun* (CarA). See MILLIONS-FISH.

hai.ma.ra *noun* (Guyn). A large, edible, fresh-water fish that lives in creeks and ponds which is said to be fierce, but is highly valued for its flesh. (An Amerindian word.)

hair.y worm *noun phrase* (Guyn). A large, yellowish-green caterpillar which is the larva of a type of butterfly; it has hairs at intervals along its body that sting sharply when touched, causing painful, itchy bumps on the skin.

har.py ea.gle *noun phrase* (Guyn). The largest, most powerful eagle in the New World, black in colour, which lives in the jungle and feeds on monkeys, sloths, parrots and macaws.

Harpy eagle

has.sar *noun* (Guyn). See CASCADU. (An Arawak word.)

hawks.bill-(tur.tle) *noun* (CarA). **Grns, USVI** ***carey.*** A large sea-turtle with a small head and hawk-like beak, with multicoloured plates on its back, much prized for both its shell and its meat, and protected by law.

Hawksbill turtle

hedge-hog fish *noun phrase* (CarA). One of several varieties of porcupine fish with spines and able to puff out its body to make its spines more prominent. It is of poor food value.

her.mit-crab *noun* (CarA). See SOLDIER-CRAB.

he.ron *noun* (CarA). Any one of several varieties of large water-birds which live in swamps and marshes.

hind *noun* (CarA). One of a few species of edible fish with a spotted, reddish-brown body.

hog-fish *noun* (CarA). A large, multicoloured fish, mostly amber, reddish and white that can change colour to match its background, with a long mouth and large spines on its back; it is considered to be of good food value.

Hog-fish

ho.ney bee *noun phrase* (CarA). Any four-winged bee which collects nectar and pollen, produces wax and honey and lives in large colonies.

hoo.ri (hu.ri) *noun* (Guyn). See GUABIN(E). (An Arawak word.)

hop.ping dick *noun phrase* (Jmca). **Jmca** ***chick-man-chick, jumping dick***. A well-known Jamaican thrush, grey and white in colour, with a prominent white spot on its wing. It is usually seen on roadsides, with its tail up, it nests in wooded areas and gardens and its song is like that of the European blackbird.

H

horse.fly *noun* (CarA). A large fly with a big head and wide body, known to suck the blood of some mammals and horses, hence its name.

house-fly *noun* (CarA). A common fly with a single pair of wings often found in human habitations. It lays it eggs in filth and often spreads disease.

house-wren *noun* (Gren, Guyn). See GOD-BIRD[1].

howl.ing mon.key *noun phrase* (Guyn). A large monkey, the male of the species having a huge neck and throat which enables it to make loud howling noises, hence its name.

Howling monkey

hum.ming.bird *noun* (CarA). **CarA *green hummingbird***. Any one of several species of small, brightly coloured birds, known by the low buzzing or humming of their wings as they fly rapidly from flower to flower.

Hummingbird

I

i.gua.na *noun* (CarA). **Belz *bamboo-chicken***. Either of two large tropical American tree-lizards, with a greyish-green body, a row of spines along the back and a large hanging dewlap under its head. It is prized for its meat.

Iguana

In.di.an rab.bit *noun phrase* (Belz). See AGOUTI.

J

jack[3]; jack-fish *noun* (CarA). A small fish resembling a herring.

Jack Span.i.ard *noun phrase* (ECar). **Dmca, StLu *djèp*; Gren *maribone*; Guyn *marabunta***. An aggressive reddish-brown wasp with a sharp sting. It usually nests in eaves and trees.

Jack Spaniard wasp

ja.guar *noun* (Guyn). A huge large wild cat with a massive body and a darkish yellow coat with black spots, which feeds on other animals, both wild and domestic.

ja.ko (par.rot)[1] (Jac.quot) *noun (phrase)* (Dmca). **Dmca *red-necked parrot***. A small, green parrot with a red patch on its neck which is native to Dominica. (French *Jacquot*, the equivalent of English 'Polly' as a pet name for a parrot.)

ja.ko (par.rot)[2] (Jac.quot) *noun (phrase)* (StLu). See ST LUCIA PARROT.

jel.ly.fish *noun* (CarA). A small sea creature with a soft, jelly-like umbrella-shaped body and sharp stinging tentacles.

Jew-fish (dew-fish) *noun* (CarA). A huge, edible brownish fish of excellent food value, with a broad mouth. It can easily be caught because it is extrememly sluggish and lies on the sea bed.

Jew-fish

John Crow *noun phrase* (Belz, Jmca). See CARRION-CROW.

jig.ger *noun* (CarA). See CHIG(G)AH.

jum.bie-bird[1] *noun* (Guyn). **Baha *death-bird*; Jmca *white-owl*; Trin *barn-owl***. A long-legged, mostly white owl which gives a piercing cry as it hunts its prey at night, hence its association with death.

jum.bie-bird[2] *noun* (Trin). **Trin *pygmy-owl***. A small, brown owl with white underparts and white spots on its wings; it makes a whistling sound, but is rarely seen.

jum.bie-bird[3] *noun* (Guyn). **Baha *dead-people bird, rain-crow*; Baha, Jmca Gren *merle-corbeau*; Guyn *ani, blackbird*; Guyn, Trin *old-witch*; Jmca, Trin *tick-bird*; VIls *black-witch***. A large, jet black bird with a long tail and a black bill. It gives a mournful cry as it flies and it usually gathers in open places near cemeteries, and feeds on insects and cattle parasites.

jump.ing dick *noun phrase* (Jmca). See HOPPING DICK.

ka.bou.ro(-fly) (ca.bou.ra, ka.bou.ra, ka.boo.ri) *noun* (Guyn). A grey fly commonly found in the interior of Guyana, especially in the wet season. Its bite causes a painful skin infection. (An Arawak word.)

ka.bwit[1] (ca.brit) *noun* (Dmca, StLu, USVI). **USVI *cabrita***. A goat. (French Creole from French *cabri* 'a young goat'.)

ka.bwit[2] (ca.brit) *noun* (StLu). See COW-FISH. (See KABWIT[1]. This fish has two small horns above its eyes.)

ka.ka.ba.wi *noun* (Dmca, Gren, StLu). See CACA-BELLY.

ka.wang *noun* (Dmca). See COBBLER.

kes.ki.dee *noun* (Tbgo, Trin). See KISKADEE.

kil.li-kil.li *noun* (Antg, Mrat, USVI). See SPARROW-HAWK.

king-fish (king.fish) *noun* (CarA). **Trin *king-mackerel***. A long round-shaped fish

K

with a dark grey back, becoming silvery at its sides and white on its belly; its meat is highly valued.

king-fish.er *noun* (CarA). A fairly large bird with a slate-blue crest and a white spot in front of its eyes; it has a harsh cry and is found in coastal areas, rivers, lakes and lagoons.

kis.ka.dee (kes.ki.dee) *noun* (Guyn, Tbgo, Trin). A medium-sized bird with a brownish back, a white throat, a yellow breast and underparts, and a black head around which there is a prominent white stripe above the eye. It is known for its call, which gives the bird its name.

Kiskadee

L

kling-kling[1] *noun* (Jmca). See BLACKBIRD[1].

kling-kling[2] *noun* (Guyn). A small, green parrot, found largely in the forests of South America.

kou.wès (snake) (cou.wès) *noun (phrase)* (Dmca, StLu). A non-venomous, slim, green snake with black and white markings on its back.

kre.ke.teh-hawk *noun* (Guyn). A dark-coloured hawk, the male of which has a largely white tail-base and it feeds on snails and hunts in swamps.

ku.rass (cui.rass) *noun* (Guyn). A medium-sized catfish found in tidal estuaries with poisonous spines on its pectoral and dorsal fins. It is of fair food value, especially when caught and cooked immediately.

kwa.byé (crab.i.er) *noun* (Crcu, Dmca, Gren). See GAULIN. (French Creole word meaning 'crab-catcher'.)

kwa.byé nwè (crab.i.er noir) *noun phrase* (Dmca, Gren, StLu). See ARSE-NICKER. (French Creole.)

L

la.ba.ri.a *noun* (Guyn). A poisonous dark-coloured, spotted snake whose bite is fatal. (An Arawak word.)

lab.ba *noun* (Guyn). See GIBNUT. (An Arawak word.)

la.belle *noun* (Dmca). See CANDLE-FLY. (French Creole word from French *la belle* 'beautiful one' (feminine).)

lamp-fly *noun* (StKt). See CANDLE-FLY.

lamp-light.er *noun* (Baha). See CANDLE-FLY.

land-ca.moo.di *noun* (Guyn). See MACAJUEL.

lappe *noun* (Trin). See GIBNUT. (Maybe from French *lapin* 'rabbit'.)

lea.ther-back tur.tle *noun phrase* (CarA). The largest member of the sea-turtle family, whose ridged shell looks like leather.

Leather-black turtle

lea.ther-bat *noun* (Bdos). See BAT[1].

li.on-fish *noun* (Bdos, Brbu, Mrat). See SCORPION-FISH.

liz.ard *noun* (CarA). A general term for any reptile, some small, some larger with an elongated, scaly body, four legs and a long tail.

lob.ster *noun* (CarA). A crustacean with a rounded shell, spines of various sizes, a pair of sharp horns over its eyes, long stiff antennae, and a powerful fan-shaped tail. It is prized for its food value. □ A different species from the lobsters of North and South America which have powerful claws.

lo.cust *noun* (CarA). A variety of African or Asian grasshopper which destroys vegetation.

Locust

log.ger-head[1] (tur.tle) *noun (phrase)* (CarA). A large sea-turtle with a big head and a reddish-brown, heart-shaped shell. It is of good food value.

log.ger-head[2] *noun* (Angu, Baha, CayI, Jmca). A member of the KINGBIRD family with a greyish-brown back, a yellow crown-patch and white or grey-tipped tail.

long-tail doc.tor bird *noun phrase* (Jmca). See DOCTOR-BIRD.

lu.ku.na.ni *noun* (Guyn). A large, fresh-water fish with small, yellowish scales and spots on the sides and tail, highly valued for its flesh. (Maybe Arawak *lokanañ* 'fresh-water scaled fish with a yellow breast'.)

ma.bou.ya *noun* (Dmca). See WOOD-SLAVE. (Maybe a Carib word.)

ma.ca.juel *noun* (Trin). **Guyn *land-camoodi*** . The BOA CONSTRICTOR, a huge snake that can grow well over 20 ft in length. (Probably from a Carib language.) This is a different snake from the ANACONDA which is also known as a ***water-camoodi***.

Macajuel snake

ma.caw[1] *noun* (CarA). Any of a number of large birds of the parrot family, which has a long tail and is usually multicoloured with a combination of red, yellow, blue and green. It is native to South America, but is found in many Caribbean islands.

Macaw

ma.caw[2](-chub) *noun* (Antg). See BLUE PARROTFISH.

ma.cla.la *noun* (Belz). Any of several types of lizards of different sizes and colours.

ma.hi-ma.hi *noun* (Bdos). See DOLPHIN.

mai.pu.ri *noun* (Guyn). See TAPIR.

ma.ko.ké-glo *noun* (Dmca). See POND-FLY.

mal.fi.ni *noun* (StLu). See CHICKEN-HAWK.

ma.na.tee (ma.na.ti) *noun* (Antg. Belz, Guyn, Jmca). **Guyn *water-cow*; Guyn, Jmca *sea-cow*.** A huge, sluggish, harmless, greyish-black aquatic mammal with flappers and a broad, flat, round tail. It usually inhabits coastal waters and river estuaries.

Manatee

man.grove-cuck.oo *noun* (CarA). See RAIN-BIRD[2].

ma.ni.cou (ma.na.koo) *noun* (Dmca, Gren, StVn, Trin). **Guyn *yawari*.** A brown, coarse-haired nocturnal rodent about the size of a cat, with a conically shaped head, a pig-like snout and big ears and eyes. It eats chickens and its flesh is considered a delicacy by some. (Maybe a Carib name.)

Manicou

man-o-war-bird *noun* (CarA). See FRIGATE-BIRD.

ma.pe.pire bal.sain *noun phrase* (ECar). See FER-DE-LANCE.

ma.pe.pire za.na.na *noun phrase* (Trin). See BUSHMASTER.

ma.ra.bun.ta *noun* (Guyn). See JACK SPANIARD.

mar.gate (fish) (mar.ga.ret/mar.get/ mar.gret (fish)) *noun (phrase)* (Angu, Baha, BrVI, Mrat, TkCa). An edible, deep water fish usually light-grey in colour, of the GRUNT family, much prized for its tasty flesh.

ma.ri.bone *noun* (Gren). See JACK-SPANIARD.

Ma.rie-su.cer *noun* (StLu). See MAWI-SOSÉ. (French Creole.)

mar.lin *noun* (CarA). See BLUE MARLIN, WHITE MARLIN.

ma.son-ma.ra.bun.ta *noun* (Guyn). **Guyn *mud-dauber*.** A yellow wasp with brown wings, which builds small separate mud nests in houses.

ma.wi-so.sé (Ma.rie su.cer) *noun* (StLu). See POND-FLY. (French Creole.)

merle-cor.beau *noun* (Trin). See JUMBIE-BIRD[1]. (French *merle* 'blackbird' + *corbeau* 'crow' together meaning a bird of ill omen.)

mi.cy-bat *noun* (Antg). See BAT **2**.

mil.lions(-fish) *noun* (CarA). **CarA *guppy*.** A variety of tiny, freshwater fish.

mon.goose *noun* (CarA). A small, meat-eating mammal with a long, slim body, and a long tail, well-known for its ability to kill snakes.

mon.key *noun* (CarA). Any of the members of the families identified including both Old World and New World primates.

Mont.ser.rat o.ri.ole *noun phrase* (Mrat). A medium-sized, mostly black bird with a yellow breast and rump. It lives largely in the mountain forests of Montserrat and is the national bird of that island.

mo.ro.coy *noun* (Dmca, Gren, Trin) **CarA** ***red-legged tortoise***. A large, slow-moving land turtle, prized for its meat and its shell. (From South American Spanish *morrocoyo* 'turtle'.)

Morocoy turtle

mos.qui.to *noun* (CarA). Any of several tiny, biting insects, the female of which punctures the skin of other animals and sucks their blood, thereby transmitting diseases such as malaria.

moth *noun* (CarA). Any variety of nocturnal flying insect, some of which are harmful to clothing.

mot.mot *noun* (Gren, Tbgo, Trin). A fairly large forest bird with a striking, long, blue tail; it is a forest bird which is known by several names such as *king-of-the-woods* or *bouhoutou*.

moun.tain-chick.en *noun* (Dmca, Mrat). A large, brown, smooth-skinned frog, usually found on mountain slopes, and prized for its meat.

Mountain-chicken

moun.tain-dove *noun* (VIls). See GROUND-DOVE[2].

mud-daub.er *noun* (Guyn). See MASON-MARABUNTA.

mul.let *noun* (CarA). An edible silver-coloured or striped fish, which is caught in nets and found either in fresh water or shallow salt-water. It is prized for its fine food value.

Mus.co.vy duck *noun phrase* (Trin). A large brownish or black duck with a purple back and rump, greenish wings, white underparts and feet, which lives in marshy swamps and is native to Trinidad.

Muscovy duck

mut.ton fish (mut.ton snap.per) *noun phrase* (CarA). A colourful edible fish with a narrow blue streak from its nostril to its eye, prized for its good food value.

M

N

nee.dle-case *noun* (Belz, Jmca). See POND-FLY.

nee.dle-fish *noun* (Baha, Dmca). See GAR-FISH.

night-bat *noun* (Bdos). See BAT[1].

night-hawk *noun* (Baha, CayI, USVI). A medium-sized bird with long, narrow, white-banded wings, usually seen flying late in the evening; it lives in open country.

night-li.zard *noun* (USVI). See WOOD-SLAVE.

numb-fish[1] *noun* (Guyn). See ELECTRIC EEL.

numb-fish[2] *noun* (Guyn). See SCORPION-FISH.

nurse shark *noun phr* (CarA). A large shark found in warm seas, which is not usually aggressive, but will fight back if provoked.

Nurse shark

O

o.cean-gar *noun* (ECar). See BILL-FISH.

o.ce.lot *noun* (Guyn). A large tawny to grey wild cat, covered in dark spots and longish paler black-rimmed spots, which is extremely aggressive and attacks poultry, pigs, etc.

Ocelot

oc.to.pus *noun* (CarA). A sea creature with eight arms, a soft body and strong beak-like jaws.

old-witch *noun* (Guyn, Trin). See JUMBIE-BIRD[3].

old-wife *noun* (CarA). **Baha, Jmca, TkCa *turbot*; Dmca, StLu *bous(s)e*; StLu *queen-triggerfish*.** A pinkish fish with bluish fins, a yellow jaw and blue stripes running from its nose and of excellent food value.

ot.ter *noun* (Guyn). **Guyn *water-dog*.** An amphibious animal like a large dog with a large, flattish head, short ears, webbed toes and a long flattened tail which lives chiefly in rivers and lakes and feeds mostly on fish.

Otter

P

pa.ca *noun* (Belz, Guyn). See GIBNUT. (A South American Indian name, probably a word in the Tupi language.)

palm-fly *noun* (Guyn). See POND-FLY.

pa.ra.keet *noun* (USVI). A medium-sized blue and yellow bird, found largely in woods and bushy thickets in the hills.

pa.ra.sol-ant *noun* (Trin). See ACCOUSHI-ANT.

par.gy (par.gie) *noun* (ECar). **Belz, Guyn, StVn *paggie*.** One of several varieties of small, silvery fish of the PORGY family; they swim in shoals near the shore and are easily caught.

par.rot *noun* (CarA). Any one of a number of green, tropical birds, that live on fruit, have a short, hooked beak, and are capable of imitating the human voice. They are usually kept as pets.

Parrot

par.rot-fish *noun* (CarA). See CHUB[1].

pat.wa (pat.ua, pot.wa) *noun* (Guyn). A freshwater fish, green with creamish spots, which lives in canals and trenches; though bony, it is considered to be of good food value. (An Amerindian name.)

pec.ca.ry *noun* (Belz, Guyn). **Belz *wari*; Guyn *bush-hog, wild hog*; Trin *quenk*.** A type of wild pig with no tail, and a gland on its back which contains an unpleasant smelling liquid. It is usually hunted for its meat.

peel-neck fowl *noun phrase* (Belz, Guyn. Jmca). See BARE-NECK FOWL.

pee.ny-wal.ly *noun* (Jmca). See CANDLE-FLY.

pee-whist.ler *noun* (Bdos, CayI, ViIs). A small, dark-greyish and yellow bird, known for its harsh whistle.

pi.lot-fish *noun* (Jmca). See SERGEANT-MAJOR.

pink conch *noun phrase* (CarA). See CONCH.

pi.ran.ha *noun* (CarA). **Guyn *pirai*.** A fierce flesh-eating fish, with strong, sharp-edged jaws that can devour larger fish and other sea creatures, as well as humans.

Piranha

pi.si.ette *noun* (StLu). See ANCHOVY.

pond-fly *noun* (Bdos, Guyn). **BrVI *Auntie Nannee*; Dmca *makoké-glo, souse-glo*; Guyn *palm-fly*; Jmca *needlecase*; StLu *mawi-sosé*; Tbgo *gully-watchman*; Tbgo, Trin *batimanmzèl*.** The dragon fly.

por.cu.pine fish *noun phrase* (CarA). A pale whitish fish tinged with green, whose body and fins are covered with many long spines.

por.gy *noun* (CarA). A silvery reef fish with blue-green spots which feeds on crabs, worms, and molluscs.

por.poise *noun* (CarA). See BOTTLENOSE DOLPHIN.

Por.tu.guese man-of-war *noun* (CarA). A poisonous JELLY-FISH which has a dangerous sting.

Portuguese man-of-war

pow.is *noun* (Guyn). A large, black and white forest bird which lives mostly on the gound in dense forest and is largely hunted for its meat.

prawn *noun* (CarA). A large shrimp, much used in Caribbean cooking.

pu.ma *noun* (Guyn). A large tan-coloured cat with a long tail, said to be usually friendly to man.

pur.ple gal.li.nule *noun phrase* (Trin). A mainly purple bird usually found in freshwater swamps and near reservoirs.

pur.ple mar.tin *noun phrase* (Baha, CayI, Tbgo). A large swallow which lives mainly in towns, but also on sea cliffs and in open country; it is a migrant in the Caribbean.

pyg.my-owl *noun* (Tbgo, Trin). See JUMBIE-BIRD[2].

Q

queen bee *noun phrase* (CarA). The fertile female in a beehive.

queen-trig.ger.fish *noun* (StLu). See OLD WIFE.

quenk *noun* (Trin). See PECCARY.

quer.i.man *noun* (Guyn). A large, edible grey fish of the MULLET family highly valued for its rich flesh. (From an Arawak word *kereme*, the name of this fish.)

R

rain-bird[1] *noun* (CarA). **Baha *chinchary*; Guyn *thrush*.** A greyish and white bird, known for its loud cry, which catches insects as it flies, nests in high places and attacks other birds.

rain-bird[2] *noun* (CarA). **CarA *mangrove-cuckoo*; Dmca *rain-crow*; Dmca, Gren *cuckoo-manioc*.** A medium-sized, brownish-grey and yellow bird with a harsh cry which lives in MANGROVE swamps and woodlands.

rain-bird[3] *noun* (Gren, StLu). See CIGALE.

rain-fly *noun* (CarA). **Bdos, Jmca** ***flying ant***. A brownish termite that swarms in wet weather, usually at dusk.

rat-bat *noun* (Belz, Jmca, Mrat). See BAT **2**.

red-ant *noun* (CarA). A reddish-brown ant with an unusually sharp bite, found in several different varieties in the Caribbean.

red-fish *noun* (Bdos, Mrat, StVn). See RED-SNAPPER.

red-hind *noun* (Dmca, Gren, Jmca, USVI). A reddish-brown fish with tiny scarlet dots that thrives in Atlantic waters and is considered to be of good food value.

Red-hind

red-leg.ged tor.toise *noun phrase* (CarA). See MOROCOY.

red-neck.ed par.rot *noun phrase* (Dmca). See JAKO (PARROT).

red-neck.ed pi.geon *noun phrase* (Jmca). **ECar** ***ramier(-pigeon)***. A dark slate-grey pigeon with a wine-coloured head, neck and chest, and red feet and bill, which lives mostly in humid rain forest, and makes a cooing sound.

red-snap.per *noun* (CarA). **Bdos** ***red-fish*****; Bdos, Mrat, Nevs** ***brim***. A large, fleshy, deep red fish found mostly in Atlantic waters and of excellent food value.

re.mo.ra *noun* (CarA). A dark-coloured fish with a vacuum cap on the top of its head which enables it to attach itself to other fish.

ro.bin *noun* (Angu, Gren, Nevs, StVn). A small, brownish-yellow fish with a pointed mouth and protruding eyes which frequents grassy shallows where shrimp trawlers operate.

rock-fish *noun* (Baha, Berm, CayI). A large, edible, olive-greenish deep-sea fish of the GROUPER family.

Rock-fish

rock-hind *noun* (CarA). A medium-sized, tawny-coloured reef fish with reddish-brown spots and prized for its good food value

round ro.bin *noun phrase* (Gren, StLu). A slender, edible, greenish-blue fish, of good food value.

roy.al tern *noun phrase* (CarA). A tern with a large orange bill, black feet, a moderately forked tail and long black feathers on its head; it nests in colonies and feeds on small fish.

Royal tern

run.ning ant *noun phrase* (Bdos, Guyn, Jmca). See SUGAR-ANTS.

R

S

sa.ki.win.ki (sack.i.win.kie) *noun* (Guyn, Trin). **Guyn** ***squirrel-monkey***. A small, olive-grey monkey with golden coloured arms and a black-tipped tail, which gives a bird-like scream when startled and is valued as a pet. (From Dutch *sagwijntje* 'a small South American monkey'.)

Sakiwinki monkey

sa.li.pen.ta (sa.lam.pen.ta, sa.lem.pen.ter, sa.li.paint.er) *noun* (Guyn, Tbgo, Trin). A yellowish-brown lizard-like reptile, with black bands on its body and dark spots on its legs. It feeds on chickens, young birds and eggs.

sand-fly *noun* (ECar). Any of many tiny, biting flies whose sting leaves a dark spot on the skin. It is normally found on beaches or other wet, sandy places.

sca.ly-breast.ed thrash.er *noun phrase* (CarA). A small, greyish-brown and white bird with a black bill which dwells in forested areas and semi-arid woodland. Its call is similar to that of a mocking-bird but softer.

scar.let i.bis *noun phrase* (Tbgo, Trin). **Guyn** ***curri-curri***. A large, scarlet swamp bird with black wing tips and a large black bill with pink legs and feet; the national bird of Trinidad & Tobago.

scis.sors-tail *noun* (CarA). See FRIGATE-BIRD.

scor.pi.on *noun* (CarA). Any member of this species with a segmented body and tail ending in a curved, poisonous sting.

scor.pi.on-fish *noun* (CarA) **CarA** ***stone-fish*****; Bdos, Brbu, Mrat** ***lion-fish*****; CayI** ***numb-fish***[2]**; Gren, StKt** ***twenty-four hour(s)***. One of several varieties of fish with big eyes at the top of its head, sharp gills and many highly poisonous spines sticking out of its head or dorsal fins. The spines can cause paralysis and death within 24 hours if the fish is stepped on.

Scorpion fish

sea-bat *noun* (Guyn). See DEVIL-FISH.

sea-cat *noun* (ECar). A small variety of octopus.

sea-cow *noun* (CarA). See MANATEE.

sea-egg *noun* (Bdos, Gren). The white sea-urchin, whose roe is much prized as a delicacy.

see-see bird *noun phrase* (Gren). See BANANAQUIT.

semp *noun* (Trin). A small bird, the male of which has a violet-blue back and an orange-yellow belly, with the female being generally greenish. It is popular as a cage bird and valued for its melodious song. (French Creole from French *simple* 'simple', maybe because it is easily caught.)

ser.geant-ma.jor *noun* (Baha, Jmca, StLu). **Jmca *pilot-fish*.** A small yellow fish with black bars which lives near docks and coral reefs and can change colour to blend in with its surroundings.

ser.pent[1] *noun* (Gren). See TREE BOA.

ser.pent[2] *noun*(StLu). See FER DE LANCE.

shell-fish[1] *noun* (CarA). Any of a number of shell-covered molluscs like oysters, or shrimp, crab, etc.

shell-fish[2] *noun* (ECar). See COW-FISH.

sher.i.ga/go *noun* (ECar). A dark-coloured, oval-shaped crab with a flat back and a hard shell, which dwells in shallow coastal waters, river-beds or marshy areas and is of poor food value.

shrimp(s) *noun (plural)* (CarA). Any of several small edible whitish or grey-green crustaceans with ten legs, which becomes pinkish when cooked.

sif.fleur mon.tagne (sif.flé-mon.tany) *noun phrase* (Dmca). **Jmca *fiddler*; StVn *Soufrière bird*.** A small, mostly grey bird with a red breast and yellow feet which dwells mostly in mountain-valleys and is famous for its flute-like whistle. (French Creole from French *siffleur de montagne* 'mountain whistler'.)

sik.yé-bird *noun* (Trin). **(su.cri.er-bird)**. See BANANAQUIT.

sis.ser.ou (par.rot) *noun (phrase)* (Dmca). A large dark green, bluish-green and violet parrot native to Dominica. It is that country's national bird.

six o'clock bee.tle *noun phrase* (Guyn). A large beetle-like insect which is known for making a high-pitched, screeching noise around nightfall, hence the name.

skin.fish *noun* (Guyn). See CATFISH.

skip.jack tu.na *noun phrase* (CarA). A dark bluish-purple fish with bands running lengthways down its body, not considered to be of good food value, although it is often sold canned or frozen.

slave-li.zard *noun* (Bdos, Trin). See WOOD-SLAVE.

slip.pery-back *noun* (Angu, BrVI). A shiny, fairly long black ground lizard.

sloth *noun* (Guyn). See TWO-TOED SLOTH, THREE-TOED SLOTH.

snail *noun* (CarA). One of several land molluscs with a spirally coiled shell, especially destructive to garden plants.

snap.per *noun* (CarA). **Bdos Mrat, StVn *red-fish*.** One of several deep-water fishes which feeds on small fishes and shrimp and are found in different colours, (red, grey, etc.). They are much prized for their good food value.

snook *noun* (CarA). A long, slender brownish-green deep-sea fish with a silvery belly and a black line running from gill to tail, prized for its delicate, flaky flesh.

sol.dier-ant (s) *noun (plural)* (Trin). See ARMY-ANT(S).

sol.dier-crab *noun* (CarA). A type of HERMIT-CRAB that covers itself with the shell of a larger mollusc.

soot.y tern *noun phrase* (CarA). A fairly large black and white bird with a forked tail, whose cry is shrill, usually found near tropical seas.

sou.flet *noun* (StLu). See TRUMPET-FISH.

Sou.frière bird *noun phrase* (StVn). See SIFFLEUR MONTAGNE.

sou.sé-glo *noun* (Dmca). See POND-FLY.

Span.ish mack.er.el *noun phrase* (Angu, Antg, Bdos, Gren, Guyn). See CARITE.

spar.row(-bird) *noun* (Angu, Bdos, Dmca, Mrat, USVI). A small, dark-coloured or greyish-brown bird with a reddish-brown chin and throat and thin legs, which hops about homes and gardens; it has a short shrill cry and feeds on crumbs, fruit, insects, etc.

spar.row-hawk *noun* (CarA). **Angu, Mrat, USVI** ***killi-killi*****; Gren** ***gri-gri***[2]. A small reddish-brown hawk with a black belly and black bars around its eyes; it lives on lizards, bats and chickens.

Sparrow-hawk

S

spi.der *noun* (CarA). An eight-legged creature with a round body which spins webs in order to capture insects as food.

spoon-bill *noun* (CarA). A large, pinkish bird usually found in swamps and lagoons.

squid *noun* (CarA). An edible, dangerous, dark-coloured sea creature with triangular tail fins and claw-like feelers, which can inflict deep wounds while the inky liquid it squirts can harm the eyes.

squir.rel.fish *noun* (CarA). A pink or reddish reef-fish with large dark eyes; it is of fine food value, comparable to that of the RED-SNAPPER.

sting.ray *noun* (ECar). A dangerous fish covered in small spines ending in a large, poisonous spine in the tail, usually found on the bottom of river beds and able to inflict serious wounds.

stink bug *noun phrase* (Guyn). A green insect with a back shaped like a shield which lives on trees, can get indoors and has a particularly unpleasant smell.

St Lu.cia par.rot *noun phrase* (StLu). A green parrot with a bluish head, a maroon belly and a red patch on its wing; it is the only parrot found in St Lucia and is the national bird of that island.

St Lucia parrot

stone-fish *noun* (CarA). See SCORPION-FISH.

stream.er-tail *noun* (Jmca). See DOCTOR-BIRD **2**.

St Vin.cent par.rot *noun phrase* (StVn). A large, colourful parrot which is the only parrot found in St Vincent and is that island's national bird.

su.gar-ant(s) *noun* (Bdos, Gren, Guyn, Jmca). **Bdos, Guyn, Jmca** r***unning-ants***. A small blackish-red ant that gets into any sweet item, especially sugar, in large quantities, many of them running in different directions.

su.gar-bird *noun* (Bdos, USVI). See BANANAQUIT.

T

tac-tac (tak-tak) *noun* (Dmca). See ACCOUSHI-ANT.

ta.pir *noun* (Guyn). **Guyn** ***bush-cow, maipuri, wild cow.*** A stout, clumsy-looking mammal with hooves, resembling a donkey, but with a long snout and short ears; it is hunted for its meat.

ta.ran.tu.la[1] *noun* (Guyn, Trin) **Trin** ***black spider***; **StKt** ***donkey-spider.*** A large, black, hairy spider with a poisonous bite.

ta.ran.tu.la[2] *noun* (Guyn, Trin). A large, black hairy spider whose bite is poisonous and severely painful, but not fatal.

tar.pon *noun* (Baha, BrVI, Guyn, Trin, USVI). A large, long, silvery blue fish which is noted for leaping high into the air when hooked.

ta.tu *noun* (Dmca, Gren). See ARMADILLO.

ten-pound.er *noun* (Antg, Brbu, Mrat, Nevs). A bony, greenish-silver fish of poor food value, which leaps into the air as soon as it is hooked.

tèt-chien (tête-chien) *noun* (Dmca, StLu). A black, non-poisonous snake of the BOA family, with a head like a dog's which is known to feed on rats. (French Creole from French *tête* 'head' + *chien* 'dog', so 'dog head'.)

thrash.er *noun* (Baha). A grey and white bird, known for its melodious song and for being a good mimic.

three-toed sloth *noun phrase* (Guyn). A slow, clumsy mammal with rough, coarse, grey and black hair, the male having a bright orange patch between its shoulders; it is usually found in the forest.

thrush *noun* (Guyn). See RAIN-BIRD[1].

tick-bird[1] *noun* (Jmca). See JUMBIE-BIRD[3].

tick-bird[2] *noun* (Trin). See CATTLE-EGRET.

ti.la.pi.a *noun* (Guyn, Trin). A herb-eating fresh-water fish much prized for its food value.

ti.ti.ri(e) (ti.ti.ree, tree-tree, tri-tri) *noun* (Dmca, Gren, StVn). Tiny fish which are caught in large numbers especially in rivers between June and August, and generally sun-dried for food.

toe-nail fish *noun phrase* (Guyn). See CASCADU.

to.bac.co-dove *noun* (Baha). See GROUND-DOVE[1].

tom.a.goff (tom.i.goff, Tom.my Goff) *noun* (Belz). See FER-DE-LANCE. (Maybe from Latin American Spanish *tamagá(s)* 'very poisonous snake of Honduras and Costa Rica'. See *Santeria Diccionario general de americanismos.*)

to.ro[1] *noun* (Guyn). See CAVALLI.

tout.wèl (tour.te.relle) *noun* (Dmca, Gren). See GROUND-DOVE[1].

tree-boa *noun* (Gren). **Gren** ***serpent*** **1.** A snake about 6 ft long, with a yellowish-brown back and yellow belly.

trig.ger.fish *noun* (Baha. Dmca, Gren, Jmca). See OLD-WIFE.

tree-duck *noun* (Trin). See WICISSI-DUCK.

tri-tri *noun* (StVn). See TITIRI(E).

trop.ic bird *noun* (CarA). A large, mostly white ocean bird with a red bill and noted for two noticably long shaft-like tail feathers; it feeds on squids and fish and its wing span is longer than its length.

trum.pet-fish *noun* (CarA). **StLu** ***souflet***. A bony reef fish with a trumpet-like mouth which feeds on tiny fishes.

tu.na *noun* (CarA). Any one of a variety of stout-bodied fish, well known for fighting against being caught, and of excellent food value.

T

tur.bot *noun* (Baha, Jmca, TkCa). See OLD-WIFE.

tur.tle *noun* (CarA). Any of several marine or fresh water reptiles whose body is protected by a shell of bony plates, and which have flippers and webbed toes for swimming.

twen.ty-four hours *noun phrase* (StKt). See SCORPION-FISH.

two-toed sloth *noun phrase* (Guyn). An animal about the size of a large dog with a shorter, smoother coat than the THREE-TOED SLOTH, chocolate-brown in colour, with arms ending in two long claws and exceedingly fierce when disturbed.

Two-toed sloth

um.brel.la-ant(s) *noun (plural)* (Belz, Guyn). See ACCOUSHI-ANT(S).

vam.pire (bat) *noun (phrase)* (Guyn). A member of the BAT family with a wide wing span and distinguished from other bats because of its extremely sharp front teeth which can cut through the skin like a razor; it sucks the blood of other animals.

vi.cis.si-duck *noun* (Guyn). See WICISSI-DUCK.

wa.hoo *noun* (CarA). A large, powerful ocean fish with a dark greenish-blue back and silver sides and belly, often confused with the KING-FISH.

wa.ri *noun* (Belz). See PECCARY.

wa.ter-cow *noun* (Guyn). See MANATEE.

wa.ter-dog *noun* (Belz, Guyn). A species of OTTER that is brownish-black, looks like a dog, eats fish and has webbed feet.

wa.ter-haas *noun* (Guyn). **Guyn *water-hare***. A large, amphibious rodent with hoofed legs, usually hunted for its meat.

wee.vil *noun* (CarA). A tiny insect that infests products made of wheat, such as flour, breadcrumbs, pasta, etc.

whale *noun* (CarA). Any of the larger mammals of this species which breathes air through a blowhole on its head.

whelk *noun* (TkCa, USVI). See WILK.

whis.tling duck *noun phrase* (Baha, Trin). See WICISSI-DUCK.

whis.tling frog *noun phrase* (CarA). A tiny brown frog with padded feet, known for its loud whistle at night, especially during the rainy season.

white-bel.ly shrimp *noun phrase* (Guyn). See FINE SHRIMP(S).

white-crown.ed pi.geon *noun phrase* (CarA). A dark-grey pigeon, with a white crown, found in the Caribbean islands and along the Caribbean Sea coast, as well as in Central America.

white e.gret *noun phrase* (Angu, Bdos, Jmca). See CATTLE-EGRET.

white gau.lin *noun phrase* (Angu, Dmca, Gren, USVI). A name loosely given to the CATTLE EGRET and other herons.

white mar.lin *noun phrase* (Baha, Berm, VIls). A bluish-black and silver fish of the BILL-FISH family and of poor food value.

white slave *noun phrase* (Bdos). See WOOD-SLAVE.

wi.chi-wi.chi *noun* (Trin). See WICISSI-DUCK.

wi.cis.si-duck (vi.cis.si, wi.si-wi.si-duck) *noun* (Guyn). **Guyn *tree-duck, whistling duck*; Trin *wichiwichi*.** Any of two types of water-bird with webbed feet, a white face, multi-coloured body and pink legs; it moves in flocks whistling as they go.

wild cow *noun phrase* (Guyn). See TAPIR.

wild hog/pig *noun phrase* (Guyn, Trin). See PECCARY.

wilk(s) (whelk(s), whilk(s)) *noun (plural)* (CarA). **Gren, StLu *brigo*.** An edible sea-snail, considered a delicacy and much sold in the Caribbean.

wind.ward sprat *n phr* (StVn). See ANCHOVY.

wood-lice *noun plural* (CarA). **CarA *wood-ants*.** A small black and white or brownish ANT, known to destroy wood or items made of wood.

wood-peck.er *noun* (Baha, CayI). A medium-sized bird with a black and white barred back and a red belly, usually found in wooded areas and groves.

wood-slave *noun* (ECar). **Bdos *white slave*; Bdos, Trin *slave-lizard*; Dmca, StLu *mabouya*; Trin *zagada*[2]; USVI *night-lizard*.** A type of gecko or house lizard with pale, translucent skin and padded toes, which moves alarmingly fast with a snake-like wriggle.

ya(c)k.man *noun* (Guyn). **1.** ARMY-ANT(S).

ya.war.rie *noun* (Guyn). See MANICOU.

yel.low-breast *noun* (Antg, Bdos, USVI). See BANANAQUIT.

yel.low-crown.ed night he.ron *noun phrase* (CarA). A large grey bird with black streaks on its back and long yellow legs which lives mostly in swamps, but is often found far from the water.

yel.low-fin tu.na *noun* (CarA). A large, ocean fish with yellow fins, prized for its flesh.

yel.low-tail(-snap.per) *noun* (CarA). A species of small SNAPPER, with a prominent yellow stripe which widens as it reaches its forked tail; its flesh is scant, but much valued.

Z

za.ga.da[1] *noun* (Gren). See GROUND-LIZARD. (French Creole from French *lézard gardant* 'watching lizard'.)

za.ga.da[2] *noun* (Trin). See WOOD-SLAVE. (French Creole from French *lézard gardant* 'watching lizard'.)

za(n).chwa (zan.chois, za.shwa) *noun* (Trin). See ANCHOVY. (French Creole from French *des-anchois* 'anchovies'.)

zan.do.li (zan.do.lee, zann.do.li) *noun* (Dmca, Gren, StLu, Trin). See ANOLE. (French Creole from French *des-anolis* 'lizards'.)

zò.fi *noun* (Dmca, StLu). See GARR[1]. (French Creole from French *des-orphies* 'gar-fishes'.)

FLORA

A

Aa.ron's rod *noun phrase* (Jmca). See GLIRICIDIA.

ab.bay *noun* (Jmca). **Guyn, Trin *oil palm*.** A tall palm tree which bears branches of reddish fruit, whose outer skin produces an oil.

a.ca.cia *noun* (TkCa, Trin). **Antg, Jmca *cassie*; Bdos *sweet briar*; Jmca *wild poponax*; Dmca *zakacha*.** A small shrub or tree covered with thorns, usually found on waste land, which bears small pods and tiny yellow flowers.

ac.kee (a.kee) *noun* (Jmca). **Jmca *ackee-apple, vegetable brain*; StVn *Jamaica-ackee*.** A large scarlet-coloured fruit with edible creamy-yellow flesh on three black seeds; it splits open when ripe but is poisonous if used before it is ripe.

Ackee

A.dam's nee.dle *noun phrase* (Angu, Trin). **CarA *yucca*; Antg *bridal wreath, sentinel*.** A plant which bears needle-like clusters or pointed, green leaves.

A.fri.can tu.lip-tree *noun phrase* (CarA). **CarA *tulip-tree*; Bdos, StKt *water-spout*.** A green, bushy tree which bears clusters of bright, orange-red flowers like tulips.

African tulip-tree (above) *and detail of flowers*

A.fri.can-vi.o.let *noun* (CarA) A small plant with velvet-green leaves and purple, blue or pink flowers only cultivated in pots.

African-violet

a.fu yam *noun* (CarA). See YELLOW-YAM.

a.ga.ve *noun* (CarA). **Antg** ***Antigua-Pride***; **Antg, Dmca, StVn** ***dagger-plant***; **Baha, CayI, Jmca** ***sisal***; **Bdos** ***maypole***; **Bdos, Trin, USVI** ***century plant***; **Belz, Dmca, Gren, Jmca** ***cactus***; **Dmca, Gren, StLu** ***lang-bèf***. Any plant of the cactus family which bears clusters of narrow, stiff, spiny leaves and tall bunches of flowers; these plants are usually used as a protective hedge.

Agave cactus

air-plant *noun* (Angu). See LEAF-OF-LIFE.

a.kee (ac.kee) *noun* (Bdos, StLu, StVn). See GUINEP.

al.fal.fa *noun* (CarA). A plant whose flowers and leaves are used as fodder for cattle.

al.la.man.da *noun* (CarA). **CarA** ***buttercup***; **Angu, Antg, Tbgo** ***yellow-bell***. An ornamental vine which bears clusters of yellow bell-shaped flowers; it is also used as a laxative and to treat malaria.

Allamanda

al.li.ga.tor-ap.ple *noun* (Dmca, Guyn, StVn, Trin). A thin, oval, yellow fruit with a glossy skin and dryish salmon-coloured, slightly acid pulp full of large, flat, light-brown seeds, which is sometimes used medicinally.

al.li.ga.tor-pear *noun* (CarA). See AVOCADO.

all.spice *noun* (CarA). **CarA** ***pimento***[1]; **Trin** ***Jamaica pepper***. Dry, fragrant berries looking like black-pepper seeds used to flavour many Caribbean dishes and also used medicinally.

al.mond *noun* (CarA). **ECar** ***Barbados almond***; **Crcu, Dmca, StLu, Trin** ***zamand / zanman***. A tough-skinned, oval-shaped fruit with an edible kernel, borne on the ALMOND-TREE.

al.mond (tree) *noun (phrase)* (CarA). A large, ornamental tree with branches spreading out evenly and horizontally and large, bright-green leaves; it bears a triangular-shaped fruit with a tough skin.

a.loe(s) *noun (plural), adjective* (CarA). **Guyn** ***bitter aloes*****; Jmca** ***sempervive*****.** A small, cactus-like shrub with thick jagged-edged leaves growing in a cluster from the base; its thick, bitter, jelly-like juice is used both medicinally and as a cosmetic, and it is also grown ornamentally.

a.ma.ryl.lis *noun* (CarA). **Bdos** ***snowdrop*****; CarA** ***wind-flower;*** **Bdos, Guyn** ***crocus*****; Jmca** ***rain-flower*****.** A small lily that grows wild along roadsides with yellow, white or pink flowers.

A

A.mer.i.can silk cot.ton *noun phrase* (BrVI). **Baha** ***silk bush*****; Bdos** ***French cotton*****; CayI** ***cotton*****[2]; Jmca** ***duppy-cho-cho*****; TkCa** ***milky bush*****.** A large shrub with large, silky leaves that give off a sticky, milky substance when crushed; it bears pink flowers and small fruit with seeds surrounded by a fine, thick, woolly fluff, often used to stuff pillows.

a.na.to (a.nat.to, ar.not.to) *noun* (CarA). **Dmca, Gren, Guyn, StLu, Trin** ***roucou*****.** A small tree with pearl-shaped leaves and white flowers that bear bunches of red, spiny, oval-shaped pods which split open when ripe, and whose pulp is used to make dye. (A Carib word meaning 'fruit used to make red dye with which Amerindians paint themselves'.)

an.ge.li.ca *noun* (USVI). **1.** A herb used for medicinal purposes. **2.** An ornamental plant which bears dark green leaves with a white margin, often used to make hedges.

an.ge.lin *noun* (CarA). **Belz, Jmca** ***cabbage bark tree*****; Jmca** ***wormwood*****; VIls** ***dog-almond*****.** A roundish tree with dark green leaves, pinkish-red flowers and a plum-like fruit, whose bark is used as a purgative and for treatment of worms, as well as for fever and other ailments.

an.gel's trum.pet *noun phrase* (Baha, Jmca, Trin). **Bdos** ***trumpet-flower*****.** A small, ornamental tree bearing trumpet-like flowers which give off a fragrance at night; its leaves are also used for headache and as a poultice, but it is poisonous if taken by humans.

Angel's trumpet

an.ise *noun* (Mrat, StKt, VIls). **Guyn** ***aniseed*****.** A small plant with white flowers carrying aromatic seeds, used in cooking and as a folk remedy.

Anne po.ta.to *noun phrase* (TkCa). See SWEET POTATO.

an.thu.ri.um (li.ly) *noun (phrase)* (CarA). An ornamental plant found in many varieties, usually in pots and bearing pink, white, yellow, smooth flowers, with a long, pointed stalk sticking out of it.

An.ti.gua black pine-ap.ple *noun phrase* (Antg). A dark-skinned PINEAPPLE with sweet, juicy, orange-coloured flesh, found only in Antigua.

An.ti.gua-heath *noun* (Bdos, Gren, Trin). **Dmca, Guyn** ***sweet willliam*****; Jmca** ***mare's tail*****; Gren** ***Chinese fire-cracker*****; Trin** ***humming-bird trumpet***. A common garden plant with long stems, bearing clusters of small, scarlet flowers; also found in cooler, more mountainous areas.

An.ti.gua-Pride *noun* (Antg). See AGAVE.

an.tro.ver (an.tro.va) *noun* (Antg, Brbu). See EGGPLANT.

ants-bush *noun* (Guyn). An annual herb with slim, lance-like leaves and tiny white, pink, or mauve flowers, found in low-lying, wet places throughout South America and used medicinally by some.

ap.ple-ba.na.na *noun* (Belz, CayI, Guyn, Jmca, TkCa). **Baha** ***dwarf banana*****; Antg, Nevs, StKt, StVn, TkCa** ***fig*****[2]; Gren** ***rock-fig*****; Antg, Brbu lady-finger[1]; Antg, Nevs, StKt, Tbgo, Trin** ***silk-fig*****; StKt** ***silk banana*****; Mrat** ***sicri***. A short, fat species of banana with firm, sweet flesh, when ripe, suitable only for eating.

ap.ple blos.som cas.sia *noun phrase* (Bdos, Gren, Trin). **Belz** ***stinking toe***. A large, ornamental tree which bears large numbers of rose-pink flowers looking like apple-blossoms and long, brown pods.

a.pri.cot *noun* (StLu). See MAMMEE-APPLE.

ar.row cane *noun* (Guyn). **Guyn** ***arrow-grass, arrow-wood*****; Jmca** ***wild cane***. A tall, thick-stemmed cane-like plant which grows well in wet, swampy areas and is also used medicinally.

ar.row.root *noun* (CarA). A plant whose roots yield a nutritious starch that is used both domestically and commercially.

asth.ma bush/weed *noun phrase* (Jmca). An erect, annual shrub with a grooved stem and compound branches; an infusion of its leaves is used to treat asthma.

au.ber.gine *noun* (Antg, Gren, StVn, Trin). See EGGPLANT.

Au.gust-flow.er *noun* (Guyn). An ornamental tree which bears large pink or white flowers and long, thin, flat brownish-yellow pods.

Au.gust-plum *noun* (Belz). See CHILLI-PLUM.

a.vo.ca.do(-pear) *noun* (CarA). **CarA** ***alligator-pear*****; Belz** ***butter-pear*****; Dmca, Gren, StLu, Trin** ***zaboca***. A green or brown pear-shaped fruit with a leathery skin and thick, creamy, smooth light-green flesh, widely used as a vegetable. (Originally Aztec via Spanish.)

a.wa.ra (a.war.ra) *noun* (Guyn). An orange-yellow fruit with tough, smooth skin and tough fibrous pulp of the same colour on a large hard black seed, which grows on a palm whose trunk and branches are covered with black spines. (An Arawak word *awara* 'spiney palm . . . bearing red, edible fruit'.)

Awara fruit

axe-mas.ter *noun* (Belz). **Bdos** ***ebony*****[4]**. A strong, black, heavy forest timber usually found in dry, rocky and warm spots.

B

baa.ji *noun* (Guyn, Trin). See CALALU.

ba.boon-cap *noun* (Belz). A shiny, yellow fruit looking like an egg, with soft, clammy, scented flesh around a hairy seed.

ba.ba.din (bar.ba.dene) *noun* (Dmca, Trin). See GRANADILLA.

ba.by-bush[1] *noun* (Nevs). See LEAF-OF-LIFE.

ba.by-bush[2] *noun* (StVn). See CHRISTMAS-BUSH.

ba.by cu.cum.ber *noun phrase* (Guyn). **Guyn *baby-pumpkin***. A small, longish fruit with a thin skin and a rich pulp which are both red when ripe; it grows on a vine that bears white flowers.

B

ba.by-lime *noun* (Guyn). **Jmca *Chinese lemon*; Trin *lime-berry***. A small, oval-shaped red berry with an oily skin with blackish dots and greenish-white pulp and seeds.

ba.ca.noe(ba.ca.nole) *noun* (Tbgo, Trin). See TRUMPET-BUSH.

ba.che.lor's but.ton *noun phrase* (CarA). **Dmca *dame-and-cavalier***. A small, white, pink, or purple flower borne on a bushy plant and easily grown in pots or gardens.

Ba.ha.ma grass *noun phrase* (CarA). **Jmca, Trin *Bermuda grass***. A low, creeping grass with narrow, pointed leaves, usually cultivated as a lawn grass.

Ba.ha.mas blue-pea *noun phrase* (Baha). See BLUE-PEA.

bai.gan (bi.gan) *noun* (Guyn, Trin). See EGGPLANT.

Ba.jan yam (Bar.ba.dos yam) *noun phrase* (Gren, Mrat). See WHITE YAM.

ba.lai-doux (bal.yé-dou) *noun* (Dmca, Gren). See SWEET-BROOM.

ba.lan.jay (ba.lan.ge(r), bo.lon.jay, bo(u).lan.ger) *noun* (Bdos. Guyn, Mrat, StVn, USVI). See EGGPLANT. (Originally fron Arabic *al be'enjen* via Spanish *berenjena* or Portuguese *berinjela*.)

ba.la.ta[1] *noun* (CarA). **Guyn, Jmca, Trin *bullet-wood (tree)***. A large, evergreen, forest tree with leathery leaves and small edible fruit which produces a very heavy, hard, strong timber and a thick, white gum.

ba.la.ta[2] *noun* (Dmca, StLu, Tbgo, Trin). The small, oval-shaped brown fruit of the balata-tree whose sticky flesh is enjoyed by children.

Balata fruit

ba.li.si.er *noun* (Dmca, Gren, StLu, Tbgo, Trin). See HELICONIA. (French Creole from French for plants of the Canna family.)

ball-and-thread *noun phrase* (Angu). See BALL-BUSH.

ball-bush (bald-bush) *noun* (Bdos, Jmca). **Antg *la-lavinton, Lord Lavinton*; Guyn *lion-bush*; Bdos, VIls *lion's tail*; Bdos, Guyn *man-piaba*; StKt *rabbit-food*; StVn *bird-honey***. A wild herb with a four-sided stalk, but no branches, with leaves entirely on the lower stalk, and bearing some ball-shaped, reddish-

Ball-bush

brown clusters of flowers, growing at intervals along the stalk; it is used both medicinally and ornamentally.

bal.sam (bush) *noun (phrase)* (CarA). Any one of a group of small shrubs with aromatic leaves and flowers of different colours; the leaves are often crushed and the juice is used medicinally and also as a herbal tea.

bal.yé-dou (ba.lai-doux) *noun* (Dmca, Gren). See SWEET-BROOM.

bam.boo *noun* (CarA). **1.** A giant tropical grass with a jointed stem, whose leaves are sometimes boiled to make a fever bath. **2.** The jointed stem of the BAMBOO plant, used to make furniture, etc. and often called a bamboo.

ba.nak *noun* (Belz). **Belz *bastard cedar*.** An extremely tall forest tree with a smooth, red-brown bark which gives a blood red sap when cut and yields a soft, straight-grained wood.

ba.na.na *noun* (CarA). A long, curved fruit with sweet pulpy flesh and yellow when ripe, which grows in bunches and of which there are many varieties.

ba.na.vis (peas) (bo.na.vist) *noun (phrase)* (CarA). See BONAVIST.

ban-ca.rai.la (ban ca.rai.li/ca.rai.lee) *noun* (Guyn, Trin). See CERASEE.

ban.ga (ban.gar) *noun* (Guyn, Trin). **2.** See GROU-GROU BÈF **2**.

ban.ner-bean *noun* (Jmca). See BONAVIST.

bar.ba.dine (ba.ba.din, bar.ba.dene) *noun* (Dmca, Gren, Trin). See GRANADILLA.

Bar.ba.dos-al.mond *noun* (ECar). See ALMOND.

Bar.ba.dos-cher.ry *noun* (CarA). **CarA *West Indian cherry;* CayI, Jmca *garden-cherry;* Nevs *cherise*.** A small bright red fruit with three seeds in acid-sweet flesh, widely used for making drink, jam and fruit preserves.

Bar.ba.dos-e.bo.ny *noun* (Bdos). See WOMAN'S TONGUE.

Bar.ba.dos-ed.doe *noun* (Gren). See DASHEEN.

Bar.ba.dos-pride *noun* (CarA). **CarA *dwarf-poinciana*; Baha, Jmca *flower-fence*; CarA *Pride of Barbados*.** A prickly shrub which bears yellow flowers and long, green pods and is popularly cultivated as a hedge.

Ba.ri.ma-plan.tain *noun* (Guyn). See BLUGGO.

bas.tard ce.dar *noun* (Belz). See BANAK.

bas.tard plan.tain *noun phrase* (StVn). See CAYENNE BANANA.

ba.teau *noun* (Guyn). See CABBAGE-BARK.

bath-net.tle *noun phrase* (Nevs). See STINGING-NETTLE.

B

bay-ber.ry tree *noun phrase* (Gren, Jmca, Trin). See BAY(-LEAF) TREE.

bay-ge.ra.ni.um(-ge.re.ni.a) *noun* (Baha). **Jmca, TkCa *bay-tansy*; Bdos *wild geranium*; Trin *wormwood* 1**. A perennial, seaside vine with rough leaves and small green flowers, widely used as a folk medicine together with other herbs.

Bay-geranium

bay(-leaf) tree *noun phrase* (CarA). **Dmca, Gren, StLu, Trin *bwa denn***. An aromatic, evergreen tree with a smooth greyish or reddish bark, bearing clusters of white flowers from which medicinal BAY-OIL and BAY-RUM are commercially made.

bay-tan.sy *noun* (Jmca, TkCa). See BAY-GERANIUM.

bead-vine (bush) *noun (phrase)* (Nevs, StKt). **Brbu, Gren, StKt, Trin, USVI *jumbie-bead vine*; Jmca *red-bead vine, wild liquorice***. The vine that bears the JUMBIE-BEAD whose leaves are sometimes used as a folk medicine.

bean-tree *noun* (Bdos). **Bdos *Judas-tree, Lent-tree*; Jmca *cutlass-bean, Spanish machete***. A tree which bears scarlet flowers and pods in which are small scarlet seeds.

beard.ed fig tree *noun phrase* (Bdos). A huge tree with many branches and many aerial roots hanging from its branches; many of these roots grow down to the ground and fuse with the main trunk, or they grow at some distance away from it.

Bearded fig tree

bed-grass *noun* (Nevs, Tbgo). See VETIVER.

beef-wood[1] *noun* (Baha). See CASUARINA.

beef-wood[2] *noun* (Bdos). A tall flowering evergreen tree with shiny leaves.

beef-wood[3] *noun* (Guyn). See BULLETWOOD.

bé.lan.jenn *noun* (StLu). See EGGPLANT.

bell-ap.ple *noun* (Guyn, Nevs, StVn, Trin, ViIs). **Bdos, Dmca, Gren, Trin** ***water-lemon*****; Guyn** ***semitu*****; Jmca** ***golden-apple*****; Dmca, StLu, Trin** ***pomme-can.nelle*****.** An oval-shaped fruit with a thick orange or yellow skin when ripe, a sweet pulp in which are seeds; it is borne on a vine.

bel.ly-ache bush *noun phrase* (CarA). **Bdos, ViIs** ***(wild) physic nut*****; Jmca** ***wild cassava*****.** A shrub with spreading branches and hairy stems, which bears a small, round fruit from whose seeds a medicinal oil is made; it is usually found on sandy ground near the sea.

bel.ly.full *noun* (CarA). See MANGO-GRAHAM.

bell-yam *noun* (Guyn). See CUSH-CUSH (YAM).

ben.ne (ben.nay, ben.neh; ben.ny) *noun* (CarA). A flowering herb (the sesame) whose seeds produce a clear oil used both for cooking and anointing; the seeds are used to make sweets. (A West African word from the Mandingo language *bene* 'sesame'.)

Be.quia-plum *noun* (StVn). See JAMAICA-PLUM. (Maybe by association with the island of Bequia in the Grenadines, where the tree grows quite abundantly.)

Ber.mu.da grass *noun phrase* (Jmca, Trin). See BAHAMA GRASS.

bha.ji *noun* (Guyn, Trin). See CALALU. (From Hindi *bhaajii* 'vegetable leaves, green or cooked'.)

big-plum *noun* (CayI). See JAMAICA-PLUM.

bi.lim.bi *noun* (Guyn, Jmca, Trin). **Guyn** ***sourie*****; Jmca** ***bimbling, jimbelin*****.** A small, pale, green, slim, cucumber-like fruit with a thin skin and acid flesh. (A plant of Asian origin which could have come into Caribbean English through Indic culture via the Tamil language *bilimbi*, or via the Swahili language *mbilimbi*, the name of the same tree).

Bilimbi

birch-gum tree *noun phrase* (Bdos, Brbu, Trin). **CayI** ***birch-tree*****; BrVI** ***log-tree*****; Gren, USVI** ***naked-Indian*****; Jmca** ***incense-tree, red birch*****; Baha, TkCa** ***gum-elemi*****.** A large tree with smooth and sometimes shiny, reddish-brown bark that scales off in papery pieces; all parts of the tree give off a turpentine-like resin and the bark yields the BIRCH-GUM.

Birch-gum tree

B

bird-hon.ey *noun* (StVn). See BALL-BUSH.

bird-pep.per *noun* (CarA). **Bdos** ***nigger-pepper, spur-pepper*****; Berm** ***guinea-pepper*****; Brbu, Jmca** ***cayenne-pepper*****; Gren, Jmca, Trin** ***chilli*****; Dmca** ***piman-zwazo***. A small, hot, pointed red pepper, cylindrical in shape that is borne on a low, bushy plant; the pepper is widely used to flavour Caribbean dishes.

bird-vine *noun* (Dmca, Gren, Guyn, Trin). **Belz, Jmca, TkCa** ***scorn-the-earth***. A parasitic shrub with small leaves and red berries whose roots burrow into host trees, finally smothering them; it is used as a folk remedy for high blood pressure, kidney-disease and other ailments.

bit.ter-a.loes *noun* (Guyn, Jmca). See ALOES.

B

bit.ter-bush[1] *noun* (Baha). **Baha** ***bitter-wood***[1]. A small, shrub or tree, bearing scarlet or reddish berries, whose leaves are used as a folk medicine.

bit.ter-bush[2] *noun* (Baha). **Baha** ***bitter-wood, snake root*****; Jmca** ***majoe-bitter***. A shrub which bears tiny, reddish-btown berries, whose leaves are used as a folk medicine.

bit.ter-bush[3] *noun* (Gren). See ZÈB-A-PIK.

bit.ter cas.sa.va *noun phrase* (CarA). See CASSAVA.

bit.ter-cup *noun* (Guyn, Jmca). A cup carved from the wood of the lignum vitae tree in which water, left in it overnight, draws the bitterness of the wood and is drunk as a medicine for fevers or poor appetite.

bit.ter o.range *noun phrase* (Angu, Bdos). See SOUR ORANGE.

bit.ter-tal.ly *noun* (Bdos, Guyn). One or more of many varieties of a twining vine that bears white or greenish flowers; its bitter juice is sometimes used as a tonic or to relieve symptoms of malaria.

bit.ter-wood[1] *noun* (Baha). See BITTER-BUSH.

bit.ter-wood[2] *noun* (Jmca). A large tree which bears sweet-smelling flowers and blackish-blue berries; it produces a wood from which the BITTER-CUP is carved.

biz.zi-biz.zi (bi.si-bi.si, bu.sy-bu.sy) *noun* (Guyn). **Guyn** ***bizzy-bizzy grass***. Any one of three or more varieties of a reed-like grass which sometimes has stalks bearing bunches of small, brown flowers, and thrives in swampy areas and is harmful to rice crops.

black ba.na.na *noun phrase* (Jmca). See BUCK-BANANA.

black.ber.ry *noun* (Belz). See JAMOON.

black-eye pea *noun phrase* (CarA). **CarA** ***cow-pea*****; Trin** ***gub-gub***. A small, creamy-white, kidney-shaped bean in long, thin pods growing on a climbing vine; the dried beans are popularly used, boiled in rice, in Caribbean cuisine.

black-man.go *noun* (Belz, Jmca). A small, tasty, thin-skinned mango with a groove running from the top halfway down the fruit.

black-sage[1] *noun* (CarA). **CarA** ***sage-bush***[1]. A sturdy shrub or small tree with a dark stem and aromatic leaves used to make a tea believed to relieve a variety of ailments; the stem is also used as a tooth-brush or to freshen the breath.

black-sage[2] *noun* (CarA). See SAGE-BUSH[2].

black-wil.low *noun* (Baha, Bdos, Gren, Jmca). A medium-sized tree with shiny, dark-green leaves and small purple flowers, slow-growing and usually found in churchyards.

blad.der-bush *noun* (Nevs). See LEAF-OF-LIFE.

bleed.ing-heart[1] *noun* (CarA). **CarA *caladium***. An ornamental plant which bears brightly coloured, heart-shaped leaves in shades of pink, red and white.

Bleeding-heart

bleed.ing-heart[2] *noun* (CarA). A small, spreading vine which bears clusters of tiny red and white flowers, the crimson part being the actual flower and the white calyx representing the 'heart'.

blim.bing (bim.bling) *noun* (Gren, Jmca). See BILIMBI.

blind-eye 1. *noun* (Mrat). **Guyn *Chinese Christmas tree*; USVI *milk-bush, pencil-bush***. A leafless, green shrub with branches resembling slim twigs which produce a milky juice that can cause temporary blindness, hence its name.

blood.wood *noun* (Guyn). A tree that grows in savannahs in tropical South America and produces a soft, light brown wood used for indoor furniture; when cut, its bark gives off a yellowish-red sap, which is used as a purgative and for skin disorders.

blue-bell 1. *noun* (Guyn). See DUPPY-GUN.

blue-pea *noun* (Jmca). **Baha *Bahamas blue-pea*; Bdos, Guyn *blue-vine*; Jmca *blue-bell* 2.** A bushy, climbing vine which bears pea-like flowers that are bright blue and other colours also, that grow into longish pods.

blue-vine *noun* (Bdos, Guyn). See BLUE-PEA.

blug.go (blo.go) *noun* (Belz, Gren, StLu, Tbgo). **Antg, Dmca *bugament*; TkCa *hog-banana*; Bdos *buffert*; Belz *flagu*; BrVI *horse-banana*; CayI *bottler-banana*; Guyn *Barima plantain*; StLu *djouboul*; Trin *moko banana*; Dmca, StLu *macambou***. A thick-skinned, tough, four-sided variety of BANANA which grows out the bunch at right angles, often used as pig fodder, and also prized for its good food value.

Bob.by-plum *noun* (Bdos, Tbgo). See BUBBY-PLUM.

bo.di (bean) *noun* (Gren, StLu, StVn, Trin). **Antg, Dmca, StKt *six-weeks*; Gren, Guyn, Trin *yard bean*; Guyn *bora***. One or more varieties of green or brownish bean encased in a long, slim pod, borne on a climbing vine, both the beans and the pod being of excellent food value.

Bodi bean

bois-bandé *noun* (Dmca, Gren, StLu, Trin). See BWA-BANDÉ.

bois-ca.not *noun* (Dmca, Gren, Tbgo, Trin). See BWA-KANO. (A French loanword.)

Bom.bay mango *noun phrase* (Gren, Jmca, Mrat). **Gren *Bombay-Ceylon*; StVn *Ceylon(-mango).*** A special variety of MANGO whose flesh is sweet and rich, with an easily removable seed when the ripe fruit is cut.

bo.na.vist (ba.na.bis, bo.na.vis) *noun* (CarA). **Antg, Berm, Trin *hyacinth-bean*; Baha, Dmca, Guyn *butter-bean* 1.; CarA *lablab-bean*; Mrat, Trin *white-bean*; StLu *saeme*; Trin *sem*; Jmca *banner-bean*.** An edible bean encased in a broad, flat pod with a beak-shaped tip which comes in many varieties and colours; the most common is an edible, light-green pod with whitish beans. (From the Spanish name Bona Vista for the Portuguese island Boa Vista from which the beans were brought to the New World.)

B

bo.ra *noun* (Guyn). See BODI-(BEAN).

bot.tler-ba.na.na *noun* (CayI). See BLUGGO.

bou.gain.vil.lea *noun* (CarA). A small tree or climbing shrub with small green leaves and thorny stems bearing clusters of flowers in a variety of colours – white, red, pink, violet, peach, orange; it is widely found in gardens in the Caribbean.

Bougainvillea

bread-and-cheese *noun* (CarA). **Brbu *goat-bush*.** A bushy shrub usually cultivated as a hedge or a medium-sized tree of the same family, both of which bear reddish pods that cover shiny black seeds in white, furry flesh, enjoyed by children.

bread.fruit *noun* (CarA). **StLu *bwa pen*; Trin *penmbwa*; Dmca *yanm pen*.** A round, green fruit with a rough skin and white, starchy flesh, much used in Caribbean cooking; it was originally brought from the Pacific to the Caribbean by Captain Bligh, captain of the ship called the *Bounty*.

Breadfruit

bri.ar *noun* (TkCa). See NICKER.

bri.dal wreath *noun phrase* (Angu). See ADAM'S NEEDLE.

broad-bean *noun* (Jmca, StVn). See LIMA BEAN.

broad-leaf thyme *noun phrase* (Bdos, Guyn). See THICK-LEAF THYME.

broom-palm *noun* (Trin). See SILVER-THATCH PALM.

brown-jolly *noun* (Jmca). See EGGPLANT.

bub.by-plum (Bob.by-plum) *noun* (Bdos, Tbgo). See JAMAICA-PLUM. (Probablly so called because of the nipple-like bottom of the fruit which looks like a female breast or BUBBY. 'Bobby' is probably a polite form of the word BUBBY).

buck-ba.na.na *noun* (Guyn). **Jmca *black banana*; Bdos *buffer(t), claret-fig*; Belz *maiden-plantain*; Trin *mataboro, red fig*.** A purple-skinned banana, similar to the APPLE-BANANA, but toughish in texture when ripe, and so not usually cultivated.

buck-bead *noun* (Guyn). See JUMBIE-BEAD[3].

buck-cot.ton *noun* (Guyn). **Guyn *brown-cotton*.** The long-fibred, brownish variety of cotton borne on a low shrub; the juice of the plant is used as a folk medicine and the lint as pillow-stuffing.

buck-yam *noun* (Guyn). See CUSH-CUSH YAM.

buf.fer(t)(-ba.na.na) *noun* (Bdos). See BLUGGO.

bu.ga.ment *noun* (Antg, Dmca). See BLUGGO.

bul.let-wood (tree) *noun (phrase)* (Guyn, Jmca, Trin). See BALATA[1].

bul.lock's heart *noun* (Jmca, StVn). See CUSTARD-APPLE.

bull-seed/-stone man.go *noun* (Jmca). See MANGO-GRAHAM.

bu.ra-bu.ra (bo.ro-bo.ro) *noun* (Guyn). **Jmca, TkCa *susumber, turkey-berry*; Jmca *gully-bean*.** A small edible berry with many seeds and a red or yellow skin when ripe, borne in clusters on a wild bush with wide, lobed leaves that have spines on their under-sides and also along the stems and branches.

bush-rope *noun* (Guyn). **1.** Any thin forest vines or aerial roots of forest trees used for binding materials together. **2.** See HAIARI.

bu.sy-bu.sy *noun* (Guyn). See BIZZI-BIZZI.

but.ter-bean **1.** *noun* (Baha, Dmca, Guyn). See BONAVIST. **2.** (StKt, StVn) See LIMA-BEAN.

but.ter-cup *noun* (CarA). See ALLAMANDA.

but.ter pear *noun* (Belz). See AVOCADO.

Bux.ton spice *noun* (Guyn). See SPICE-MANGO.

bwa-ban.dé (bois ban.dé) *noun* (Dmca, Gren, StLu, Tbgo, Trin). A medium-sized tree usually found on hillsides, with leathery leaves and small white flowers. (French Creole *bwa* + *bandé*.)

bwa-denn (bois d'Inde) *noun* (Dmca, Gren, StLu, Trin). See BAY(-LEAF) TREE. (French Creole from French *bois d'Inde* 'wood/tree of India'.)

bwa-ka.no (bois ca.not) *noun* (Dmca, Gren, Tbgo, Trin). See TRUMPET-BUSH. (A French Creole item from French *bois canot* 'canoe wood' The variants *bwa-kano* or *bois canon* are found in Dominica and St Lucia.)

bwa kwa.ib; Ca.rib wood *noun phrase* (Dmca). A small tree with thin, whip-like branches and compound leaves, all of which fall off when the tree blooms with abundant scarlet flowers. (French Creole from French *bois caraïbe* 'Carib wood'.)

Bwakwaib tree

bwa-pen *noun* (StLu). See BREADFRUIT.

byre *noun* (Guyn). See DUNKS.

B

C

cab.bage *noun* (CarA). **Dmca, StLu *tjé-palmis*.** The edible, white, inner leaf-bud of the CABBAGE-PALM, used in salads, as a side dish or a pickle preserved in vinegar.

cab.bage-bark *noun* (CarA). **Guyn *bateau*.** The boat-shaped dried stalk of the flowers of the same tree, used for making baskets, and also by children for making toy 'boats'.

cab.bage-bark tree *noun phrase* (Jmca). See ANGELIN.

cab.bage-palm *noun* (CarA). **CarA *cabbage-tree*; Antg, Jmca, StVn *mountain-cabbage*; Baha *pond-top*[2]; Dmca, Gren, StLu, Trin *palmis(te)*.** A very tall palm with a straight, grey trunk crowned by horizontal branches.

ca.cao-plum *noun* (Trin). See COCO-PLUM.

ca.chi.man *noun* (Dmca, StLu). See CUSTARD-APPLE (small caps).

cac.tus *noun* (CarA). A general name loosely applied to plants of many different types that have in common green, often spiny stems, but no true leaves and may not belong to the CACTUS family as such.

cac.tus (hedge) (hedge cac-tus) *noun (phrase)* (CarA). **USVI *monkey-puzzle*.** One of two different varieties of CACTUS type plant, one with triangular-shaped stems, the other with five-angled green stems which grow close together and can form an impassable hedge.

cac.tus (plant) *noun phrase* (CarA). **CarA *night- blooming cactus*.** A climbing garden plant with thick spiny stems and dull, spiny edges, which bears at their ends large, yellowish or whitish-yellow flowers that bloom only at night.

cai.mite (cai.mi.to) *noun* (Dmca, Gren, StLu, Tbgo, Trin). See STAR-APPLE. (A word that is probably of Carib origin as the tree is indigenous to South and Central America.)

ca.la.bash *noun* (CarA). The large, dried, round, brown fruit of the calabash-tree.

Calabash tree

ca.la.di.um *noun* (CarA). See BLEEDING-HEART.

ca.la.lu (cal.(l)al.loo (ou, u), ka.la.loo) *noun* (CarA). **Guyn, Trin *baaji, bhaji*; Tbgo, Trin *calalu-bush, dasheen-bush*; CarA *spinach*; StLu *zèbaj*; Dmca *zépina*.** Any one of a number of plants with edible leaves cooked as green vegetables. (Probably from the African language Malinke *kalalu* 'many things' or Mandingo *colilu* 'an edible herb resembling spinach'.)

cam.pesh (cam.peche, kan.pèch) *noun* (Dmca, Gren, Trin). **Belz, BrVI, Gren, Jmca, Trin *logwood*.** A small, spreading, slow-growing tree with spiny branches, highly valued for its heavy heart-wood which yields a deep red dye.

can.dle-bush *noun* (Dmca). See BALL-BUSH.

can.dle-flow.er *noun* (CayI). See CHRISTMAS-CANDLE.

can.dle-stick *noun* (Jmca). See CHRISTMAS-CANDLE.

can.dle.wood *noun* (Bdos). A hard, light-brown wood, used in construction and boat-building, produced by a tree that bears whitish flowers and a golden-brown fruit, which is also used medicinally.

cane-li.ly *noun* (Bdos). A large, bushy shrub with long, slim, greenish-grey, sharp-edged leaves used to make baskets and mats.

ca.nep (ca.nip) *noun* (Baha, TkCa). See GUINEP.

can.ker-ber.ry (kan.ka-ber.ry) *noun* (CarA). **Angu *corberry*; Angu, BrVI *ka-berry.*** A bright-red, smooth, shiny berry borne in clusters on a thorny shrub with dark green leaves.

can.na (li.ly) *noun (phrase)* (CarA). One of many varieties of garden-lily bearing red, pink, yellow or spotted flowers growing at the end of slim, cane-like stalks with broad, green leaves and spiny fruit encasing many round black seeds.

Canna lily

can.nelle *noun* (StLu). See CINNAMON (TREE).

can.non-ball tree *noun phrase* (CarA). **Gren, StVn *comb-and-brush.*** A tall, ornamental tree which bears inedible, hard, round fruit about the size of a cannonball.

Cannon-ball tree

ca.rai.la (ca.ril.la, ka.rai.la) *noun* (Guyn, StVn, Trin). See CERASEE.

ca.ram.bo.la *noun* (CarA). **Gren, Trin *coolie-tamarind*; Guyn, Mrat, Trin *five-finger*.** A five-winged, yellow, juicy and extremely acid fruit, borne in clusters on a small tree; the fruit is popularly used in the Caribbean for making jams and jellies, as well as dried fruit.

Carambola

Ca.rib wood *noun phrase* (Dmca) See BWA KWAIB.

car.pen.ter-grass *noun* (Jmca). See GARDEN-BALSAM.

car.pet-dai.sy *noun* (Bdos). **Guyn *daisy*; Jmca, TkCa *marigold*; Mrat *church-yard-grass*; Bdos *zèb-a-fanm*[2]**. A low, spreading herb with branches rooting at each joint in the stem, bearing small, light-green leaves and bright yellow flowers at the end of each stem; the plant is used as a tea and is often taken for colds.

Carpet daisy

ca.ri.on-crow bush *noun phrase* (Guyn). See CHRISTMAS-CANDLE.

ca.sha(w)[1] (ka.sha, ku.shu) *noun* (Angu, Jmca, Nevs, StKt, ViIs). **TkCa, Trin *acacia*; Bdos *sweet briar***. The name of more than one variety of a thorny, evergreen shrub bearing tiny, yellow flowers and usually growing wild. (Probably a combination of Carib and African items, and also possibly from the British English botanical name *acacia*; also possibly from Twi *kasɛ* 'thorn'.)

ca.sha(w)[2] (ka.sha) *noun* (Angu, Jmca, Nevs, StKt, ViIs). **Antg, Jmca *cashew*; Trin *mesquit tree***. Another variety of the CASHA(w), either a shrub or a large tree, usually found in dry areas and used medicinally by some.

ca.shew[1] *noun* (CarA). **Jmca, Mrat *cashew-apple*; Mrat *cashew-cherry*; Antg, Brbu *cashew-nut***. A small, yellow, pear-shaped fruit with a brown nut looking like a large bean at one end, with juicy flesh, and borne on a medium-sized tree. (Originally from the Tupi language *acaju*.)

Cashew

ca.shew[2] *noun* (Guyn). See MALACCA-APPLE/PEAR.

cas.sa.va *noun* (CarA). **ECar *manioc*; Guyn *cassava-stick***. A root vegetable with stiff, rough, brown, leathery skin and hard white flesh of which there are two kinds, SWEET CASSAVA and BITTER CASSAVA; the first kind is used as a vegetable and the second kind is used to make starch or grated and used as a poultice. (Probably coming from Arawakan language via Spanish and Portuguese. Compare Spanish variants *casabe, cazaba* 'cassava'.)

Cassava

Castor oil plant

cas.tor-oil (bush/plant/tree) *noun (phrase)* (CarA). **Bdos *oil-leaf tree*; Belz, Jmca, TkCa *oil-nut tree*.** A small shrub or tree with large, light-green leaves, with male flowers growing towards the base and female flowers towards the tip; it bears round, green pods and its seeds yield a powerful oil, which is used as a laxative.

cas.u.a.ri.na (cas.u.ri.na) *noun* (CarA). **Baha *beef-wood*[1]; Bdos *mile-tree*; Gren, Jmca, StVn, Trin *whistling pine/willow*; Guyn *needle-and-thread*; Jmca *willow*.** A tall, narrow, cone-shaped tree with long branches bearing many needle-like leaves, often used as a Christmas tree, or for other ornamental purposes. (A Malayan loanword coming from Australia, and also called *Australian pine* by some botanists.)

cat-claw *noun* (StKt). See FIT-WEED.

ca.ter.pil.lar-ca.la.lu *noun* (BrVI, Guyn). Either one of two similar-looking, tall, erect, bushy herbs with smooth, reddish-brown or green stems, yellow flowers and pale-green spoon-shaped leaves used as CALALU.

cat's claw creep.er *noun phrase* (Trin). See GOLDEN-SHOWER.

cat-tail *noun* (CarA). **Trin *chenille (plant)*.** A tall, garden shrub that bears long, red, velvety, tail-like flowers, hence the name.

cat.tle-tongue *noun* (Antg, Brbu, Mrat, Nevs, StKt). **Bdos, Guyn *cure-for-all*; Jmca *wild tobacco*; StLu *tabak-djab*; Dmca *tabak-zonbi*; Nevs, USVI *ram-goat bush* 2.** A shrub with light-green, aromatic leaves whose leaves are widely used medicinally.

ca.yenne-ba.na.na *noun* (Guyn). **StVn *bastard plantain, short banana, Trinidad banana*.** A short, blunt-ended species of BANANA, oblong-shaped and smaller and shorter than the regular species, often cooked when not ripe.

ca.yenne-pep.per (ca.yan-pep.per) *noun* (Brbu, Jmca). See BIRD-PEPPER.

cei.ba *noun* (CarA). See SILK-COTTON. (From Arawak *shiba-dañ* 'a large hard-wooded tree'; *-dañ* is a suffix meaning 'tree'.)

cen.tu.ry-plant (sen.try-plant) *noun* (Bdos, Trin, VIls). A variety of AGAVE which has sharp prickles on its elongated spine-tipped leaves and grows a central pole with flowers, after which it dies.

ce.ra.see *noun* (Baha, Bdos, CayI, Jmca, TkCa). **Baha, Belz *sorosse, sorossi*; Tbgo *sorrow-seed*; Bdos *circe(e) bush, miraculous bush, miraculous vine, sersee, sersey*; Bdos, Nevs, StKt *lizard-food*; Dmca, Mrat *pomme coolie*; Guyn, StVn, Trin *caraila, carilla, karaila*;**

Cerasee bush

Gren *coolie papaw*; Guyn, Trin *ban-caraila*. A slender, vigorously spreading vine which bears a bumpy, ribbed yellow fruit, that splits open when ripe, yielding bright red, sweet, sticky seeds, although the skin is bitter; the leaves and the fruit are widely used for medicinal purposes. (Probably of African origin.)

C

ce.rise[1] *noun* (Trin). See GOVERNOR-PLUM, JAMAICA-PLUM, SOUR CHERRY.

ce.rise[2] *noun* (StLu). See BARBADOS-CHERRY.

Cey.lon(-man.go) *noun* (StVn). See BOMBAY-MANGO.

cha.co.ni.a *noun* (Tbgo, Trin). **Tbgo, Trin *Pride of Trinidad & Tobago, Trinidad's Pride, wild poinsettia*.** A slender forest tree which bears very long sprays of flaming red flowers, which bloom every year around late August, near the independence anniversary of Trinidad & Tobago, and is its national flower.

Chaconia flowers

cha.po.ti *noun* (Dmcs, StLu). See SAPODILLA.

che.nep; che.nip *noun* (Gren, Tbgo). See GUINEP.

che.net(te) (chen.nette, tjennèt, quenette) *noun* (Dmca, StLu, Tbgo, Trin). See GUINEP. (From French *quénette, quenette* in St Lucia from *quénèpe* in Haiti from Arawakan *kenepa*.)

che.nille (plant) *noun (phrase)* (Trin). See CAT-TAIL.

che.ra.mi.na (che.ra.mi.la, cher.ry.mi.na) *noun* (Jmca). See GOOSEBERRY.

che.rise *noun* (Nevs). See BARBADOS-CHERRY.

cher.ry-nut *noun* (Angu, BrVI, StKt). See CASHEW[1].

cher.ry-pep.per *noun* (Baha, Trin). **Guyn *wiri-wiri pepper*.** A variety of the PEPPER family cultivated as a pot plant.

chic.le; chic.le-gum tree, chic.le tree *noun (phrase)* (Belz). The name commercially used for the SAPODILLA/SAPADILI tree as the producer of gum, the original name of which is *chicle*. (A Spanish word coming from Nahuatl *tzictli*, the name of the gum.)

chil.li *noun* (Gren, Jmca, Trin). See BIRD-PEPPER.

chi(l).li-plum *noun* (Antg, Bdos, Gren, Tbgo, Trin). **Belz *August-plum*; Gren, StVn *Jamaica-plum*; StLu *pwinn*; Belz, CayI, Jmca, Trin *yellow plum*.** A small, yellow, oval-shaped fruit, with a hard, thick seed and yellow, juicy flesh, borne in clusters on a low tree.

chi.nee ca.la.lu (Chi.nese ca.la.lu) *noun phrase* (Guyn). A green, succulent, climbing vine which bears a small, purple berry and smooth roundish edible leaves used as a CALALU.

Chi.nese cab.bage *noun phrase* (CarA). **Guyn, Jmca, Tbgo, Trin** ***pakchoy.*** A thick-leaved species of CABBAGE with a thick, white stem, much used as a vegetable in Caribbean dishes.

Chi.nese Christ.mas-tree *noun phrase* (Guyn). See BLIND-EYE.

Chi.nese ed.doe *noun phrase* (CarA). See DASHEEN.

Chi.nese lem.on *noun phrase* (Jmca). See BABY-LIME.

Chi.nese yam *noun phrase* (Guyn, Trin). **Trin** ***potato-yam.*** A variety of YAM which bears a number of smaller yellowish ones on a large tuber.

chi.qui.to ba.na.na *noun phrase* (Trin). See SIKYÉ (SUCRIER)-FIG.

chive(s) *noun* (Trin). See ESCHALLOT.

cho.cho *noun* (Baha, Belz, Jmca, TkCa). See CHRISTOPHENE.

chou ca.ra.ibe *noun phrase* (StLu). See TANNIA.

Christ.mas-bush[1] *noun* (CarA). **Gren** ***Mary-Magdalene*****; Jmca** ***jack-in-the-bush***. A shrub that is sometimes erect that can grow higher than 6 ft, with slender stalks, spear-shaped leaves and bearing white to light mauve flowers which bloom in December; both the leaves and the flowers are used for colds and the leaves as poultices.

Christ.mas-bush[2] *noun* (StKt). See SNOW-ON-THE-MOUNTAIN.

Christ.mas can.dle *noun phrase* (Bdos, Dmca, Nevs, StLu). **CayI** ***candle-flower*****; Jmca** ***candlestick*****; Guyn** ***carrion-crow bush*****; Jmca** ***king-of-the-forest*****; Bdos, Gren, Jmca, Trin** ***ring-worm bush*****; StLu** ***sené-mawon*****; Trin** ***wild-senna*****; VIls** ***sasparila*** A sprawling shrub with compound leaves and round, golden-yellow flowers growing in clusters at the end of erect stalks; the leaves are used for various ailments and the flowers sometimes give off an unpleasant smell.

Christ.mas can.dle.stick *noun phrase* (Baha, Jmca). See BALL-BUSH.

Christ.mas flow.er[1] *noun phrase* (Dmca, Jmca, StVn, Tbgo). See POINSETTIA.

Christ.mas flow.er[2] *noun phrase* (Nevs). See LEAF-OF-LIFE.

chris.to.phene (chris.to.phine) *noun* (ECar). **Baha, Belz, Jmca, TkCa** ***cho-cho***. A green, pear-shaped vegetable with a furrowed and slightly hairy skin and flesh of the texture of squash, borne on a climbing vine with rough, roundish leaves.

chuk-chuk (chook-chook) *noun* (Dmca). See FIT-WEED.

church.yard-grass *noun phrase* (Mrat). See CARPET-DAISY.

cin.na.mon (tree) *noun (phrase)* (CarA). **StLu** ***cannelle*****; Bdos, Dmca, Gren, Guyn** ***spice***. A small tree with long, leathery, green, strongly aromatic leaves, or pieces of its dried bark, both used to flavour food and drink.

Cir.cas.sian bead/bean/seed *noun phrase* (Jmca, Trin, USVI). See JUMBIE-BEAD[3]. (A European name, probably imported from the United States where it is one of the names given to the RED SANDALWOOD TREE.)

cir.ce(e) bush *noun phrase* (Bdos). See CERASEE.

cive(s) *noun* (Gren, Trin). See ESCHALLOT.

clam.my-cher.ry (clam-/clam.(m)a-/ clam.man-cher.ry *noun* (CarA). **Antg** ***sticky berry*****; Antg, Mrat** ***turkey-berry*****; Dmca** ***kaka-poul***[1]**; Jmca** ***duppy-cherry*****; StLu** ***gum-tree, kaka-poul***. A round, creamish fruit with sweet, sticky flesh, covering a single seed, borne in clusters on a small tree with no flowers.

clar.et-fig *noun* **(Clarke-fig)** (Bdos). See BUCK-BANANA.

clar.et-nut (Clara-nut) *noun* (Guyn). See DWARF-COCONUT.

co.chi.neal (cac.tus) *noun (phrase)* (Guyn, Jmca, Trin). **Bdos** ***flat-hand dildo*****; Baha, Bdos, CayI, VIls** ***prickle/ prickler/prickly-pear*****; Trin** ***rachette.*** A cactus resembling a small tree made of many-jointed, pad-like, oblong green stems, which when mature bear a yellowish-red flower and edible red fruit; the pulp of the younger ones is used medicinally.

cock-and-hen tree *noun phrase* (Angu, Antg, Nevs, StKt). See FLAMBOYANT.

cock.roach-grass[1] *noun* (Gren, StKt, Trin). **BrVI** ***French weed*****; Baha, Jmca, USVI** ***wandering Jew.*** A trailing plant with succulent leaves, purplish-green, with two pale green bands above and purplish below, used as an ornamental plant and usually found in shady places.

cock.roach-grass[2] *noun* (Tbgo). See VETIVER.

cock.spur *noun* (TkCa). See BREAD-AND-CHEESE.

co.coa *noun* (Dmca, Gren, Trin). **CarA** ***cocoa-beans.*** The brown beans contained in the pods of the cocoa tree, which are dried and polished before being sold and made into the brown powder from which the beverage COCOA is made.

Cocoa-bean and pod

co.coa-shade *noun* (Trin). See GLIRICIDIA.

co.co.nut *noun* (CarA). **1.** The fruit of the COCONUT-TREE. **2.** The hard white flesh of the mature fruit usually grated for use in cooking.

co.co-plum[1] *noun* (CarA). **ECar** ***fat-pork*****; Berm** ***pork-fat apple*****; Trin** ***cacao-plum*****; Dmca, StLu** ***zikak.*** A brownish-red fruit with white pulp on a single seed, borne on a shrub or small tree.

co.co-plum[2] *noun* (CayI). See DUNKS.

co.co-plum[3] *noun* (TkCa). See JAMAICA-PLUM.

Coco-plum

co.cor.ite (co.kor.ite, ko.ker.ite) *noun* (Guyn). A brown, oval-shaped fruit with a pointed tip and tough skin over sweet, creamy flesh around a hard, black seed.

con.go peas *noun phrase* (CayI). See PIGEON-PEAS.

con.go-pump *noun* (Guyn). See TRUMPET-BUSH.

cook.ing-fig *noun* (Trin). See GOOSEBERRY.

coo.lie-pa.paw *noun* (Gren). See CERASEE.

coo.lie-plum 1. *noun* (Jmca). See DUNKS. **2.** See CHILI-PLUM.

coo.lie-ta.ma.rind *noun* (Gren, Trin). See CARAMBOLA.

co.ra.li.ta *noun* (CarA). **Jmca** ***coral-vine*; Antg** ***honey-bee bush*.** A climbing vine with large heart-shaped leaves which bears bright pink flowers in hanging clusters; it is usually cultivated as an ornamental plant.

cor.di.a (red cor.di.a, scar.let cor. di.a) *noun (phrase)* (Angu, Bdos, CayI, StKt). A shrub or small tree with dark green leaves that bears clusters of red trumpet-like flowers throughout the year; it is usually grown in gardens as an ornamental plant.

cot.ton[1] *noun* (CarA). **VIls** ***cotton-bush***. The native Caribbean shrub with green or brownish, leaves, large yellow or purplish flowers, and a ball-shaped capsule that bursts open when ripe, showing the soft white fibre that is used commercially; the best known variety is SEA-ISLAND COTTON.

cot.ton[2] *noun* (Guyn). See AMERICAN SILK COTTON .

cot.ton-bush *noun* (VIls). See COTTON[1].

cow-foot (bush) *noun (phrase)* (Belz, Guyn). A shrub in two or three varieties which has large, shiny, dark-green leaves and which is said to be of great medicinal value.

Cowitch plant

cow.itch (cow.hage) *noun* (CarA). **Baha** ***monkey-tambran*.** A pod covered with hairs that strongly irritate the skin and which grows in clusters on a climbing vine.

cow-pea *noun* (CarA). See BLACK-EYE PEA.

crab-eye (crab's-eye(s) *noun* (Guyn, Jmca, StKt). See JUMBIE-BEAD[1].

crab-eye vine *noun phrase* (Guyn, Jmca, StKt). See BEAD-VINE (BUSH).

crab-grass *noun* (Guyn, Trin). A creeping wayside grass which roots at the nodes and bears long, slender, hairy stems and leaves.

crab.wood *noun* (Guyn). A tall tree with a dense crown which yields a light-brown or pinkish wood much used in joinery and construction; the seeds yield an oil which is used as a skin lotion and for the relief of pain, swelling and itching.

cro.cus *noun* (Guyn, Jmca, Trin). See AMARYLLIS.

cro.ton *noun* (CarA). A small tree or large shrub of which there are many varieties, all bearing coloured ornamemtal leaves, widely grown as a garden or potted plant in the Caribbean.

cush-cush (yam) *noun (phr)* (ECar). **Guyn** ***bell-yam; buck-yam*; StLu** ***couche-couche*.** An oval-shaped variety among several varieties of YAM, growing in clusters and slightly sweetish and pink when cooked, considered the most delicious of yams grown in the Caribbean. (From Hausa *kush-kush*; Arabic *kus-kus* 'a food made of wheat'.)

cus.tard-ap.ple *noun* (CarA). **Jmca, StVn** ***bullock's heart*; Dmca, StLu** ***cachiman*; Gren** ***snat-apple, tjè-bèf*.** A pinkish-cream or brownish fruit, about the size of the human fist, with grainy, yellowish, sweet custard-like flesh.

cut.lass-bean *noun* (Jmca). **1.** See JUMBIE-BEAD[2]. **2.** See BEAN-TREE.

C

D

dag.ger-plant *noun* (Antg, Dmca, StVn). See AGAVE and CENTURY-PLANT.

dai.sy *noun* (Guyn). See CARPET-DAISY.

dame-and-ca.va.lier *noun* (Dmca). See BACHELOR'S BUTTON.

dam.sel *noun* (Gren, StVn, Trin). See GOOSEBERRY.

dam.son *noun* (Belz). See JAMOON.

dan.de.lion *noun* (Jmca). See WILD COFFEE.

da.sheen (da.chine) *noun* (CarA). **Bdos** ***eddoe-head*****; Berm** ***eddoe*****[2]; Gren** ***Barbados eddoe*****; Gren, Guyn, Trin** ***Chinese eddoe***. A low-growing stemless plant with edible tubers that produce a number of smaller, smoother SUCKERS called EDDOES; it has large, edible, purplish leaves which grow on tall stalks branching directly into the tuber.

da.sheen-bush *noun* (Tbgo, Trin). See CALALU[1].

date-palm *noun* (CarA). A tall palm, found in many varieties, with a rough trunk and long, bluish-green branches that curve outwards and downwards; it is usually a decorative tree, but bears no fruit in the Caribbean.

Date-palm

de.vil-grass *noun* (Bdos, Guyn, Trin). See BAHAMA-GRASS.

de.vil's horse.whip *noun phrase* (Jmca). See MAN-BETTER-MAN.

de.vil's tree *noun phrase* (Bdos). See BEAN-TREE.

de.vil's trum.pet *noun phrase* (Jmca). See THORN-APPLE.

dew-plum *noun* (CayI). See JEW-PLUM[2].

dil.do *noun* (CarA). **Bdos** ***(columnar) cactus*****; VIls** ***pipe-organ cactus***. An erect, leafless cactus with a columnar stem and many branches with ribs and sharp spines, which bears greenish-purple flowers and round, purplish fruit with many black seeds.

dil.ly (dil.lie) *noun* (Baha, TkCa). See SAPODILLA.

di.té-pé.yi (di.tay-pay.ee) *noun* (Dmca, Gren, StLu, Tbgo, Trin). **Guyn** ***wild-tea*****; Jmca** ***goatweed***. An erect, bushy, roadside herb with hairy stems and long leaves bearing small pinkish-white flowers, used to make tea to help in treating colds, fevers and as an internal cleanser. (French Creole from French *du thé (du) pays* 'country tea'.)

djou.boul (ju.boule) *noun* (StLu). See BLUGGO. (French Creole name, used mostly in rural St Lucia.)

dod.der *noun* (Antg, BrVI, Jmca, Mrat, Trin). See LOVE-VINE.

dog-al.mond *noun* (VIls). See ANGELIN.

dog-dump.lings *noun* (Bdos). See PAIN-KILLER (BUSH).

dog.wood[1] *noun* (Baha, Jmca, USVI). A tall tree which bears whitish, greenish or purplish flowers and light-golden pods; it is used in construction and its crushed bark is also said to cure mange in dogs.

dog-wood[2] *noun* (Baha, Jmca, USVI). A tall tree, bearing pinkish and sometimes yellow flowers that are papery in texture; it usually grows in thickets and on limestone and bauxite-bearing soil.

don.key-cac.tus *noun* (USVI). See SPANISH NEEDLE.

don.key-eye *noun* (Gren, Tbgo, Trin). See NICKER.

duck-weed[1] *noun* (Guyn). See WATER-HYACINTH.

duck-weed[2] *noun* (Bdos). A flat, green, pond-plant with broad leaves and small flowers.

duck-weed[3] *noun* (Bdos). A herb with many branches growing out of its base in the shape of 'mats' with spiny leaves and small, yellow flowers which flourishes on lawns, on the seashore and on wasteland.

dunk(s) *noun (plural)* (Bdos, Guyn, StKt, StVn). **Angu, Nevs, StKt** ***pomme-surette*; Antg *dumbs, dumps*; Baha, Jmca *juju(be)*; Belz *governor-plum***[2]**; CayI *coco-plum***[2]**, *Jew-plum***[2]**; Guyn *dungs*; Jmca *coolie-plum* 1**. A small, round, plum-like fruit, yellow to yellowish, or light-brown when ripe with a single, hard seed, covered by white, dryish sourish-sweet flesh; some varieties of the tree give off an unpleasant smell when in bloom.

Dunk

dup.py-ba.sil *noun* (Bdos). **CarA *mosquito-bush*; Jmca *wild-basil/bassley*.** An aromatic, annual, erect, bushy herb, bearing white or lavender flowers with purple spots with black seeds; it is sometimes used medicinally for colds and stomach disorders.

dup.py-cap *noun* (Jmca). See DUPPY-PARASOL.

dup.py-cher.ry *noun* (Jmca). See CLAMMY-CHERRY.

dup.py-cho-cho *noun* (Jmca). See AMERICAN SILK-COTTON.

dup.py-gun *noun* (Jmca). **CarA *minnie-root*; Guyn *blue-bell***[1]. A sturdy, perennial bush with erects shoots and bearing mauve or bluish-purple, trumpet-shaped flowers and long thin pods which split in wet weather; the plant is used a folk remedy for kidney problems and general debilitation.

dup.py-nee.dle *noun* (Bdos). **Bdos *monkey-needle, needle-grass*; Jmca, StKt, StVn, USVI *Spanish needle*.** An annual herb with a straight, square stem, leaflets and long, yellow, daisy-like flower-heads and spiny seeds which stick to clothing.

dup.py-pa.ra.sol *noun* (Bdos). **CarA *jumbie-umbrella*; Jmca *duppy-umbrella, duppy-cap*.** A poisonous, wild mushroom with a soft, cup-like top on a short stem, or a harder, ruffled, semicircular outgrowth from rotting wood; both types are found in damp, shady places.

dup.py-um.brel.la *noun* (Bdos, Jmca). See DUPPY-PARASOL.

dwarf-ba.na.na[1] *noun* (Baha, Trin). See APPLE-BANANA.

dwarf-ba.na.na[2] *noun* (Trin). A short, stout variety of BANANA which grows on a short, tough tree.

dwarf-co.co.nut *noun* (Belz, Dmca, Gren, StKt). **Bdos *yellow-boy*; Guyn *claret-nut*; StLu *yellow-dwarf (coconut)*.** A yellow-skinned species of COCONUT which is much smaller than the regular green-skinned ones, grows in clusters on a short tree, and is much valued for the sweetness of its water.

dwarf-poin.ci.a.na *noun* (CarA). See BARBDOS-PRIDE.

E

East.er-flow.er *noun* (Bdos, Trin). A tough, climbing shrub that bears quantities of small, reddish-mauve, pea-like flowers around Easter, hence the name.

East.er-li.ly[1] *noun* (Berm, Trin). A large, white, sweet-smelling, trumpet-shaped lily, borne in horizontal clusters on upright stalks.

East.er-li.ly[2] *noun* (Bdos, Dmca, Guyn). A bright red lily growing in clusters of two or three together on short stalks.

East-Ind.i.an man.go *noun phrase* (Jmca). See BOMBAY-MANGO.

e.bo.ny[1] *noun* (Bdos). See WOMAN-TONGUE TREE.

e.bo.ny[2] *noun* (Baha, CayI, Jmca). **Baha *red-wood*; Jmca *ketto*.** A tall, slender tree which produces a tough, sturdy wood.

e.bo.ny[3] *noun* (Guyn). A very tall forest tree with an erect, grooved trunk which yields a deep purple, extremely tough wood.

e.bo.ny[4] *noun* (ViIs). See AXEMASTER.

e.bo.ny-ber.ry *noun* (Angu). See JAMOON.

ed.doe[1] *noun* (CarA). **Bdos *pulp(-ing)-eddoe, white eddoe*.** A low-growing plant with heart-shaped leaves and upright stalks which yields edible tubers, each about the size of a potato, much prized as a vegetable, particularly for making soup.

ed.doe[2] *noun* (Berm). See DASHEEN.

ed.doe-head *noun* (Bdos). See DASHEEN.

egg-fruit *noun* (CarA). See EGGPLANT.

egg.plant (egg-plant) *noun* (CarA). **CarA *egg-fruit*; Antg, Gren, StVn, Tbgo, Trin *aubergine*; Antg, Brbu *antrover (antrova)*; Dmca, Gren *balangene*; Bdos, Guyn, Mrat, StVn, Trin, USVI *bo(u)langer*; Dmca, StLu, Trin *melongene*; Guyn, Trin *baigan*; CayI, Jmca, TkCa *garden-egg*.** A smooth-skinned, oval-shaped or round, purple fruit with soft creamish flesh in which there are many tiny seeds; it is much used as a vegetable in the Caribbean.

el.der (el.der-ber.ry) *noun* (Bdos, Belz, Brbu, Jmca, USVI). A small tree, with a thickish trunk that bears fragrant, abundant, circular clusters of white, round, juicy, purple-black fruits; it is used medicinally by some.

el.der-bush *noun* (Bdos, Guyn). A shrub which bears yellow, bell-shaped flowers, the leaves of which are used as a cure for various ailments.

e.le-phant-grass *noun* (CarA). **Jmca *Napier grass*.** A coarse, fast-growing, grass with sugar-cane like stems used for cattle fodder.

e.le.phant's ear (e.le.phant-ear(s) *noun phrase* (Baha, Bdos). An ornamental plant bearing large, triangular-shaped, shiny, green leaves usually found in moist areas.

Eng.lish plum *noun phrase* (Nevs). See GOVERNOR-PLUM.

Eng.lish po.ta.to *noun phrase* (CarA). **CarA *potato*; Antg, Bdos, Guyn, Mrat, StVn *white potato*; Guyn, Jmca *Irish potato*.** The internationally known potato which was originally imported from England.

es.chal.lot *noun* (Bdos, Guyn). **Bdos, Guyn *seasoning*; Gren, Trin *chives, cive*; Jmca *escallion, skellion*.** A plant of the onion family with long, slender hollow green leaves growing from a small, onion-like bulb, much valued as a seasoning in the Caribbean. (From French échalote 'shallot, scallion'.)

eu.phor.bi.a *noun* (Gren). See SNOW-ON-THE-MOUNTAIN.

e.ver.green *noun* (CarA). **1.** Any one of several bushy shrubs or large shade trees that are green and keep their leaves throughout the year. **2.** (Bdos, Jmca) Several varieties of large, bushy, green shade tree, bearing pea-like fruit and putting down aerial roots.

F

false mam.mee *noun phrase* (USVI). See PITCH-APPLE.

fan-leaf palm *noun phrase* (Bdos). See SILVER-THATCH PALM.

fat-pork *noun* (ECar). See COCO-PLUM[1].

fence-post tree *noun phrase* (USVI). See BIRCH-GUM TREE.

fe.ver-grass *noun* (CarA). **Bdos, Dmca, Gren, Guyn, TkCa, Trin *lemon-grass*; TkCa *tea-grass*.** An aromatic grass that grows in tufts with tapering, rough-edged leaves and a longer stalk in the centre bearing a cluster of flowers; the leaves have a strong lemony scent and are widely used as a remedy for the relief of fever, colds, etc.

fid.dle-wood *noun* (CarA). A hard, pale wood produced by about four varieties of tall trees with a papery, flaky bark and bearing clusters of small, white flowers and small, reddish fruit. (The name comes from the use of this wood to make fiddles and guitars.)

fig[1] *noun* (CarA). The word generally used for BANANA in the Caribbean.

fig[2] *noun* (Bdos, StKt, StVn, TkCa, USVI). See APPLE-BANANA.

fin.ger-pep.per *noun* (Baha, Bdos). See BIRD-PEPPER.

fit-weed *noun* (CarA). **Dmca *chuk-chuk*; Gren, StLu, StVn, Tbgo, Trin *shado-beni*; StKt *cat-claw*; StVn *shadow-vinnie bush*.** A stong-smelling wild herb with long leaves growing in bunches from its base, and a central stalk bearing green flowers with stiff, pointed petals; it is used for relief of epileptic fits and also for colds.

Fit-weed

five-fin.ger[1] *noun* (Guyn, Mrat, Trin). See CARAMBOLA.

five-fin.ger[2] *noun* (Angu, StKt, USVI). **Jmca *ink-berry (tree)*.** A stiff, erect shrub or small tree with a smooth, grey bark and spiny leaves which bears a blue berry that stains; it is also used folk-medicinally.

fla.gu-plan.tain *noun* (Belz). See BLUGGO.

flam.boy.ant (tree) *noun (phrase)* (CarA). **Angu, Antg, Nevs, StKt *cock-and-hen tree*; Antg, BrVI, StLu, StVn *shack-shack tree*; ECar *poinciana*, *royal poinciana*; Trin *flame-of-the-forest*, *flame tree*.** A medium-sized, umbrella-shaped tree with feathery leaves which fall leaving the tree bare, with long, dry, hanging pods for a few months, which then bust into clusters of bright red flowers, that can also be orange, white or golden in less well known varieties. (From French *flamboyer* 'to flame', *flamboyant* 'flaming' to describe the striking redness of the flowers in full bloom).

Flamboyant tree

flat-hand dil.do *noun phrase* (Bdos). See COCHINEAL (CACTUS).

flat-o-the-earth *noun* (Guyn). A low growing annual herb with thin stems bearing small, white flowers, and greenish, spiny fruit, found in pastures; the entire plant is used to make a cooling tea to relieve heat rash and it is also said to be good for heart palpitations.

flow.er-fence *noun* (Baha, Jmca). See BARBADOS-PRIDE.

for.bid.den fruit[1] *noun phrase* (Belz). See GRAPEFRUIT.

for.bid.den fruit[2] *noun phrase* (Guyn). See SHADDOCK.

for.bid.den fruit[3] *noun phrase* (Guyn). See PASSION FRUIT and CANNON-BALL TREE.

four o'clock (bush) *noun phrase* (Angu, Baha, Bdos, Gren, Jmca, Trin). One of several varieties of a small plant usually found in shady, moist places; it bears pink, yellow, scarlet, or purplish flowers that open around 4:00 p.m.; it is also used as a folk medicine and the leaves as a poultice for sprains.

Four o'clock bush

fowl-foot grass *noun phrase* (CarA). An annual grass, growing quite high with erect, smooth leaves growing from the base and a central stem, topped by a small cluster of small, hairy spikes, spread out in the shape of a hen's foot.

Frangipani tree

fran.gi.pa.ni *noun* (CarA). An ornamental, small tree, with stiff branches, forking at the tips from which grow clusters of pink, red, white or yellow flowers; it gives off a milky substance.

French ca.shew *noun phrase* (Guyn). See MALACCA-APPLE.

French cot.ton *noun phrase* (Bdos). See AMERICAN SILK-COTTON.

French thyme *noun phrase* (StVn). See THICK-LEAF THYME.

French weed[1] *noun phrase* (BrVI). See COCKROACH-GRASS[1].

French weed[2] *noun phrase* (Antg). See WATER-GRASS.

fresh-cut *noun* (Jmca). See GARDEN-BALSAM.

fu.fu man.go *noun phrase* (Guyn). See MANGO GRAHAM.

G

ga.la.ba *noun* (StVn). See GALBA.

gal.ba *noun* (Dmca, Gren, StVn, Trin). **StVn *galaba***. A tall, evergreen tree, with large, glossy green leaves, small, white flowers and bearing an inedible fruit with one large seed; it yields a tough, yellow, durable timber used in woodwork.

gan.ja *noun* (CarA). **CarA *marijuana***; **Jmca *holy herb***. A highly potent, narcotic herb, the leaves of which are usually smoked; its use is largely illegal in the Caribbean, except for Jamaica where small quantities are legally allowed for personal or medicinal use.

gar.den-bal.sam *noun* (Bdos, Jmca, Trin, USVI). **Guyn *toyo*; Jmca *fresh-cut*; Trin**

carpenter-grass. A small, shrub with slender stems and small pink, white or pale-blue flowers, usually cultivated for its leaves, and often used as a cold remedy.

gar.den-cher.ry *noun* (CayI, Jmca). See BARBADOS-CHERRY.

gar.den-egg *noun* (CayI, Gren, Jmca, TkCa). See EGGPLANT.

gar.den-grapes *noun plural* (Nevs, StKt). Locally grown purple grapes.

gar.den-peas *noun plural* (Trin). A variety of peas enclosed in short pods, growing on an annual, climbing vine, and of good food value.

gar.den-plum *noun* (Guyn). See CHILLI-PLUM.

G

gar.den-pump.kin *noun* (Bdos). See BELLY-PUMPKIN, PUMPKIN.

ge.nip *noun* (CarA). See GUINEP.

gé.ri.tout (ge.ri.tou, gué.rir-tout, gué. rit-tout) *noun* **1.** (Trin). See CATTLE-TONGUE. **2.** (Gren). See LEAF-OF-LIFE.

ghaut (gut)-apple *noun* (Antg). See MONKEY-APPLE[2].

ghaut (ghut)-plum *noun* (Angu, Antg BrVI, Nevs). See HOG-PLUM.

gi.ant fig *noun phrase* (Gren). See LACATAN BANANA.

gin.ger *noun* (CarA). A low-growing shrub whose hot, spicy roots are popularly used for medicinal and flavouring purposes; the roots are also made into powder and used for the manufacture of preserved ginger.

gin.ger-li.ly[1] *noun* (Bdos). **Bdos *red ginger-lily***. A bright crimson or red, cone-shaped, upright floral head borne at the end of a tall, erect stalk, made up of large, open red petals, growing between large, green, blade-like leaves and widely used ornamentally.

gin.ger-li.ly[2] *noun* (Guyn, Jmca, Trin). A sweet-smelling lily of different varieties – white, pink, yellow, cream – growing in clusters of three or four flowers on stems from a fleshy stalk.

Gin.ger Tho.mas *noun phrase* (USVI). A small, funnel-shaped, yellow flower about 2 in. in diameter growing on a shrub or small tree which also bears long pods containing many winged seeds; the national flower of the USVI.

gli.ri.ci.di.a (gli.ri.ci.da) *noun* (Angu, Bdos, StLu, StVn). **Angu, Dmca, Gren *glory-cedar*; Jmca *Aaron's rod, quick-stick*; Mrat, StVn *rain-bush*; StKt *wind-break*; Trin *cocoa-shade***. A small tree which loses its leaves in the dry season and bears abundant clusters of lilac-coloured flowers and flat pods; the plant is much used as a shade tree for cacao and for making fence posts.

Gliricidia

(glo.ri.ci.da, glo.ri.si.di.a) *noun* (Angu, Dmca, Gren). See GLIRICIDIA.

goat-bush *noun* (Brbu). See BREAD-AND-CHEESE.

goat's foot creep.er *noun phrase* (Guyn). See IPOMEA.

goat-rose *noun* (Trin). See OLD-MAID BUSH.

goat-weed *noun* (Jmca). See DITÉ-PÉYI.

god-bush *noun* (Jmca). See BIRD-VINE.

gold.en-ap.ple[1] *noun* (CarA). **Belz *golden-plum*; Gren, StLu, Trin, VIls *ponm-sité*; Jmca *Jew-plum*.** A round, edible fruit, shaped like an apple, but golden in colour when ripe, and with veined flesh on a single spiny seed.

gold.en-plum *noun* (Belz). See GOLDEN-APPLE.

gold.en-show.er *noun* (Bdos). **Bdos *shower of gold*; Trin *cat's claw creeper*.** A large climbing vine which usually grows on the branches of trees or on walls, and bears masses of long, striking, yellow flowers; it has hooked tendrils which enables it to cling on to trees and has earned it the name of 'cat's claw'.

Golden-shower vine

goose.ber.ry *noun* (CarA). **Jmca *cheramina, jimbelin, jimbling, sour barge*; Gren, StVn, Trin *damsel*; Trin *Otaheiti gooseberry*.** A small, ribbed, greenish-yellow fruit with scanty, white, acid flesh on a single seed, borne in clusters on a small tree.

gos.pò *noun* (Dmca, Gren, Trin). See SOUR ORANGE.

gourd[1] (gou(r)ge) *noun* (StKt, StLu, Trin). **Guyn *lauki*; CarA *marrow*; CarA *squash*; Bdos, Jmca *vegetable marrow*.** Any one of a few varieties of a green, smooth-skinned, bottle-shaped vegetable, sometimes long, sometimes shorter, borne on a climbing vine with heart-shaped leaves, and firm white flesh.

gourd[2] *noun* (Jmca). See CALABASH.

gov.er.nor-balls *noun* (Bdos). See BALL-BUSH.

gov.er.nor-fig *noun* (Trin). **Trin *cooking-fig, dwarf-banana*.** A short, stout variety of BANANA, growing on a short tree and used as a vegetable.

gov.er.nor-plum[1] *noun* (CarA). **CarA *cerise*; Nevs *English plum*; StLu *miwiz*; Guyn *psidium*.** A small, round, purple fruit, like a marble, with many seeds in sour-sweet brown flesh, softened by squeezing before it is eaten, and borne on a small tree, covered in spines.

gov.er.nor-plum[2] *noun phrase* (Belz). See DUNKS.

graft.ed man.go *noun phrase* (CarA). **Angu, Bdos, Gren, Guyn, Jmca *Julie-mango*.** A variety of mango with a chin-shaped end, a flat seed, and sweet, juicy flesh.

Gra.ham(-man.go) *noun* (StLu). See MANGO-GRAHAM.

graine-en-bas-feuille *noun* (Dmca, Gren, Trin). See GWENN-ANBA-FÈY.

G

gran.a.dil.la (gren.a.dil.la) *noun* (CarA). **Dmca, StLu, Trin *barbadine*.** A large, yellowish-green fruit, with slightly acid pulp, borne on a vine and much used to make drinks and punches.

gra.na.di.ta *noun* (Jmca). A type of PASSION-FRUIT with a hard skin that is purple when ripe.

gran.ny-back.bone *noun* (Guyn). A woody, forest climbing-vine, with flat stems, often used as a folk medicine for pains. (A medicinal plant referred to in the 'Weed Song' from Guyana that became famous in the Caribbean during the 1930s.)

grape.fruit *noun* (CarA). **Belz *forbidden fruit*[1]**. A fruit like a large variety of orange with pale yellow skin and flesh, the latter sometimes pink, and usually tasting bitter-sweet, although there are other varieties that are sweet.

G

grape-tree *noun* (Bdos, CayI, Guyn, Jmca). The tree that bears the SEASIDE-GRAPE.

grat.er-wood *noun* (Trin). See SAGE-BUSH[2].

greas.y-bush *noun* (Baha, Jmca). **1.** See WOMAN-PIABA. **2.** (Tbgo, Trin) A weedy shrub which grows into a climbing-vine with hairy stems and leaves, and white flowers which become dry nuts; it is used to make a tea for cooling the blood or for baths for the sick.

green ba.na.na (green fig) *noun phrase* (CarA). The young BANANA, cooked as a vegetable and often eaten with saltfish.

green fig *noun phrase* (CarA). See GREEN BANANA.

green.heart *noun* (Guyn). A very tall forest tree which yields a hard, heavy, brown to yellowish-green wood, which is extremely strong and termite and water-resistant and much used in construction.

gri.chi-gri.chi (grit.chee-grit.chee) *noun* (USVI). See SENSITIVE PLANT. (A folk name prob from Dutch Grietje 'Peggy'.)

gri-gri (palm) *noun (phrase)* (Trin). **Guyn *pimple-palm*.** One of two varieties of a slim palm with a pale bark whose trunk and leaves are full of sharp, black spines and bearing clusters of small, edible fruit with a hard seed and scanty pulp.

Gros Mi.chel (ba.na.na) (Gwo Mi.chèl) *noun (phrase)* (CarA). The largest and most valued of all cultivated varieties of BANANA, borne on a huge bunch and most suitable for export. (French meaning 'big Michael' referring to the size of the tree, the fruit and the bunch which can grow up to about 5ft long.)

gros-pom-pom; gros-tête *noun* (StLu). See GWO PON PON; GWO-TÈT.

grou-grou (gru-gru, gwou-gwou, gwu-gwu) *noun* (Gren, StVn, Tbgo, Trin). **Antg, Bdos, StKt *macaw*[1]; Bdos *macaw-palm*; Belz, Jmca *macca-palm*.** An erect palm with a tough trunk and leaves covered at intervals in long, stout, black spines, which bears clusters of edible, reddish fruit on a hard seed.

grou-grou bèf (gru-gru bèf, grou-grou bèf, gwu-gwu bèf) *noun phrase* (Trin). **Jmca *macca-fat*. 1.** A tougher variety of the GROU-GROU, but used to refer to its much bigger fruit which has a very hard nut. **2.** (Guyn, Trin) ***banga(r)*** The dried, hard seed of the palm, used by boys as a marble. (French Creole from French *bœuf* 'bull, cow', often used to indicate large-sized fruit.)

grudge-pea *noun* (Gren). **Bdos, Jmca, Trin *horse-bean*; Jmca, Trin *jack-bean*; Gren, Trin *maldjo*; Bdos, Jmca *overlook-bean*; Bdos *sword-bean*.** A green, bushy plant with long stems which tend to climb and which bears purple flowers and long, stiff, green pods that can be used as a vegetable.

gru-gru bèf (gwou-gwou bèf, gwu-gwu bèf) *noun phrase* (Trin). See GROU-GROU BÈF.

guan.go *noun* (Jmca). See SAMAN (TREE).

gua.va *noun* (CarA). A roundish, yellow fruit, with sweet or sour pink or white flesh in which there are many seeds, borne on a tough-limbed tree.

gua.va.ber.ry *noun* (VIls). A purple, smooth-skinned juicy berry borne on a tree that resembles the GUAVA tree, but has smaller leaves; the fruit is used to make a syrup that is often added to rum to make a Christmas drink.

gub-gub *noun* (Trin). See BLACK-EYE PEA.

guér.ir-tout (guér.it tout) *noun* (Trin, Gren, USVI). See GÉRITOU.

gui.nea-corn *noun* (CarA). One of many varieties of a strong, erect, annual grass which yields a small-grained corn of different colours – black, white, red, yellow – which are ground to make GUINEA-CORN FLOUR.

gui.nea-grass *noun* (CarA). A coarse grass with long blades and flowering shoots above the leaves, that grows in thick clumps and is used as cattle fodder.

gui.nea-hen weed *noun phrase* (Baha, Bdos, Jmca). See GULLY-ROOT.

gui.nea-pepper *noun* (Berm). See BIRD-PEPPER.

gui.nea-yam *noun* (Dmca, Gren, Jmca, Tbgo, Trin). **Baha *white-yam*.** A yam of which there seem to be two closely similar varieties, one yellow and one white.

gui.nep (ge.nip, gi.nep) *noun* (CarA). **Bdos, StLu, StVn *akee*; Baha, TkCa

Guinep

canep, canop; Mrat *canop*; Dmca, StLu, Tbgo, Trin *chennette*; Gren, Guyn, StKt *skinip, skinop*; Dmca, StLu *quenette, tjènnet*.** A small, round fruit with a tough green skin over scant, salmon-coloured, pleasant-tasting flesh on a single hard seed and which grows in bunches on a tall tree.

G

gul.ly-bean *noun* (Jmca). See BURA-BURA.

gul.ly-plum *noun* (Bdos). See HOG-PLUM[1].

gul.ly-root *noun* (CarA). **Baha, Bdos, Jmca *guinea-hen weed*; Dmca, Gren, StVn *kojo-root*; Jmca *strong-man weed*.** An erect weed about 3 ft tall which bears tough stems ending in little tufts of tiny white flowers; the leaves are long and pointed and the plant, which smells like garlic, is popularly used as a cure for fevers, aches and skin complaits.

Gully-root

gum-e.le.mi (ga.ma.la.mi) *noun* (Baha, TkCa). See BIRCH-GUM.

gum-tree *noun* (StLu). See CLAMMY-CHERRY.

gun.go(-peas) *noun* (Belz, CayI, Jmca). See PIGEON-PEAS. (An African word from the Kikongo language *ngungu* 'peas'.)

Gungo peas

gwenn-an-ba-fèy (graine-en-bas-feuille) *noun* (Dmca, Gren, Trin). **StVn, Tbgo, Trin** ***seed-under-leaf.*** One of about three varieties of a short, green weed with a single stem, branching at intervals, the branches looking like compound leaves; the seeds are green or reddish and borne on the underside of each leaf-stalk which gives the plant its name; it is also used folk medicinally. (French Creole from French – 'seed under leaf'.)

Gwo Mi.chel (gros Mi.chel) *noun phase* (Dmca, StLu). See GROS MICHEL.

gwo pon pon *noun phrase* (StLu). See BALL-BUSH. (French *gros pompon* 'big pompom'.)

gwo-tèt *noun* (Dmca). See BALL-BUSH. (French Creole from French *gros tête* 'big head'.)

gwou-gwou (grou-grou, gwu-gwu) *noun* (Dmca, StLu). See GROU-GROU.

gwou-gwou bèf (grou-grou bèf, gwu-gwu-bèf) *noun phrase* (Trin). See GROU-GROU BÈF.

gwu-gwu (gwou-gwou, grou-grou, gru-gru) *noun* (StLu). See GROU-GROU.

gwu-gwu bèf *noun phrase* (Trin). See GROU-GROU BÈF.

ha.ba.ne.ro *noun* (Belz). A fiery hot, red, yellow or green pepper, popularly used in cooking. (Sp *habanero, noun and adjective,* 'a person or thing from Cuba', but the reason for it being connected with heat is not obvious.)

ha.i.a.ri (ha.i.ar.ry) *noun* (Guyn). **Guyn** ***bush-rope*** **2.** A sturdy, parasitic, forest vine, the roots of which are ground up and thrown into the river in order to drug fish and catch them more easily. (An Arawak word which is the name of this vine.)

hair.y man.go *noun phrase* (Belz, Gren, Jmca, Mrat, Nevs, StVn). **Guyn, Tbgo, Trin** ***long mango*****; Dmca** ***mango-bab*****; StLu** ***mango-fil*****; Bdos** ***mango-long.*** A well-known variety of MANGO with a greenish skin, which is juicy, but its flesh is extremely stringy and tends to stick between the teeth when sucked, thereby giving it its name.

hait.i-hai.ti (tree) *noun (phrase)* (USVI). See SEASIDE-MAHOE.

hard co.co *noun phrase* (Jmca). See TANNIA.

hard-yam *noun* (Guyn). See YELLOW-YAM.

head.ache-bush *noun* (Angu, Baha, Jmca). A shrub or small tree about 20 ft tall on rocky slopes, the leaves of which are used by some to cure headache.

hedge-cac.tus *noun* (CarA). See CACTUS-HEDGE.

he.li.co.ni.a *noun* (CarA). **Bdos** ***lobster-claw*****; Dmca, Gren, StLu, Tbgo, Trin** ***balisier, balayé*****; Guyn, Trin** ***wild plantain.*** A variety of WILD-BANANA, growing brightly coloured clusters of large, yellow or scarlet, or scarlet and yellow flowers in large sheaths shaped like boats, on a central stem, either growing straight up, or hanging down.

hi.bis.cus *noun* (CarA). A flowering shrub which bears large, brightly coloured pink, red, yellow, purple or peach flowers; it is often used to make hedges.

Hibiscus – pink and purple

hog-ap.ple *noun* (Jmca). See JUMBIE SOURSOP.

hog-ba.na.na *noun* (Baha, TkCa). See BLUGGO.

hog-plum[1] *noun* (CarA) **Angu, Antg, BrVI, Nevs** ***ghaut-plum*****; Bdos** ***gully-plum*****; Belz, CayI** ***yellow-plum*****; Guyn, Trin** ***plum*****[1]; Jmca** ***yellow-coat (plum)***. A round fruit made up of acid pulp around a large seed, borne on a tree with long leaves and small, yellowish-white, sweet-smelling flowers. (Maybe from Arawak *hobo* 'hog-plum', Carib *oubou* and Spanish *jobo*, the name widely used for this frut in Latin America.)

hog-plum[2] *noun* (Baha, Belz, Jmca, TkCa). See CHILLI-PLUM.

hol.ly-hock *noun* (Bdos, Gren), See THISTLE.

ho.ly herb/weed *noun phrase* (Jmca). See GANJA.

ho.ney-bee bush *noun phrase* (Antg). See CORALITA.

horse-ba.na.na *noun* (BrVI, Nevs). See BLUGGO.

horse-bean *noun phrase* (Bdos, Jmca, Trin). See GRUDGE-PEA.

horse-man.go *noun* (Belz). See MANGO-GRAHAM.

horse-nick.er *noun* (Bdos). See NICKER.

horse-plan.tain (horn-plan.tain) *noun* (Guyn, Jmca, Trin). The largest variety of PLANTAIN.

hum.ming-bird trumpet *noun phrase* (Trin). See ANTIGUA HEATH.

hy.a.cinth-bean *noun* (Angu, Berm, Trin). See BONAVIST.

I

I.bo yam *noun phrase* (Mrat). See YELLOW YAM.

im.mor.tel(l)e *noun* (CarA) **Gren** ***mortel***. A tall, spreading tree with flame-coloured flowers, borne profusely early in the year, and usually grown as a shade tree for COCOA plants.

in.cense-tree *noun phrase* (Jmca). See BIRCH-GUM TREE.

in.crease-peas *noun* (Bdos). **Bdos** ***rouncival (rounceval, runciful)***. Small, bean-shaped peas in pods about 8 ins long, borne on a wild vine; they are cooked either when green or dried pale brown.

In.di.an al.mond *noun phrase* (ECar). See ALMOND.

In.di.a-rub.ber plant/tree *noun phrase* (CarA). **CarA *rubber-plant*.** A pot-plant or small, ornamental tree with large, shiny, brownish-green leaves and aerial roots, which help it to spread widely.

in.flam.ma.tion-bush (in.form.a.tion-bush) *noun* (CarA). Any one of two or more herbs, which can be used for the relief of swelling, inflammation and pains.

ink.ber.ry (tree) *noun (phrase)* (Jmca). See FIVE-FINGER[2].

i.po.me.a *noun* (CarA). **Guyn *goat's-foot creeper*; Jmca *morning-glory*; Bdos *seaside-yam*.** An attractive, creeping vine with ribbed, fleshy, green leaves and crimson-purple flowers, which thrives on sandy beaches, growing thickly on the ground.

i.xo.ra *noun* (CarA). A flowering, bushy shrub with smooth, leathery, green leaves which bears bunches of bright red flowers in round clusters throughout the year.

J

jack-bean *noun* (Jmca, Trin). See GRUDGE-PEA.

jack.fruit *noun* (CarA). A large, oddly shaped yellowish-green fruit resembling a BREADFRUIT, borne on a large tree and eaten either raw when ripe or cooked before it is ripe.

jack-in-the-beanstalk *noun* (USVI). See AUGUST-FLOWER.

Jack-in-the-box *noun* (Bdos, Guyn). A large, forest tree which yields timber for boat-building and flooring.

Jack-in-the-bush *noun* (Jmca). **CarA *Christmas-bush*.** A shrub with pointed, oval-shaped leaves and white to pale mauve flowers which usually blooms in December.

Ja.cob's coat *noun phrase* (Bdos, Guyn). See JOSEPH'S COAT.

Ja.mai.ca-ac.kee *noun* (StVn). See ACKEE.

Ja.mai.ca-ap.ple *noun* (Baha). See CUSTARD-APPLE.

Ja.mai.ca-plum *noun* (Bdos, BrVI, Gren, Tbgo, Trin). **Antg, Bdos, Gren, Tbgo, Trin *chilli-plum*; Baha *sweet-plum*; Baha, TkCa *hog-plum*[2], *scarlet-plum*; Bdos, Tbgo *bubby-plum*; Belz *May plum*; CayI *big-plum*, *red-plum*; CayI, Jmca *leather-coat plum*; Dmca, Gren, Nevs *plum*[2]; Jmca *red-coat plum*; StLu *pwinn Mowis*, *pwinn-tété*; StVn *Bequia-plum*; Tbgo, Trin *cerise*[1], *governor-plum*; TkCa *coco-plum*[3].** A small, round red or purplish fruit with a single seed, covered by scanty, sweet flesh.

Jamaican plum

ja.moon *noun* (Guyn). **Angu *ebony-berry*; Antg, Jmca *Java-plum*[1]; Bdos *jamur*; Belz *black-berry*, *damson*.** A round, dark-purple fruit like a plum with one seed and juicy, sweetish-sour, purple flesh, borne in clusters on a tall tree. (From Hindi *jaaman* 'black plum'.)

ja.mur *noun* (Bdos). See JAMOON.

Ja.va-plum[1] *noun* (Antg, Jmca). See JAMOON.

Ja.va-plum[2] *noun* (Dmca, Mrat, StVn). See ROSE-APPLE.

Jew-plum[1] **(dew-plum, June-plum)** *noun* (Jmca). See GOLDEN-APPLE.

Jew-plum[2] **(dew-plum, June-plum)** *noun* (CayI). See DUNKS.

jhin.gie *noun* (Guyn). A type of green squash with tough, ridged skin and green pulp; the green fruit is used in Caribbean cooking to make curry and the dried fruit is used as a scrubber. (A Bhojpuri word from Hindi *jhinggii* the name of this fruit.)

jim.be.lin *noun* (Jmca). See GOOSEBERRY.

jim.bling (jim. be.lin) *noun* (Jmca). See GOOSEBERRY.

Job's tears *noun phrase* (Bdos, Guyn, Jmca, Trin). **Guyn** ***buck-bead, jumbie-bead***[5]. A smooth, hard, glossy, oval seed that is green when young, but pale blue, grey or purple when ripe. (The reference to Job may be to the shape of the seed and the mournful looking colour.)

John-Crow bead *noun phrase* (Belz, Jmca). See JUMBIE-BEAD[1].

Jo.seph's coat *noun phrase* (Bdos, Brbu, Jmca). **Bdos, Guyn** ***Jacob's coat***. A bushy plant with variegated leaves, which grows in many, different colours, from deep purple and red, to green and yellow, and widely popular as an ornamental plant. (A reference to the biblical Joseph's 'coat of many colours', Genesis 38:23.)

Joseph's coat

Ju.das-tree *noun* (Bdos). See BEAN-TREE.

ju.ju *noun* (Baha). See DUNKS.

ju.jube *noun* (Baha, Jmca). See DUNKS.

Ju.lie-man.go *noun* (Angu, Bdos, Gren, Guyn, Jmca). See GRAFTED-MANGO.

jum.bie-bal.sam *noun* (Guyn). **Guyn** ***jum.bie-ba.sil, tulsie***; **Trin** ***toonsie***. An annual, aromatic herb with small, hairy leaves and stems, tiny, brownish flowers and fruit, which is used to treat colds and digestive ailments.

jum.bie-ba.sil *noun* (Guyn). See JUMBIE-BALSAM.

jum.bie-bead[1] *noun* (Brbu, Gren, StKt, Trin, USVI). **Belz, Jmca** ***John-Crow bead***; **Guyn** ***buck-bead***; **Guyn, StKt** ***crab-eye, crab's-eyes***; **Nevs** ***jumbie-bead seed***. The small, hard, shiny red seed with a dark spot, growing four to five in a pod on a climbing vine bearing pale pink flowers, sometimes used to make jewellery or as a folk medicine. (Called 'jumbie' because these 'seeds' or 'beads' are believed by some to bring bad luck if they are kept in the home.)

jum.bie-bead[2] *noun* (Bdos, Gren, Tbgo, Trin). **Bdos, Tbgo** ***crab-eye***; **Gren** ***coral bean***; **Guyn** ***buck-bead***[2]; **Jmca** ***cutlass-bean***. The glossy, scarlet bean, sometimes with a black spot, growing in a pod with several other beans, and borne on a tree with tough spines and bright red flowers.

jum.bie-bead[3] *noun* (Gren, Trin, USVI). **Gren, Jmca, Trin** ***red sandalwood***; **Guyn** ***buck-bead***; **Jmca** ***red-bead***; **Jmca, Trin, USVI** ***Circassian bean/seed***; **USVI** ***kokreko***. A shiny red seed, encased in a pod with many others, and borne on a medium-sized tree which produces reddish wood and bears long, spiky flowers.

jum.bie-bead[4] *noun* (Guyn, Trin). A hard, spiny red and black seed, found in

J

a short, roundish or oblong pod, borne on a forest tree whose younger branches, leaves and pods are covered with brownish hairs.

jum.bie-bead[5] *noun* (Guyn). See JOB'S TEARS.

jum.bie-bead seed *noun phrase* (Nevs). See JUMBIE-BEAD[1].

jum.bie-bead vine *noun phrase* (Brbu, Gren, StKt, USVI). See BEAD-VINE (BUSH).

jum.bie-bean *noun* (Baha, Berm). See WILD TAMARIND.

jum.bie-bub.by *noun* (Guyn). See BURA-BURA.

jum.bie-cho.cho *noun* (Jmca). See JUMBIE-SOURSOP.

jum.bie-cof.fee *noun* (StKt, Trin, USVI). See WILD COFFEE.

jum.bie-pa.ra.sol *noun* (Gren, Tbgo, Trin, TkCa). See DUPPY-PARASOL.

jum.bie-pep.per *noun* (BrVI). See BIRD-PEPPER.

jum.bie-sour.sop *noun* (Antg, Nevs, StVn). **Bdos *Cain-fruit, forbidden fruit, pain-cure*; Bdos, Nevs *monkey-apple*; Dmca *kòwòsòl-djab, pomme-killer*; Guyn *pain-killer fruit, yaws(-bush) fruit*; Jmca *hog-apple, jumbie-chocho, monkey-berry, pig-apple*.** A soft fruit, like a PINEAPPLE, that smells unpleasant when ripe, borne on a small tree with large, shiny, green leaves, a poultice of which is used for headaches.

jum.bie-um.brel.la *noun* (CarA). See DUPPY-PARASOL.

jump-up-and-kiss-me *noun* (CarA). **Bdos, Jmca, StKt, Trin, USVI *purslane, pussley*; Dmca, Jmca *kiss-me-quick*.** Any one of three varieties of a low-growing, spreading herb, with tiny leaves and reddish-purple, yellow or white flowers, used as a poultice in folk-medicine.

June-plum *noun* (Jmca). See JEW-PLUM.

K

ka-ber.ry *noun* (Angu, BrVI). See CANKER-BERRY.

ka.chi.man (ca.chi.man, ca.chi.ment) *noun* (Dmca, StLu). See CUSTARD-APPLE.

ka.ka-poul[1] **(ca.ca-poule, ko-ko-poul)** *noun* (Dmca, StLu). See CLAMMY-CHERRY. (Creole *kaka* 'dung' + French Creole *poul* 'hen' = English Creole 'fowl dung', but the connection between the fruit and the name is not clear.)

ka.ka-poul[2] **(ca.ca-poule, ko-ko-poul)** *noun* (Dmca, StLu). See OLD-MAID.

ka.ki.te-bwa *noun* (Gren). See BIRD-VINE. (A French Creole item.)

kan.ka-ber.ry *noun* (ECar). See CANKER-BERRY.

ka.ya.kit *noun* (Trin). See SAGE (-BUSH)[2].

ket.to *noun* (Jmca). See EBONY[2].

khus-khus (grass) (cus-cus, kuss-kuss) *noun (phrase)* (CarA). See VETIVER.

kid.ney-bean *noun* (Baha, Jmca). See STRING-BEAN.

kid.ney-man.go *noun* (Antg, Belz, Jmca, VIls). A sweet and kidney-shaped variety of MANGO.

king-of-the-for.est *noun* (Jmca). See CHRISTMAS-CANDLE.

king-o.range *noun* (Jmca, StLu, Trin). A large, sweet orange of which there are several varieties.

kiss-me-quick *noun* (Dmca, Jmca). See JUMP-UP-AND-KISS-ME.

knuck.le-seed *noun* (Nevs). See NICKER.

ko.jo-bush/root *noun* (Brbu, Gren, StVn). See GULLY-ROOT.

ko.ker.ite *noun* (Guyn, Trin). See COCORITE.

ko.ko-bèf (co.co-boeuf) *noun* (Dmca, StLu). One of the largest and most fleshy of the MANGOES cultivated in the Caribbean.

ko.ko-poul *noun* (Dmca). See CLAMMY-CHERRY.

ko.kre.ko *noun* (USVI). See JUMBIE-BEAD[3].

kò.wò.sòl *noun* (Dmca, StLu). See SOURSOP.

kò.wò.sòl-djab (co.ro(s).sol-di.able) *noun* (Dmca, StLu). SEE JUMBIE-SOURSOP.

ku.shu (ca.shew) *noun* (Antg, Bdos, Gren, StVn, Tbgo). See CASHEW[1].

kuss-kuss (grass) *noun phrase* (Bdos). See VETIVER.

L

lab-lab (bean) *noun (phrase)* (CarA). See BONAVIST.

La.ca.tan ba.na.na *noun phrase* (CarA). **Gren *giant fig*.** A large blunt-ended banana that remains green when ripe, and which spoils easily.

Lacatan banana

la.dy-fin.ger[1] *noun* (Nevs). See APPLE-BANANA.

la.dy-fin.ger[2] *noun* (Guyn). A variety of pointed, yellow pepper.

la.dy-fin.ger[3] **(la.dy's-fin.ger)** *noun* (Antg, Guyn, Trin). A type of OKRA that is extremely slim.

la-la.vin.ton (law-la.ving.ton, Lord-La.ving.ton) *noun* (Antg). See BALL-BUSH.

lamp.shade bush *noun phrase* (Nevs). See LEAF-OF-LIFE.

lang-bèf (langue-boeuf) *noun* (Dmca, Gren, StLu). See AGAVE. (French Creole from French *langue de bœuf* 'ox's tongue' with loss of *de* because of its position in the middle of the phrase.)

lang-fanm *noun* (StLu). See WOMAN('s)-TONGUE TREE. (French Creole from French *langue de femme* 'tongue of woman' with loss of *de* because of its position in the middle of the phrase.)

lau.ki *noun* (Guyn, Trin). See GOURD.

la.tan.yé (la.tan.ier) *noun* (ECar). See SILVER-THATCH PALM.

lau.ri.er *noun* (Dmca, Gren). See LOWYÉ.

la.ven.der-grass *noun* (Guyn, StVn). See VETIVER.

lead-tree *noun* (Jmca). See WILD-TAMARIND.

leaf-of-life *noun* (Bdos, Dmca, Guyn, Jmca). **Angu *air-plant*; Angu, StKt, StVn *luck-bush*; Angu, Antg, Bdos, StKt, StVn *love-bush*[2]; Bdos, Gren, Tbgo, Trin *wonder-of-the-world*; Nevs *baby-bush, bladder-bush, Christmas flower, lampshade-bush*; Gren *géritout* 2.; Nevs, StKt, Trin *never-dead*.** An erect herb with fleshy leaves from whose curved edges new plants spring, even when the leaves are cut off; the juice from the leaves is used as a folk medicine and the leaves are used as a poultice.

Leaf-of-life

leath.er-coat plum *noun phrase* (CayI, Jmca). See JAMAICA-PLUM.

lem.on-grass *noun* (CarA). See FEVER-GRASS.

Lent-tree *noun* (Bdos). See BEAN-TREE.

let.tuce *noun* (CarA). **CarA *salad*.** A short plant with bright green leaves, growing in the shape of a rosette; it is cultivated as a salad and much used in Caribbean cuisine.

lig.num-vitae *noun* (CarA). A medium-sized, evergreen tree with a slim trunk and scaly brown bark, with bright blue flowers and yellow pods, so that it is also grown as an ornamental plant; it yields a hard wood and its leaves and sap are also used in folk medicine.

L

Li.ma bean *noun* (CarA). **CarA *white bean*; Dmca *white pea*; Jmca, StVn *broad bean*; StKt, StVn *butter-bean* 2.** A whitish, kidney-shaped bean encased in a crescent-shaped pod, borne on a climbing vine, and found in many varieties.

lime-ber.ry *noun* (Trin). See BABY-LIME.

li.on-bush *noun* (Guyn). See BALL-BUSH.

li.on's-tail *noun* (Bdos, ViIs). See BALL-BUSH.

lis.bon yam *noun phrase* (CarA). **Belz, Guyn, Jmca, StVn *water-yam*; Dmca *white yam*[2].** A large yam with usually three or four sections, widely cultivated in the Caribbean with floury flesh that can be white, cream or yellow.

li.zard-food *noun* (Bdos, Nevs, StKt). See CERASEE.

lob.ster-claw *noun* (Bdos, Gren). See HELICONIA.

lo.cust[1] *noun* (CarA). See STINKING-TOE[1].

lo.cust[2] *noun* (Guyn). A very tall tree which yields a tough, hard, reddish wood, used for furniture-making.

log-tree *noun* (BrVI). See BIRCH-GUM TREE.

log.wood *noun* (Belz, BrVI, Gren, Jmca, Trin). See CAMPESH.

long-man.go *noun* (Guyn, Tbgo, Trin). See HAIRY MANGO.

loo.fah *noun* (Gren, Jmca). **Guyn *nenwah*; Trin *torchon*.** A long, green fruit, looking like a CUCUMBER, with ridges running along it and soft, cream flesh full of seeds; it is cooked particularly by the East Indians; when dry it is used as a scrubber.

Lord-La.ving.ton *noun* (Angu). See BALL-BUSH.

love-ap.ple *noun* (StLu). See MALACCA-APPLE.

love-bush[1] *noun* (Jmca). See LOVE-VINE.

love-bush[2] *noun* (Angu, Antg, Bdos, StKt). See LEAF-OF-LIFE.

love-vine *noun* (CarA). **Angu *yellow-dad/dod*; Jmca *love-bush*[1]; Nevs *yellow-dodder*; ViIs *yellow-love*.** A yellow, twining, parasitic vine whose stems smother any plants to which it attaches itself; it then leaves its roots to die and lives off the sap of the host plant or tree; it is declared a pest by law, but is also used as a folk-medicine.

Love-vine

lòwyé *noun* **(lau.ri.er)** (Dmca, Gren). Several varieties of a large forest tree, with leathery leaves and small flowers; they yield wood much valued in construction, furniture-making and cabinet work. (French Creole from French *laurier* 'laurel'.)

Lu.cea-yam (Jmca). See WHITE YAM1.

luck-bush (Antg, StKt, StVn). See LEAF-OF-LIFE.

ly.chee (CarA). A small, round, or oval-shaped fruit with thin, leathery, rough skin and thick, glossy, translucent flesh which can be pinkish or greyish on a single seed; it has a special flavour and is used in Caribbean cuisine as a dessert.

ma.cam.bou *noun* (Dmca, StLu). See BLUGGO.

ma.caw *noun* (Antg, StKt). **Gren, StVn *grou-grou*.** A round, yellowish-brown fruit with a hard outer skin, soft flesh and a hard seed with a kernel inside which yields a valuable oil, borne on a tall, spiny palm.

ma.caw-palm *noun* (Bdos). See GROU-GROU.

mac.ca(-palm) (mac.ca-fat (palm)) *noun (phrase)* (Belz, Jmca, Mrat). See GROU-GROU.

ma.ho(e) *noun* (CarA). See SEA-SIDE MAHOE. (From Arawak *maho* 'a tree whose strong, pliable bark is used to make rope'.)

ma.ho.ga.ny *noun* (CarA). A tall, upright tree with small leaves and pods which yields a rich, dark-brown wood much used and much valued in furniture-making.

mai.den-ap.ple *noun* (Mrat, Nevs, StKt, VIls). See CERASEE.

mai.den's blush (mai.den's bush) *noun phrase* (Angu, Antg, Mrat, StKt, Trin). See CERASEE.

mai.den-plan.tain *noun* (Belz). See BUCK-BANANA.

ma.kam.bou (ma.cam. bou) *noun* (Dmca, StLu). See BLUGGO. (Maybe of African origin from Bantu or Kikongo *mankondo*, a general term for plantain.)

ma.lac.ca-ap.ple/-pear *noun* (Antg, Guyn). **Bdos, Dmca, Trin *pommerac*; Belz, Berm *Malay-apple*; CayI, Jmca *otaheite-apple*; Dmca, StLu *pomme-rose*[2], *ponm-wòz*; Gren, Guyn *French cashew*[2]; Guyn *cashew*[2]; StLu *love-apple*; StLu, StVn, Trin *plum-rose*[1]; Trin *pomme-malac*.** A red, pear-shaped fruit with white, fluffy, juicy flesh around a single seed, and borne on a bushy tree with long, pointed, leathery leaves. (Probably from the Moluccas, islands in the East Indies from which the fruit was introduced to the Caribbean.)

Malacca-apple

ma.mee(-ap.ple) (ma.mey/mam.my-ap.ple) *noun* (CarA). **Dmca, StLu *zabwiko*; StLu *apricot*.** A large, fruit, in the shape of a sphere, with a tough, brown skin and sweetish orange flesh which contains a few seeds, borne on a tall tree with sweet-smelling flowers and large, shiny leaves. (From the Amerindian name of the fruit *mami* + English *apple*, a name often given to edible fruit of a similar shape and size in Caribbean English.)

mam.mee-sa.pote *noun* (CarA). A roundish, brown fruit with fragrant flesh on a single seed; the flesh is stewed or used to make fruit preserves, the seed for flavouring and making scent and the fruit is borne on a tree similar to the MAMMEE-APPLE TREE. (From *mammee* because it resembles the mammee-apple + *sapote* from Spanish *zapote* from Aztec *tzapotl* 'sapodilla' from its shape and size.)

Mammee-apple

man-bet.ter-man *noun* (Dmca, StLu, Trin). **Jmca, StLu, Trin *devil('s) horsewhip*; Guyn *devil-whip*; Bdos *hug-me-close*; Guyn *soldier-rod*.** An erect herb with long, thin branches bearing long, spiny leaves which cling to the clothing or skin of passers-by or animals; it is also used as a folk medicine by some to cure high blood pressure, colds and fever.

man.chi.neel (man.chi.neal) *noun* (CarA). An evergreen tree usually found near the sea or on sandy ground; its bark, leaves and fruit all give off a toxic, milky juice that irritates the skin. (Probably from French *mancenille* or Spanish *manzanilla*, 'a small apple' a version of Spanish *manzana* 'apple', referring to its fruit.)

man.da.rin(-o.range) *noun* (Dmca, Gren, StLu, Trin). See TANGERINE.

man.ger.ine *noun* (Belz, Guyn, Jmca). A citrus fruit resembling a TANGERINE, but a lighter yellow in colour. (A blend of *mandarin* and *tangerine*.)

man.gle *noun* (Dmca, USVI). See MANGROVE.

man.go-bab (man.go-barbe) *noun* (Dmca). See HAIRY MANGO. (French Creole *bab* from French *barbe* 'beard' referring to the long hairy fibres that cling to the seed once the mango is sucked.)

man.go-bèf *noun* (Dmca, Gren, StLu). The name given to two or three varieties of a very large mango.

man.go-ca.bane *noun* (Dmca). See MANGO-KABANN.

man.go-Cey.lon *noun* (Dmca). See BOMBAY-MANGO.

man.go-fil *noun* (StLu). See HAIRY MANGO.

man.go-Gra.ham; Gra.ham(-man.go) *noun* (StLu). **Antg, Belz, Dmca, Gren, Tbgo *bellyful*; Jmca *bull-seed/stone mango*; Guyn *fufu-mango*; Dmca, StLu *mango-koko-bèf*; Belz *horse-mango*.** A huge mango, the type of which is called MANGO-BÈF.

man.go-ka.bann (man.go-ca.bane) *noun* (Dmca). A mango ripened under cloth either in a box or a basket. (From English *mango* + French Creole *kabann* from French *cabane*, 'a hut or a shack', used as an adjective and put after the noun.)

man.go-ko.ko-bèf *noun* (Dmca, StLu). See MANGO-BÈF.

man.go-long (long-man.go) *noun* (Bdos). See HAIRY MANGO.

man.go-mou.chach/(-mou.chasse) *noun* (Dmca, StLu). (French Creole *mouchach* 'starch'.)

Mangrove

man.go-par.lui/pal.wi/pe.lo.wie *noun* (Dmca, Gren, StLu, StVn). **Bdos** ***palwi/ parwi-mango*****; Dmca** ***Pierre Louis.*** A sweet, roundish mango, which is yellow to yellowish-red and either small or large, fibrous in texture and often tapers to a point. (From *Pierre Louis* or *Père Louis* probably after the person who produced this plant.)

man.go-rose *noun* (Dmca, Gren, StLu, Tbgo, Trin). See MANGO-WÒZ.

man.go.steen (man.go.stain) *noun* (CarA). A small, round, dark to red-purple fruit with a thick skin with a bitter latex and staining purple juice; its white flesh is sweetish to slightly acid and it is divided into 4 or 5 segments which are either seedless or have between 1 and 5 seeds which cling to the flesh.

man.go-té.té *noun* (Dmca). A mango shaped like a breast, with a point at the end from which the juice is sucked when ripe. (French Creole from English *mango* + French *tété* from French *téter* 'to suck at the breast'.)

man.go-wòz (man.go-rose, rose man. go) (Dmca, Gren, StLu, Tbgo, Trin). A small, sweet, juicy mango which has a rosy look when ripe. (A French Creole item. The pronunciation ***-wòz*** is used in Dominica and St Lucia, ***-rose*** in Grenada, Tobago and Trinidad.)

man.grove (man.gro) *noun* (CarA). **Dmca** ***mangle***. The general name given to a family of tropical plants growing in water and which have stilt roots, are usually found in muddy coastal swamps, and are covered by sea water at high tide.

ma.ni.cole-palm *noun* (Guyn). A palm with stems growing clumped together, each with a crown or branches in the shape of an arch; the stems and bark are used in construction, the dried branches as brooms, and the young shoots are cooked as 'cabbage'.

man.i.oc *noun* (ECar). See CASSAVA.

man.ja(c)k *noun* (Dmca, Gren, Tbgo, USVI). See CLAMMY CHERRY.

man-pi.a.ba *noun* (Bdos, Guyn). See BALL-BUSH.

ma.ny-roots *noun* (CarA). See MINNIE-ROOT.

ma.ri.gold *noun* (Jmca, TkCa). See CARPET-DAISY.

mar.ried-man pork *noun phrase* (Guyn). A bushy, pleasant-smelling herb with tiny leaves, much used in Guyana for seasoning food.

Married-man pork

mar.row *noun* (CarA). See GOURD[1].

Ma.ry-Mag.da.lene *noun* (Gren). See CHRISTMAS-BUSH.

mas.tic *noun* (Baha, Bdos, Belz, Gren, Trin). A tall, forest tree which bears bunches of small, yellow flowers and a pale yellow fruit; it yields a hard, heavy, strong yellowish-brown timber much used in construction.

ma.ta.bo.ro (ma.ta.bur.ro) *noun* (Tbgo, Trin). See BUCK-BANANA.

match.wood *noun* (Gren, Guyn, Trin). A large tree with leaves resembling palm leaves and many small flowers bunching at the tips of the stalks; it yields a soft, white wood used for making match-sticks, thus giving the tree its name.

May-plum *noun* (Belz). See JAMAICA-PLUM.

ma.vi.sou *noun* (Dmca). See SAGE-BUSH[2].

may.pole (male-pole) *noun* (Bdos). See AGAVE.

me.lon cac.tus *phr* (Trin). See TURK'S CAP CACTUS.

me.lon.gene (me.lon.gae, me.lon.ger) *noun* (Dmca, StLu, Trin). See EGGPLANT.

me.now-weed *noun* (Jmca). See MINNIE-ROOT.

mes.ple (mes.pel) *noun* (VIls). See SAPODILLA. (From the Dutch word *mispel* 'a fruit resembling the sapodilla'.)

mes.quit tree *noun phrase* (Trin). See CASHAW[2].

Me.xi.can pop.py *noun phrase* (Jmca). See THISTLE.

mè.zè-ma.wi (Mè.sè Ma.rie) *noun* (Dmca). See SENSITIVE PLANT.

mi.a.mol *noun* (Guyn, Trin). See WILD-COFFEE.

mi.a.mos.si *noun* (Bdos). See WILD-TAMARIND.

mile-tree *noun* (Bdos). See CASUARINA.

milk-bush *noun* (USVI). See BLIND-EYE[1].

milk.y-bush *noun* (Jmca). See ANTIGUA-HEATH.

mi.mo.sa (mi.a.mos.si) *noun* (Bdos). See WILD-TAMARIND.

min.nie-root (many-root, min.ny-root) *noun* (CarA). **Bdos *monkey-gun*; Jmca *duppy-gun, menow-weed*; VIls *iron-root*.** A short weed, with light-green leaves, which bears blue funnel-shaped flowers and small pods; its roots are crushed and used in folk medicine.

mi.ra.cu.lous bush (mi.ra.cu.lous vine) *noun phrase* (Bdos). See CERASEE.

mis.tle.toe *noun* (Gren, Jmca, Trin). See BIRD-VINE.

mi.wiz (mee.rese) *noun* (StLu). See GOVERNOR-PLUM. (French Creole from French *merise* 'wild cherry'.)

mo.ka-mo.ka (mo.ca-mo.ca, moc. co-moc-co) *noun* (Guyn). A small herb with flat, heart-shaped leaves and a juicy, prickly stem, which is sometimes pounded and used for cuts, or for colds in children; it grows in swamps or along river-banks. (From Arawak *mokomoko* 'spiny plant with fleshy insides found on river banks'.)

mo.ko-ba.na.na *noun* (Tbgo Trin). See BLUGGO.

mo.ney-bush *noun* (Bdos, Gren, Guyn, Tbgo, Trin). A small bushy herb with small, round leaves, yellow flowers and pods which grows wild; the juice from its leaves is used folk medicinally to treat skin infections. (So called because its leaves look like coins and maybe also because it is believed to bring good luck if grown in yards.)

mon.key-ap.ple[1]. (Nevs). See JUMBIE-SOURSOP.

mon.key-ap.ple[2] *noun* (Bdos, Guyn). **Antg *ghaut-apple*; Jmca *pond-apple*.** An edible, roundish, yellowish-brown fruit with brown seeds, growing on a small tree usually found in swampy areas.

mon.key-ber.ry *noun* (Jmca). See JUMBIE-SOURSOP.

mon.key's din.ner-bell *noun phrase* (Guyn). See SANDBOX-TREE.

mon.key-fid.dle *noun* (TkCa). See WOMAN('S) TONGUE.

mon.key-gun *noun* (Bdos). See MINNIE-ROOT.

mon.key-nee.dle(s) *noun* (Bdos). See DUPPY-NEEDLE.

mon.key-pis.tol (tree) *noun* (USVI). See SANDBOX-TREE.

mon.key-puz.zle *noun* (USVI). See CACTUS-HEDGE.

mon.key-sha(c) k-sha(c)k *noun* (Guyn). See WOMAN'S TONGUE.

mon.key-tam.bran/-ta.ma.rind *noun* (Guyn). See COWITCH.

mo.ra (tree) *noun phrase* (Guyn, Tbgo, Trin). A huge forest tree with large, dark-green leaves and tiny, sweet-smelling, white flowers; it bears a dry pod with a large, heavy seed, and its tough, heavy wood is used in ship-building. (An Arawak word which is the name of this tree.)

morn.ing-glo.ry *noun* (Jmca). See IPOMEA.

mor.tel(le) *noun* (Gren, Trin). See IMMORTELLE. (A shortened form of IMMORTELLE).

Mo.ses-in-the-bul.rushes *noun* (Jmca. USVI). See OYSTER-PLANT.

mos.qui.to-bush *noun* (Bdos). See DUPPY-BASIL.

mo.ther-in-law-tongue *noun* (Guyn) See SANSEVERIA.

moun.tain-cab.bage *noun* (Antg, Jmca, StVn). See CABBAGE-PALM.

moun.tain sweet-cup *noun phrase* (Jmca). See PASSION-FRUIT.

mung(-bean) *noun* (Belz, Guyn, Trin). **Guyn, Trin *urdi*; Trin *woolly pyrol*.** A yellowish-green bean in a short, stout, very hairy pod growing on a trailing plant; the beans are used mostly by East Indians to make DAAL, a popular dish. (The word *mung* is probably the Bhojpuri or Hindi name of this bean.)

myr.tle-lime *noun* (Antg, Mrat). See SWEET-LIME.

M

N

na.ked-In.di.an *noun* (Gren, Trin, USVI). See BIRCH GUM TREE.

na.ked-wood *noun* (Baha). A small tree with a smooth trunk that is flesh-coloured, bearing fragrant, white or yellow flowers and small, round, purplish-red fruit; the leaves are sometimes boiled to reduce fever.

na.pi.er grass *noun* (Jmca). See ELEPHANT GRASS.

nase.ber.ry *noun* (Jmca). See SAPODILLA.

nee.dle-and-thread *noun* (Guyn). See CASUARINA (TREE).

nee.dle-grass *noun* (Bdos, Trin). See DUPPY-NEEDLE.

neem (nim(e) *noun* (Guyn, Jmca, Mrat, Trin). An evergreen, dense leafy tree with small leaves, used by some to treat diabetes, jaundice and other ailments; the leaves are also used in East Indian religious ceremonies. (From a Hindi word *niim* 'the name of this tree'.)

ne.gro cof.fee *noun phrase* (Guyn, Trin). See WILD COFFEE.

Ne.gro-yam *noun* (Jmca, Trin). See WHITE-YAM1.

nen.wah *noun* (Guyn). See LOOFAH.

ne.roo yam *noun phrase* (Guyn). See YELLOW-YAM.

ne.ver-dead *noun* (Nevs, StKt, Trin). See LEAF-OF-LIFE.

nick.er *noun* (Angu, BrVI, Jmca). **Baha, Jmca, Mrat, Nevs *nickal, nickle*; Bdos, Gren *horse-nicker*; Gren, Tbgo, Trin *donkey-eye*; Nevs *knuckle-seed*; TkCa *briar*.** A hard, roundish, brown, grey, or yellow seed, borne on a prickly brown pod growing on a prickly bush, and usually used as a marble, but also sometimes in the preparation of folk medicine.

nig.ger-pep.per *noun* (Bdos). See BIRD-PEPPER.

night-bloom.ing cac.tus *noun phrase* (CarA). See CACTUS PLANT.

night-shade *noun* (Bdos). See THORN-APPLE.

nu.nu-bal.sam/-bush (noo-noo) *noun* (Antg, Brbu, Jmca). A low-growing aromatic plant which bears tiny mauve flowers, and is used as a BUSH-TEA.

nut-grass *noun* (CarA). A fast-growing grass with three-angled stems whose roots bear many small, nut-like tubers, which help it to spread and make it difficult to get rid of.

nut.meg *noun* (CarA). The hard, round fruit borne on an evergreen tree, which bursts open to reveal the scarlet mace covering the brown shell, in which the round, dry seed is encased.

o.chro *noun* (CarA). See OKRA.

oil-leaf (bush)/tree *noun phrase* (Bdos). See CASTOR-OIL (BUSH).

oil-nut tree *noun phrase* (Belz, Jmca, TkCa). See CASTOR-OIL (BUSH, PLANT, TREE).

oil-palm *noun* (Guyn, Trin). See ABBAY.

o.kra (o.chro) *noun* (CarA). **Antg, Guyn, Trin *lady-finger*[1], *ladies-fingers*.** A young, green, pointed pod with many ridges and slimy flesh and seeds, widely used as a vegetable in the Caribbean, and borne on a hairy plant with large leaves. (Probably from West African Igbo dialectal form *okworo* 'okra'.)

old-maid (bush) *noun (phrase)* (CarA). **CarA *periwinkle*; Jmca *ram-goat rose*; Dmca, StLu *kaka-poul*[2]**. A small garden plant, bearing small, white, reddish-violet or blue flowers all year round, and growing in dry, sandy places, usually near the sea.

o.le.an.der *noun* (CarA). A tall, attractive but poisonous shrub with grey stems that bears clusters of double or single cream, white, pink, rose or red flowers.

Oleander

or.tan.ique *noun* (CarA). A type of citrus fruit that is a blend of the orange and the TANGERINE with sweet, juicy pulp. (A blend of three words *or(ange)* + *tan(gerine)* + *un(ique)*. The fruit was developed by agriculturalists in Jamaica.)

o.ta.hei.te-ap.ple *noun* (CayI, Jmca, USVI). See MALACCA-APPLE. (From the South Pacific island Otaheite or Tahiti from which it was introduced to Jamaica.)

o.ta.hei.te-goose.ber.ry *noun* (Jmca, Trin). See GOOSEBERRY.

o.ver.look-bean *noun* (Bdos, Jmca). See GRUDGE-PEA.

oys.ter-plant *noun* (ECar). **Jmca, USVI *Moses-in-the-bulrushes*; USVI *sangria***. A low, decorative plant with stiff, pointed leaves, dark green inside and purple outside, about 10 in. long, bearing small white flowers encased in purple leaves which look like oysters in half a shell.

P

pain-bush *noun* (Tbgo). See PAIN-KILLER (BUSH).

pain-kill.er (bush) *noun (phrase)* (Guyn, Mrat, Nevs, USVI). **Bdos *dog-dumplings, pain cure, wild pine*[3]; Tbgo *pain-bush***. A shrub with large, glossy, green leaves used by some as a poultice for the relief of pains about the body; its fruit is known as the JUMBIE-SOURSOP.

Pain-killer bush

pain-kill.er fruit *noun phrase* (Guyn). See JUMBIE-SOURSOP.

pak.choy (pat.choi) *noun* (Guyn, Jmca, Tbgo, Trin). See CHINESE CABBAGE. (From Cantonese and Hakka Chinese *pakchoy* 'white vegetable'.)

pal.met.to *noun* (Baha, Berm, TkCa). See SILVER-THATCH PALM.

pal.mist(e) *noun* (Dmca, Gren, StLu, StVn, Trin). See CABBAGE-PALM.

P

pal.wi-man.go *noun* (Bdos). See MANGO-PARLUI.

pan.go.la-grass *noun* (CarA). A bushy, pasture grass grown especially as cattle fodder, because of its nutritious qualities. (From Pongola in South Africa for which the grass is named.)

pa.paw (pa.pa.ya, paw-paw) *noun* (CarA). A round or oblong fruit, yellow when ripe, with a thick skin and sweet, thick, yellowish flesh in which are found many tiny black seeds; it is much valued as a dessert, and is also used to tenderize meat, as well as for medicinal purposes. (From Arawak *papaia* through Spanish *papaya*, the name of the fruit.)

pa.ra-grass *noun* (CarA). A coarse grass with large, flowering shoots and which puts out roots at the joints in its stem; it is used as cattle fodder. (The grass originated in Pará, a province in Brazil for which it is named.)

pas.sion-fruit *noun* (CarA). **Jmca** ***mountain sweet-cup*****; StKt** ***cocktail-fruit***. A smooth, round fruit, yellow when ripe, which has a sweetish-sour, yellowish, gluey pulp with dark-brown seeds, and is borne on a climbing vine.

peach *noun* (Guyn). A brownish, yellow, or pink fruit, covered with short brown hairs and whitish, unpleasant-smelling mealy pulp, borne on a tall tree with leathery, dark-green leaves and bunches of white flowers.

pen.cil-bush *noun* (USVI). See BLIND-EYE.

penm.bwa *noun* (Trin). See BREADFRUIT.

pep.per *noun* (CarA). Any one of a variety of highly spicy fruits used to flavour Caribbean cooking, such as BIRD-PEPPER, CAYENNE PEPPER, HABANERO, WIRI-WIRI PEPPER, etc.

pe.ri.win.kle *noun* (CarA). See OLD-MAID.

phy.sic-nut *noun* (CarA). **Angu, StKt** ***white barricader***. A large shrub with large leaves and small yellow flowers; the fruit is roundish and its seeds are used as a purgative, and both the fruit and the plant are used to treat many ailments.

pi.geon-pea(s) *noun (plural)* (CarA). **Bdos, Gren, Guyn, Trin** ***green peas*****; Belz, CayI, Jmca** ***gungo-peas*****; CayI** ***congo peas***. Yellowish-green peas contained in small, green pods which grow in clusters on an upright green shrub, and are much used in Caribbean cooking.

pi.man zwa.zo *noun phrase* (Dmca). See BIRD-PEPPER. (French Creole from French *piment* 'pepper' + '*z*' + *oiseau* 'bird'.)

pi.men.to[1] *noun* (CarA). See ALLSPICE.

pi.men.to[2] *noun* (Belz). See SILVER-THATCH PALM.

pim.pler-palm *noun* (Guyn). See GRI-GRI (PALM).

pine-(ap.ple) *noun* (CarA). **Dmca, StKt** ***zanana***. A large, ridged, prickly, yellow, reddish-yellow or green fruit growing on a short ground plant with long, narrow, spiny leaves.

ping-wing *noun* (Belz, Jmca, USVI). A variety of wild PINEAPPLE plant, often used to build fences.

pipe-or.gan cac.tus *noun phrase* (VIls). See DILDO[1].

piss-a-bed *noun* (Guyn, Jmca). See WILD COFFEE. (The plant was often used to cure bed-wetting in children which gives it this name.)

pitch-ap.ple *noun* (VIls). **USVI** ***false mammee; strangler fig***. A round, tough-skinned, yellowish fruit which gives off a yellowish latex that hardens and turns black and can be used like pitch to seal boats.

plan.tain *noun* (CarA). A large, horn-shaped fruit, resembling a large BANANA, but which is less sweet and less starchy, used widely as a vegetable in the Caribbean.

plum[1] *noun* (Guyn, Trin). See HOG-PLUM.

plum[2] *noun* (Dmca, Gren, Nevs). See JAMAICA-PLUM.

plum[3] *noun* (Antg, Mrat, StVn). See CHILLI-PLUM.

plum-rose[1] *noun* (Gren, Mrat, StVn, Trin). See MALACCA-APPLE.

plum-rose[2] *noun* (Dmca, Guyn). See ROSE-APPLE.

poin.ci.a.na *noun* (CarA). See FLAMBOYANT.

poin.set.ti.a *noun* (CarA). **Dmca, Jmca, StVn, Tbgo** ***Christmas-flower***[1]. An ornamental garden shrub that bears large, abundant, bright, scarlet bunches of flowers.

Poinsettia

po.ke.no.boy (pork-and-dough-boy) *noun* (Belz). A palm with many stems and long leaves armed with sharp, black spines which bears bunches of red nuts with a rough skin and sticky pulp that are sometimes used to feed animals.

po.me.lo *noun* (Trin). The smaller, rounder variety of SHADDOCK.

pomme (ponm) *noun* (Dmca, StLu). See CASHEW[1].

pomme-can.nelle (ponm-ka.nèl) *noun* (Dmca, StLu). See SUGAR-APPLE.

pomme-cool.ie (ponm-koul.i) *noun* (Mrat, StKt). See CERASEE.

pomme-cy.thère (ponm-si.tè) *noun* (Gren, StLu, Trin, VIls). See GOLDEN-APPLE.

pomme-(de)-li.ane (ponm-di-ly.ann) *noun* (Dmca, StLu, Trin). See BELL-APPLE.

pomme-ma.lac *noun* (Trin). See MALACCA-APPLE.

pomme-rose[1] **(ponm-wòz)** *noun* (Dmca). See ROSE-APPLE.

pomme-rose[2] **(ponm-wòz)** *noun* (Dmca, StLu). See MALACCA-APPLE.

pomme-su.rette *noun* (Angu, Nevs, StKt). See DUNKS.

pond-ap.ple *noun* (Jmca). See MONKEY-APPLE[2].

pond-thatch (pond-top) *noun* (Baha). A palm with a thick trunk, topped by fan-shaped leaves that are dried, stripped and used for straw-work or thatch-work.

pond-top[1] *noun* (Baha). See POND-THATCH.

pond-top[2] *noun* (Baha). See CABBAGE-PALM.

poor man's tears *noun plural* (Bdos). See THICK-LEAF THYME.

pork-and-dough.boy *noun* (Belz). See POKENOBOY.

pork-fat-ap.ple *noun* (Baha, Berm). See COCO-PLUM[1].

por.tu.gal *noun* (Trin). See TANGERINE.

po.ta.to *noun* (CarA). See ENGLISH-POTATO.

po.ta.to-yam *noun* (Trin). See CHINESE YAM.

P

prick.le-/prick.ler-/prick.ly pear *noun phrase* (Baha, Bdos, GayI, ViIs). See COCHINEAL-CACTUS.

pou.i *noun* (CarA). A large tree which flowers when it has no leaves, and bears clusters of pale-pink, trumpet-shaped flowers that make it supremely attractive to look at. (A word of Carib origin.)

prick.le-yam *noun* (Tbgo, Trin). See YELLOW-YAM.

Pride of Bar.ba.dos *noun* (CarA). See BARBADOS-PRIDE.

psi.di.um *noun* (Guyn). See GOVERNOR-PLUM.

pulp(.ing)-ed.doe *noun* (Bdos). See EDDOE[1].

pur.ple al.la.man.da *noun phrase* (CarA). A spreading shrub with stems that yield a milky sap, pale, green leaves and bearing pinkish-mauve flowers and pairs of pods with small, brown seeds.

pur.ple.heart *noun* (Guyn, Trin). A huge tree which yields a hard, heavy, strong, dark-purple wood, much valued in construction, particularly furniture-making.

purs.lane (purs.ley) *noun* (Jmca). See JUMP-UP-AND-KISS-ME.

puss.ley *noun* (Bdos, Jmca, StKt, Trin, USVI). See JUMP-UP-AND-KISS-ME.

pwa-ga.té *noun* (Dmca, Gren, StLu). See COWITCH. (French Creole from French *pois* 'pea(-pod) + *gratter* 'to scratch' and in the Caribbean sense means 'itch'.)

pwin (prune) *noun* (StLu). See CHILLI-PLUM.

pwin-Mo.wis; pwin-tété *noun* (StLu). See JAMAICA-PLUM.

pyé-poul *noun* (Dmca). See FOWL-FOOT GRASS. (From French pied 'foot' + *poule* 'chicken, fowl.)

queen-of-flow.ers[1] *noun* (ECar). A bushy, garden shrub in several varieties, with slender, erect branches, bearing clusters of tiny pink, white, crimson or purple flowers.

queen-of-flow.ers[2] *noun* (Trin). **Jmca** ***queen's flower-tree***. A large tree with pointed, oblong leaves, bearing clusters of round mauve flowers.

Queen-of-flowers

que.nette (tjènn.èt) *noun* (StLu). See GUINEP.

quick-stick (Jmca). See GLIRICIDIA.

rab.bit-food *noun* (StKt). See BALL-BUSH.

rab.bit-meat *noun* (Gren, Trin). A spreading weed, usually found in moist places, with hairy stems and bearing white flowers; it is used to feed rabbits and goats.

ra.chette (wa.chèt, wa.tjèt) *noun* (Dmca, Trin, StLu). See COCHINEAL-CACTUS. (From French *raquette* 'prickly pear' with a racket-shaped stem which became *rachette* in French Creole.)

rain-bush (rain.fall-bush) *noun* (Mrat, StVn). See GLIRICIDIA.

rain-drops *noun* (StKt). See GLIRICIDIA.

rain-tree (CarA). See SAMAN.

ram.bu.tan *noun* (CarA). A small red or orange fruit, covered with long spines on the outside, which has white, soft, slightly acid pulp over a single large seed; it is borne on a large tree.

Rambutan

ram-goat bush *noun phrase* (StKt).**1. Jmca *ram-goat dashalong*.** A strongly scented bushy shrub with crinkled, dark-green, glossy leaves which usually bears yellow flowers, although other colours are found in different varieties; it is used as a folk medicine to relieve colds, and also as a laxative. **2.** (Nevs, USVI). See CATTLE-TONGUE.

ram.goat rose *noun phrase* (Jmca). See OLD-MAID.

rasp.ber.ry *noun* (Antg, Brbu). See GOOSEBERRY.

ra.zor-grass *noun* (CarA). One of many varieties of grasses growing in clumps, with blades that have edges like a fine-toothed saw that cut the skin, if it rubs againt them.

red-bead *noun* (Jmca). See JUMBIE-BEAD[1].

red-bead vine *noun phrase* (Jmca). See BEAD-VINE BUSH.

red-bean *noun* (BrVI, Dmca, TkCa). See STRING-BEAN.

red birch *noun phrase* (Jmca). See BIRCH-GUM TREE.

red ce.dar *noun phrase* (Bdos, Dmca, Gren, Guyn, Nevs). A large forest tree with huge branches and a wide crown that yields a fragrant, tough, smooth brownish-pink wood, much valued for its being able to resist termites.

Red cedar

red-coat plum *noun phrase* (Jmca). See JAMAICA-PLUM.

red cor.di.a *noun phrase* (Angu, Bdos, CayI, StKt). See CORDIA.

red-fig *noun* (Trin). See BUCK-BANANA.

red gin.ger-li.ly *noun phrase* (Bdos). See GINGER-LILY[1].

red-plum *noun* (CayI, Trin). See JAMAICA-PLUM.

red-sage (Bdos). See BLACK-SAGE[2].

red san.dal.wood *noun phrase* (Gren, Jmca, Trin). The wood of the tree which bears the JUMBIE-BEAD[3].

red-wood *noun* (Baha). See EBONY[2].

red-yam *noun* (Baha, Gren, Jmca, Nevs, StKt). A yam whose inner skin is red when peeled; some varieties have pinkish flesh, while others have white flesh.

ring-worm bush *noun phrase* (Bdos, Gren, Jmca). See CHRISTMAS-CANDLE.

ri.ver-ta.ma.rind *noun* (Bdos). See WILD TAMARIND.

roast-pork (cac.tus) *noun (phrase)* (Jmca). A variety of CACTUS with flat, fleshy leaves that look like meat.

rock-bal.sam *noun* (Bdos, Guyn, Mrat, USVI). Any one of many types of BALSAM BUSH that grow in damp, rocky places, used as a folk-medicine for colds.

rock-fig *noun* (Guyn, StVn). See APPLE-BANANA.

rope-bush *noun* (Guyn). See AGAVE.

rose-ap.ple *noun* (CarA). **Dmca *pomme rose*[1]; Dmca, Mrat, StVn *Java-plum*; Guyn *plum-rose*[1]**. A small, round fruit about the size of a marble with a single seed, yellow when ripe, sweetish flesh and borne on a evergreen tree.

Rose-apple

ro.seau *noun* (Dmca, Gren, Tbgo, Trin). A tall reed looking like a bamboo with saw-like edges, usually used for thatching roofs and basket making. (From French *roseau* 'a weed'.)

rose-man.go *noun* (Dmca, Gren, Tbgo, Trin). See MANGO-WÒZ.

rose.ma.ry(-weed) *noun* (Bdos, Brbu, CayI, Jmca, USVI). An evergreen, aromatic shrub whose leaves and twigs are used to flavour food and to tone the skin; it yields a perfume-like oil and its twigs are sometimes burned as incense.

rou.cou *noun* (Dmca, Gren, Guyn, StLu, Trin). See ANATO.

roun.ci.val (roun.ce.val, run.ci.ful) *noun* (Bdos). See INCREASE PEAS.

ro.yal palm *noun phrase* (CarA). **Baha *Victoria-palm***. An erect palm, similar to the CABBAGE-PALM, but somewhat shorter, which stands out because of the bulge at the base of its trunk and the way in which its branches droop.

Royal palm

round-the-world *noun* (Bdos). See LEAF-OF-LIFE.

ro.yal poin.ci.a.na *noun phrase* (ECar). See FLAMBOYANT.

rub.ber-plant/tree *noun* (CarA). See INDIA RUBBER-PLANT/TREE.

S

saeme *noun* (Guyn). **Jmca** ***yam-bean***. An edible, green bean encased in a pod with a pointed tip, borne on a climbing vine with heart-shaped leaves, and immensely popular as a vegetable in Guyanese cooking.

sage *noun* (Bdos). See SAGE-BUSH.

sage(-bush)[1] *noun* (CarA). See BLACK-SAGE[1].

sage(-bush)[2] *noun* (CarA). **Baha, Bdos, Jmca, Trin** ***pink, red, white or wild sage*****; CarA** ***black-sage***[2]**; Dmca** ***mavisou*****; Guyn** ***sweet-sage*****; Jmca** ***wild mint*****; Trin** ***grater-wood, kayakit***. An erect, aromatic shrub with rough or prickly stems and rough, saw-edged leaves with a minty smell; it bears small, blackish berries, and it is also used folk-medicinally for colds, high blood pressure and malaria.

sai.jan *noun* (Guyn). A long, triangular, greenish-brown pod, full of many seeds and commonly used as vegetable, especially in curries, etc.

sa.lad *noun* (Bdos, Guyn). Lettuce.

sa.lad-bean *noun* (Trin). See STRING-BEAN.

salve-bush *noun* (Baha, TkCa). See CATTLE-TONGUE.

sa.man (sa.maan, saa.man) *noun* (CarA). **CarA** ***rain-tree*****; Jmca** ***guango*****; Trin** ***tamarind***. A huge shade-tree with a short, thick trunk and long branches, bearing bunches of pale pink flowers and dark pods, like those of the TAMARIND, and which have a sweet, sticky pulp around the seeds; the pods are eaten by children and cattle and the wood is used for furniture-making.

Saman tree

sand-box(-tree) *noun* (CarA). **Guyn** ***monkey's dinner-bell***; **USVI** ***monkey-pistol***. A large forest-tree with a huge, prickly trunk and branches and round, smooth leaves, which bears round, grooved, dark-brown pods in which there are seeds containing an oil that can be used as a purgative; the tree gives off a poisonous, milky sap, and the wood is used in construction.

san.gri.a *noun* (USVI). See OYSTER-PLANT.

san.se.vi.e.ri.a *noun* (VIls). **Guyn** ***mother-in-law tongue, snake-bush***. Any one of several varieties of an ornamental plant, usually grown in pots, consisting of a cluster of spotted green or white, stiff, sword-shaped leaves.

S

Sansevieria

sa.po.dil.la *noun* (CarA). **Baha, TkCa** ***dilly***; **Dmca, StLu** ***chapoti, sapotie, shapotie***; **Jmca** ***naseberry***; **VIls** ***mesple (mespel)***. A light-brown, roundish fruit with a thin skin and creamish-brown, juicy flesh covering a few shiny, black seeds; the bark of the tree on which it grows produces a white, milky substance from which chicle gum is made. (Probably from its original Aztec name *tzapotl* which gave rise to the Spanish name *sapotilla* with the 't' becoming 'd' in the English pronounciation of the word.)

sa.po.tie *noun* (StLu, Trin). See SAPODILLA.

sas.pa.ril.la *noun* (VIls). See CHRISTMAS-CANDLE.

sa.van.na(h)-grass (Bdos, Gren, Jmca, Trin). A dark-green creeping grass with flattened shoots and leaves that have crinkled and hairy edges; it is also known as 'carpet-grass' because of its smooth leaves and the way it looks when it is moved flat.

sa.wa.ri (sa.wa.ree, sou.a.ri) *noun* (Guyn). A large palm tree that bears clusters of hard-shelled, brown nuts with a soft, sweet kernel. (Probably from an Arawak word *sawarama* 'cabbage palm'.)

scar.let plum *noun* (Baha, TkCa). See JAMAICA-PLUM.

scorn-the-earth/ground *noun* (Belz, Jmca, TkCa). See BIRD-VINE[1].

scor.pi.on-tail/-weed *noun* (CayI, Jmca). See WILD CLARY.

Scotch-bon.net pep.per *noun phrase* (Jmca). A type of red pepper looking like a tam (worn by RASTAFARIANS) from which it gets its name; it is highly valued as a seasoning in Jamaican cooking.

Scotch-bonnet pepper

scratch-bush *noun* (Tbgo). See STINGING-NETTLE.

screw-pine *noun* (Bdos, Dmca, Nevs, Tbgo, Trin). **Baha, CayI, Jmca, StKt *thatch*; Gren *wild pine*[2].** A large variety of CANE-LILY looking like a PINEAPPLE plant, which is the reason for its name; its leaves are used to make 'straw' for hats, mats, etc.

sea moss *noun phrase* (CarA). **Belz *sea-weed*.** A type of seaweed that yields a thick, cream-coloured liquid, which is sweetened and flavoured and highly valued as a health drink.

sea.side-grape *noun phrase* (CarA). **CarA *sea-grape*; Bdos, CayI, Guyn, Jmca *grape*.** A small fruit, the size of a marble, which is purple when ripe and has sweetish-sour flesh around a hard seed.

Seaside-grape

sea.side-ma.hoe *noun* (Bdos, Guyn, Jmca). **CarA *mahoe*; USVI *haiti-haiti*, *seaside-hibiscus*.** A bushy, spreading tree with a small trunk, rounded or heart-shaped leaves, and yellow hibiscus-like flowers which change colour to almost brown during the day; it usually grows near sea coasts.

sea-side-yam *noun* (Bdos). See IPOMEA.

sea.son.ing *noun* (Bdos, Guyn). See ESCHALLOT.

sea-thyme *noun* (Baha). See BAY-GERANIUM.

sea-weed *noun* (Belz). See SEA-MOSS.

se.cret-fig *noun* (Gren). See SIKYÉ-FIG. (From French *sucrier*, adjective and easier for Caribbean folk to pronounce than the original French.)

seed-un.der-leaf *noun* (StVn, Tbgo, Trin). See GWENN-ANBA-FÉY.

se.mi-con.tract (se.men-con.tra bush) *noun phrase* (Gren, Jmca). **Dmca *simé-kontwa*; Dmca, Gren, Jmca *worm-bush/-weed*.** A bushy, aromatic herb bearing clusters of greenish flowers with long yellow or white stamens, and usually found on open, waste land; it is widely used as a folk remedy for worms, and other intestinal complaints. (From SEMEN CONTRA, a Latin name that became 'semi-contract', which was easier for Caribbean folk to prounounce.)

se.mi.tu (si.mi.too) *noun* (Guyn). See BELL-APPLE.

sem.per.vive (si.em.pre.vi.vi, sim.pre.vi.vy) *noun* (Angu, Jmca, USVI). See ALOES. (From Latin *semper-vivens* 'ever-living' but now obsolete in Standard English.)

se.ne.bone *noun* (Guyn). See STRING-BEAN.

sé.né-ma.wòn *noun* (StLu). See CHRISTMAS-CANDLE.

sen.si.ble weed *noun phrase* (Belz). See SENSITIVE-PLANT.

sen.si.tive plant *noun phrase* (Bdos, Gren, Guyn, Tbgo, Trin, USVI). **Belz *sensible weed*; Dmca, Trin *mézé-mawi*; Guyn *shame-baby*; Guyn, Trin *shame-bush*; Jmca *shame-lady/-weed, shame-mi-lady*; USVI *grichi-grichi*.** A weed which bears round clusters of pink flowers on slightly prickly greenish-mauve stems, noted for the closing of its leaves at the slightest touch, which gives the plant its name; it is used as a folk remedy for some for stomach complaints.

sen.ti.nel *noun* (Angu). See ADAM'S-NEEDLE.

sen.try-plant *noun* (Bdos). See CENTURY-PLANT.

shack-shack[1] *noun* (Bdos). See WOMAN(S)-TONGUE.

S

shack-shack[2] *noun* (Trin). See WILD-TAMARIND[1].

shack-shack tree *noun phrase* (Antg, BrVI, StLu, StVn). See FLAMBOYANT-TREE.

shad.dock *noun* (CarA). **Gren, Guyn, Trin *forbidden-fruit*[2]; Trin *pomelo*.** A large, round or pear-shaped greenish-yellow or pale yellow fruit with thick, tough, easy removable skin and greenish, pale-yellow, pink or red pulp; it can be sweet or mildly acid or bitter.

Shaddock

sha.do-beni (cha.do(n)-be. ni) *noun* (Gren, StVn, Tbgo, Trin). See FIT-WEED. (From French Creole *chardon béni* 'blessed thistle'.)

shame-ba.by *noun* (Guyn). See SENSITIVE PLANT.

shame-bush *noun* (Guyn, Trin). See SENSITIVE PLANT, SHAME-BABY.

shame-la.dy/-weed *noun* (Jmca). See SENSITIVE PLANT.

sha.po.tie *noun* (Dmca, StLu). See SAPODILLA.

shell gin.ger *noun phrase* (Dmca). See SHELL-PLANT/FLOWER.

shell-plant/flow.er *noun* (CarA). **Dmca *shell ginger*.** A large, bushy plant with juicy stems, alternate dark-green leaves and fragrant, pink-tipped, white or scarlet flowers with yellow markings; the leaves and flowers are used as a folk remedy for a number of complaints.

she.lot *noun* (Guyn). See ESCHALOT.

shine (shin.ing, shi.ny) bush *noun phrase* (Bdos, StVn, Tbgo, Trin). A low weed with light-green stems, shiny, heart-shaped leaves, and terminal spikes of greenish-white flowers; it is widely used as a folk remedy for colds in children.

short ba.na.na *noun* (StVn). See CAYENNE BANANA.

show.er of gold *noun phrase* (Bdos). See GOLDEN-SHOWER.

si.cri *noun* (Mrat). See APPLE-BANANA.

si.kyé-fig (su.crier-fig) *noun* (Gren, Trin). **Gren *secret-fig*; Trin *chiquito-banana*; Angu, Gren, Nevs, StKt, Tbgo, Trin *silk-fig*.** A small, thin-skinned, excessively sweet fruit, golden-yellow with brown spots when ripe. (French Creole from French *sucrier* adjective meaning 'sugar' + Caribbean French *figue* 'banana'.)

silk-ba.na.na *noun* (Nevs, StKt). See APPLE-BANANA.

silk-cot.ton tree *noun phrase* (CarA). **CarA *ceiba;* Baha, Belz, Jmca *cotton-tree;* VIls *kapok tree.*** A massive tree that grows to over 100 ft in height, with a spreading crown and thick, high buttresses; the trunk and the branches are covered with prickles; the tree bears 4-in. long pods filled with seeds embedded in a light-brown silky, cotton-like fibre that is carried by the wind.

Silk-cotton tree

silk-fig[1] *noun* (Angu, Gren, Nevs, StKt, Tbgo, Trin). See APPLE-BANANA.

silk-fig[2] *noun* (Angu, Gren, Nevs, StKt, Tbgo, Trin). See SIKYÉ-FIG.

sil.ver-thatch palm *noun phrase* (Baha, Trin). **Baha, Berm, TkCa *palmetto*; Baha, TkCa *silver-top palm*; Bdos *fan-leaf palm*; Belz *pimento*[2]; CayI, Jmca *thatch (palm)*; ECar *latanyé*; Trin *broom-palm*.** A palm with slender stems and shiny, green leaves, each growing from a smooth, slender stalk, wrapped together at the base in a brown, netted fibre; the dried leaves are used in basket-making, but the palm is also cultivated as an ornamental pot palm or tree.

sil.ver-top (palm) *noun (phrase)* (Baha, TkCa). See SILVER-THATCH PALM.

si.mé-kont.wa *noun* (Dmca, Gren, StLu). See SEMI-CONTRACT. (French Creole rendering of the original plant known as SEMENCONTRA (BUSH).)

six-weeks *noun* (Antg, Dmca, StKt). See BODI-BEAN. (The plant is ready to be reaped within six weeks of being planted which accounts for the name.)

skin.(n)ip (skin.(n)up, skin.op) *noun* (Gren, StKt). See GUINEP.

skin.op (skin.(n)up, skin.(n)up) *noun* (Gren, Guyn, StKt). See GUINEP.

snake-bush/-cham.pi.on/-plant *noun* (Bdos, Belz, Guyn, USVI). See SANSEVERIA.

snake-root *noun* (Baha). See BITTER-BUSH[2].

snat-ap.ple *noun* (Gren). See CUSTARD-APPLE.

snow.drop *noun* (Bdos). See AMARYLLIS.

snow-on-the-moun.tain *noun* (Antg, Bdos, Dmca, Jmca, StVn). **Dmca, Guyn *snow-tree*; Gren *euphorbia, white poinsettia*; StKt *Christmas-bush*; Trin *snow-poinsettia*.** An erect garden shrub with many branches, and abundant tiny, spaced leaves which bloom into lush, white, leaf-like flowers throughout the Christmas and New Year seasons.

snow-poin.set.ti.a *noun* (Trin). See SNOW-ON-THE-MOUNTAIN.

snow-tree *noun* (Dmca, Guyn). See SNOW-ON-THE-MOUNTAIN.

sol.dier-rod *noun* (Guyn). See MAN-BETTER-MAN.

sor.rel *noun* (CarA). A red, fleshy, cup-like fruit widely used to make a refreshing drink, particularly during the Christmas season; the drink made from this fruit is also called SORREL.

sor.row-seed *noun* (Tbgo). See CERASEE.

Sou.fri.ère tree *noun phrase* (StVn). A tree with pale-green, spear-shaped leaves, bearing clusters of small pink flowers, which are the National Flower of St Vincent. (The tree was first reported in 1804 found on the slopes of ths Soufrière volcano, which accounts for the name.)

sour cher.ry *noun phrase* (Trin). See CHILLI-PLUM.

sour fig *noun phrase* (Gren). A small, sour-sweet variety of BANANA.

sour grass *noun phrase* (Bdos, Tbgo, Trin). A bushy type of pasture grass with silky brown spikelets which is sometimes also cultivated.

sour.ie *noun* (Guyn). See BILIMBI.

sour o.range *noun phrase* (CarA). **Antg, Bdos, BrVI** ***bitter orange***; **Gren, Guyn, Trin** ***gospo***; **StLu** ***zowanj-gòspo***. A rough-skinned variety of orange with a bitter rind and acid pulp, which is rarely eaten.

sour.sop *noun* (CarA). **Dmca, StLu** ***kòwòsòl***. A fairly large, green-skinned, heart-shaped, prickly fruit with a thick, white pulp, covering many shiny, black seeds; it is either eaten fresh or made into ice-cream or a refreshing drink.

Span.ish bay.o.net *noun phrase* (VIls). See ADAM'S NEEDLE.

Span.ish ma.chete *noun phrase* (Jmca). See BEAN-TREE.

Span.ish nee.dle[1] *noun phrase* (Bdos). **USVI** ***donkey cactus***. A variety of AGAVE with white-edged, blade-like leaves, each tipped with a sharp spine which prevents animals from passing; it is also grown as a decorative plant.

Span.ish nee.dle[2] *noun phrase* (Jmca, StKt, StVn, USVI). See DUPPY-NEEDLE.

Span.ish net.tle *noun phrase* (Jmca). See DUPPY-NEEDLE.

spice-man.go *noun* (Guyn). **Guyn** ***Buxton spice***. A medium-sized mango with sweet, yellow, cheese-like flesh and a definitely spicy smell and taste, prized as a delicacy.

spur-pep.per *noun* (Bdos). See BIRD-PEPPER.

squash *noun* (CarA). See GOURD.

star-ap.ple *noun* (CarA). **Dmca, Gren, StLu, Tbgo, Trin** ***caimite (caimito)***. A round fruit, like an apple, sometimes with a purple skin when ripe and sweet, slighty stainy, purplish-white pulp covering shiny, black seeds in a star shape, when the fruit is cut across; the skin gives off a white, milky latex. (There is also a green-skinned variety.)

starch man.go *noun phrase* (Gren, StLu, Tbgo). **Dmca, StLu** ***mango-mouchach/ (-mouchasse)***. A small and very sweet mango with a pink or rosy patch on the skin and pale yellow flesh. (Probably so called because of the thick texture of its flesh which is like that of a starchy vegetable).

sta.tia yam *noun phrase* (Baha, Nevs, StKt, StLu). A very large, round, tasty yam with white flesh and a smooth, thick, brown skin.

stick.y ber.ry *noun* (Antg). See CLAMMY-CHERRY.

sting.ing-net.tle[1] *noun* (CarA). **Nevs** ***bath-nettle***; **Tbgo** ***scratch-bush***; **StLu** ***zouti***. A shrub with juicy stems and stinging hairs on both its heart-shaped saw-edged leaves and reddish stems.

sting.ing-net.tle[2] *noun* (Trin). See ZOUTI.

stink.ing-bush/-weed *noun* (CarA). See WILD COFFEE.

stink-ing-toe *noun* (Guyn). **Bdos, Guyn, Trin** ***locust*** **1**. A woody, brown pod containing several seeds encased in a sweet-tasting, but unpleasant-smelling pulp much liked and eaten by children.

St John('s) bush *noun (phrase)* (ECar). A low-growing roadside herb, with flower-like shoots, commonly used as a folk remedy, especially for female complaints.

strang.ler fig *noun phrase* (USVI). See PITCH-APPLE.P

string-bean *noun* (CarA). **Baha, Jmca, Trin** ***kidney-bean*****; BrVI, Dmca, TkCa** ***red bean*****; Guyn** ***senebone*****; Trin** ***salad-bean***. A kidney-shaped bean in different varieties and colours (the most common being reddish-brown), encased in narrow green or yellow pods which grow on a bushy plant, that sometimes climbs. The beans are cooked either green or dry.

strong-back/bark (weed) *noun (phrase)* (Baha, Gren, Jmca). Any one of several varieties of plant whose leaves, fruit or flowers are used as a folk remedy to strengthen the back.

strong-man weed *noun phrase* (Jmca). See GULLY-ROOT.

su.gar-ap.ple *noun* (CarA). **Antg, Baha, Belz, CayI, Jmca** ***sweet sop;*** **Dmca, StLu** ***pomme-can.nelle***. A green, heart-shaped fruit with many segments with very sweet, white flesh in which there are many hard, shiny, black seeds, which grows on a small, leafy tree.

su.gar-ba.na.na *noun* (Baha, TkCa). See APPLE-BANANA.

su.gar-cane *noun* (CarA). A coarse perennial grass with tall, stout, jointed stems that yield sugar, cultivated chiefly in the CarA.

Sur.i.nam cher.ry *noun phrase* (CarA). A ribbed, red, cherry-like fruit, growing on

Sugar-apple

a large shrub with small pointed leaves and white flowers, highly valued for its pleasant taste, and either eaten raw or used to make jellies and preserves.

su.sum.ber *noun* (Jmca). See BURA-BURA.

sweet bar.zey *noun phrase* (Bdos, BrVI, Jmca, StKt, Tbgo, Trin). See ZÈB-A-FANM.

sweet bri.ar *noun phrase* (Bdos). See ACACIA.

sweet broom *noun phrase* (CarA). **Dmca, Gren** ***balyé-dou***. A large, thickly branched, erect herb with slender stems, tiny, white flowers and globe-shaped capsules; the entire plant is dried and used to make a 'tea' and also to purify the blood; it is a folk remedy for many complaints.

sweet-cas.sa.va *noun* (CarA). See CASSAVA.

sweet-cup *noun* (Jmca). See PASSION-FRUIT.

sweet grass *noun phrase* (Antg, Mrat, Trin). See VETIVER.

sweet-lime *noun* (ECar). **Antg** ***myrtle-lime***. A small, oval-shaped shiny red fruit which has a sticky juice and one green

S

seed, and is borne on a spiny shrub with fragrant, white flowers, usually grown as a hedge.

sweet mar.gar.et *noun phrase* (Baha). A large shrub bearing pink flowers and edible berries, found near the sea.

sweet plum *noun phrase* (Baha, Jmca). See JAMAICA-PLUM.

sweet po.ta.to *noun phrase* (CarA). **TkCa *Anne potato*.** A sweet, edible root plant with pinkish, purple or creamy skin, and creamish-grey starchy flesh, much used in CarA cooking, which grows on either an erect bush, or a rambling vine.

sweet-sage *noun* (Guyn). See SAGE-BUSH.

sweet-sop/-sap *noun* (Antg, Baha, Belz, CayI, Jmca). See SUGAR-APPLE.

sweet-wil.li.am *noun* (Dmca, Guyn, Jmca). See ANTIGUA-HEATH.

sword-bean *noun* (Bdos). See GRUDGE-PEA.

syve *noun* (Gren). See CIVE.

T

ta.bac-dia.ble *noun phrase* (StLu). See CATTLE-TONGUE.

ta.bak-djab (ta.bac-dia.ble) *noun* (StLu). See CATTLE-TONGUE. (French Creole from French *tabac-diable* 'devil tobacco', 'devil' meaning 'wild' when referring to plants.)

ta.bak-zon.bi (ta.bac-zom.bie) *noun* (Dmca). See CATTLE-TONGUE.

ta.ma.rind (tam.(b)ran, tam.brin) *noun* (CarA). A hard, brown pod containing a number of seeds surrounded by an acid, reddish-brown pulp.

tan.ge.rine *noun* (CarA). **Dmca, Gren, StLu, Trin *mandarin*; Trin *Portugal*.** A small variety of orange, with thin, loose, orange-reddish skin and many segments which are easily removed.

tan.ni.a *noun* (CarA). **Bdos *tannia-eddoe*; Jmca *eddoe, (hard) coco, taya*; StLu *chou caraïbe*.** A root vegetable, pink or yellowish in colour which is usually boiled and sliced and is often used in soup.

tan.nia-ed.doe *noun* (Bdos). See TANNIA.

tea-grass *noun* (TkCa). See FEVER-GRASS.

te.yer (palm) *noun (phrase)* (ViIs). A slender variety of the THATCH-PALM.

thatch *noun* (Baha, CayI, Jmca, StKt). **Bdos *cane-lily*; Bdos, Jmca *ping-wing*; Dmca, Tbgo, Trin *screw-pine*; Gren *wild-pine*.** The name given to different varieties of palm and also to one or more cane-like shrubs with long, blade shaped coloured leaves, which, when dry, are used for thatching roofs, or for straw-work.

thatch-ber.ry (palm) *noun (phrase)* (Baha). A medium-sized palm that bears bunches of edible berries and has large, fan-shaped leaves, used for thatching roofs.

thatch palm *noun phrase* (Baha, Guyn). **Guyn *troolie*.** A type of palm with low, spreading leaves, usually used for thatching roofs and the walls of houses.

thick-leaf thyme *noun phrase* (Bdos, Guyn). **Bdos, Guyn *broad-leaf thyme*; Bdos *poor man's tears*; StVn *French thyme*.** An erect, spreading, aromatic herb with juicy stems and heart-shaped, saw-edged leaves with tiny hairs, much used as a seasoning, and also to treat a number of complaints.

this.tle (StKt, ViIs). **Bdos, Gren *hollyhock*; Jmca, Trin *Mexican poppy*.** A herb with grey-green, spiny leaves on which are white veins, and spiny stems; it gives off a yellow milky juice and is used as a folk-medicine.

thorn-ap.ple *noun* (Bdos, Gren, Guyn, Trin). **Bdos *night shade*; Jmca *devil's trumpet*.** A common, weedy herb with sturdy stems and coarse leaves, which bears white or purplish trumpet-shaped flowers with claw-like petals that open at night; its ftuit is prickly and oval-shaped and splits open when ripe sending out poisonous seeds.

thorn-tree *noun* (Angu). See MACCA (-PALM).

ti-ko.kom (ti.con.combre) *noun* (StLu). See WILD CUCUMBER.

ti.mite *noun* (Trin). See TROOLIE-PALM.

tjè-bèf (chè-boeuf) *noun* (Gren). See CUSTARD-APPLE.

tjen.nèt (chen.nette) (Dmca, StLu). See GUINEP.

tjè-pal.mis(chè-pal.mis (Dmca, StLu). See CABBAGE.

ton.ka-bean (ton.ca-bean) *noun* (Guyn, Trin). The dry, black, glossy seed found in the pod of a large forest tree and used to flavour food, and also perfume.

to.pi-tambo(o) *noun* (Dmca, Gren, StLu, Trin). The round tubers of a plant similar to the CANNA which are like small white potatoes and are boiled and eaten.

tor.chon *noun* (Trin) See LOOFAH. (French Creole, French *torchon* 'a duster'.)

tou.la.ma *noun* (Dmca, Gren, Mrat, StLu, Trin). See TOULEMWA.

tou.lé.mwa (tou.la.ma, tous-les-mois, tou.lo.mon) *noun* (Dmca, Gren, Mrat, StLu, Trin). A small variety of the CANNA whose roots yield a rich starch similar to ARROWROOT. (From French *tous-les-mois* 'all months' 'throughout the year' referring to the plant which grows all year round.)

tous-les-mois *noun* (Dmca, Gren, Mrat, StLu, Trin). See TOULÉMWA.

to.yo *noun* (Guyn). See GARDEN-BALSAM.

Tri.ni.dad-ba.na.na *noun* (StVn). See CAYENNE BANANA.

Tri.ni.dad-fig (Gren). A small, extremely sweet variety of BANANA, only used in the territory where it is found.

Tri.ni.dad's Pride (Pride of Tri.ni.dad and To.ba.go) *noun phrase* (Tbgo, Trin). See CHACONIA.

troo.lie(-palm) (Guyn). *noun* **Trin *timite*.** A local palm with broad leaves much valued by Amerindians for thatching roofs and making mats.

trum.pet-bush *noun* (CarA). **Bdos, Jmca, StVn, USVI *trumpet-tree*; Guyn *congo pump*; StVn *trumpet-bush tree*; Tbgo, Trin *bacano*; Trin *bacano(e), bwa-kano*; USVI *trumpet-wood*.** A fast-growing, medium-sized tree with one of more hollow, greyish trunks and large leaves with a silvery underside, that are used for colds, chest complaints and other ailments.

trum.pet-flow-er *noun* (Bdos). See ANGEL'S TRUMPET

trum.pet-tree/-wood *noun* (Bdos, Jmca, StVn, USVI). See TRUMPET-BUSH.

try.sil *noun* (Guyn). A large forest tree which yields wood that is used as fuel, as well as in construction; its bark and leaves are used folk-medicinally.

tu.lip-tree *noun* (Bdos, StVn). See AFRICAN TULIP-TREE.

tur.key-ber.ry *noun* (Antg, Mrat). See BURA-BURA, CLAMMY-CHERRY.

Turk's cap (cac.tus) (Turk's head (cac. tus)) *noun (phrase)* (CarA). **Trin *melon cactus*.** A small variety of CACTUS, covered with rows of stiff spines and topped by a circular mass of white wool with brownish bristles and small pink flowers.

Tur.pen.tine-man.go *noun* (Belz, Guyn, Jmca, StVn, Trin). One of a few varieties of fleshy MANGO of different sizes, smelling strongly like turpentine, thus giving the fruit its name.

tur.pen.tine-tree *noun* (Angu, Antg, VIls). See BIRCH-GUM TREE.

tur.tle-grass *noun* (Bdos, USVI). A variety of grass which grows in shallow salt-water and is used to feed turtles.

tu.ru-palm *noun* (Guyn). A type of palm whose leaves are used by Amerindians to thatch huts. (From Arawak *toro* 'a type of palm'.)

Ug.li (fruit) *noun (phrase)* (CarA). A large, hybrid of TANGERINE–GRAPEFRUIT, with thick, greenish-yellow, strangely shaped rind covering orange-like, acid-sweet flesh. □ This name is officially a trademarked proper name in Jamaica for this variety of citrus fruit.

up.side-down ba.na.na *noun phrase* (Bdos). See JUMBIE-BANANA.

vage *noun* (Trin). See BIRD-VINE.

ve.ge.ta.ble-brain *noun* (Jmca). See ACKEE.

ve.ge.ta.ble-mar.row *noun* (Bdos, Jmca). See GOURD[1].

ve.ti.ver *noun* (Dmca, Gren, Mrat, StLu, Trin). **CarA *khus-khus, kuss-kuss (grass)*; Antg, Mrat, Trin *sweet grass*; Guyn, StVn *lavender-grass*; Nevs, Tbgo *bed-grass*.** A coarse grass growing in thick clumps much used in soil conservation and mat-making; its pleasant-smelling roots are sometimes used to make tea to relieve fever.

Vic.to.ri.a-palm *noun* (Baha). See ROYAL-PALM.

Vic.to.ri.a Re.gi.a *noun phrase* (Guyn). A large plant growing in water, with huge, round, floating leaves with upturned edges, rich green on the surface and bearing huge pink or white rosette-shaped lilies, each sticking out of the water on a stout stalk.

wal.la.ba *noun* (Guyn, Trin). A huge forest tree, native to Guyana, much prized for its tough, durable timber which is widely used in construction, especially for utility poles.

wa.ma.ra *noun* (Guyn). A large forest tree, which yields a tough, heavy wood that is dark-brown and yellow in colour, and much valued in furniture-making and woodwork.

wan.der.ing Jew *noun phrase* (Baha, Jmca, USVI). See COCKROACH-GRASS[1].

wan.gla *noun* (Belz, Jmca). The sesame plant; sesame seeds used to flavour food and make sweets.

wa.ter-grass *noun* (CarA). **Antg *French weed*; Dmca *zèb-gwa(s)*; Guyn *zep-grass*.** A creeping, leafy weed with abundant lance-like leaves and bearing clusters of small, blue flowers which fade in the midday sun, usually found in cool, damp places and used as a folk medicine.

wa.ter-hy.a.cinth *noun* (Bdos, Guyn, Jmca, Trin). **Guyn *duck-weed*[1], *water-lily*.** A plant with a cluster of lily-like, reddish flowers, with blue and yellow spots growing from a large, separate, upright, purplish, waxy leaf about one foot high; it grows in still or slow-moving water, and sometimes chokes drains.

wa.ter-le.mon *noun* (ECar). See BELL-APPLE.

wa.ter-li.ly *noun* (CarA). **Bdos, Guyn, Jmca, Trin *water-hyacinth.*** Any one of a variety of plants that grow in water with flat leaves that float and produce beautiful, wax-like, white or brilliantly coloured flowers that grow on single stalks.

wa.ter-spout *noun* (Bdos, StKt). See AFRICAN TULIP.

West In.di.an al.mond *noun phrase* (BrVI, Jmca, Trin). See ALMOND.

West In.di.an birch *noun phrase* (Trin). See BIRCH-GUM TREE.

West In.di.an cher.ry *noun phrase* (CarA). See BARBADOS-CHERRY.

West In.di.an e.bo.ny *noun phrase* (Trin). See WOMAN'S TONGUE.

West In.di.an mi.mo.sa *noun phrase* (Trin). See WILD TAMARIND[1].

West In.di.an sas.pa.ril.la *noun phrase* (ViIs). See SASPARILLA.

whisk *noun* (CarA). See WISK.

whist.ling bean *noun phrase* (Baha). See WOMAN'S TONGUE.

whist.ling pine/wil.low *noun phrase* (Gren, Jmca, StVn, Trin). See CASUARINA.

white back *noun phrase* (Jmca). A bushy shrub with long, hairy leaves, which bears a yellow flower and silky pods, and which is used to make a 'bush-tea' in Jamaica, but is proved to be harmful to both humans and animals.

white bar.ri.ca.der *noun phrase* (Angu, StKt). See PHYSIC-NUT.

white-bean[1] *noun* (CarA). See LIMA BEAN.

white-bean[2] *noun* (ViIs). See BONAVIST.

white cap *noun phrase* (ViIs). See WHITE HEAD BROOM/BUSH.

white-ce.dar *noun* (BrVI, Guyn, Nevs, StLu, Trin). A tall evergreen tree which yields a hard, creamish wood with tiny, dark patches that is used to make paddles, handles, etc.

White-cedar

white clair.ie *noun phrase* (Guyn). See WILD CLARY.

white-eddoe *noun phrase* (Bdos). See EDDOE.

white.head broom/bush *noun phrase* (CarA). **ViIs *white cap*.** A short, aromatic herb that bears loose clusters of tiny, white flowers on long slender stalks and is widely used as a folk medicine for colds, skin diseases and other complaints.

white man.grove *noun phrase* (CarA). A fairly large tree which produces a reddish-brown wood used to make fence posts and house frames; it bears white flowers and is found largely in coastal swamps.

white pea *noun phrase* (Dmca). See LIMA-BEAN.

white poin.set.tia *noun phrase* (Gren). See SNOW-ON-THE-MOUNTAIN.

white po.ta.to *noun phrase* (Antg, Bdos, Guyn, Mrat, StVn). See ENGLISH POTATO.

white sage *noun phrase* (Baha, Bdos, Guyn, StKt). **Jmca, Trin *wild sage*.** A sweet-smelling variety of SAGE-BUSH, topped by a crown of pink, lavender, purple or sometimes white flowers, the leaves of which are used to make a folk-medicinal tea.

white wood[1] *noun phrase* (Bdos, CayI, Jmca). A medium-sized tree with a whitish bark, evenly spaced branches, and bearing lilac flowers noticed when the tree loses its leaves in the dry season.

white wood[2] *noun phrase* (Jmca). A small tree with a slender trunk and drooping branches which bears bunches of fragrant flowers and orange-scarlet, oval-shaped fruit.

white yam[1] *noun phrase* (CarA). **Dmca, Jmca, Tbgo, Trin *Guinea-yam*; Gren, Mrat *Bajan yam, Barbados yam*; Jmca *lucea yam, negro yam*.** A YAM with a white, mealy texture, much valued in Caribbean cooking.

White yam

white yam[2] *noun phrase* (Dmca). See LISBON YAM.

wild ba.na.na[1] *noun phrase* (Dmca, Jmca, StLu, Trin). See JUMBIE-BANANA.

wild ba.na.na[2] *noun phrase* (Baha, Jmca, Trin). See BIRD-OF-PARADISE.

wild ba.sil/bass.ley *noun phrase* (Jmca). See DUPPY-BASIL.

wild cane *noun phrase* (CarA). See ARROW-CANE.

wild cas.sa.va *noun phrase* (Jmca). See BELLY-ACHE BUSH.

wild cher.ry *noun phrase* (Belz, Guyn). See CLAMMY-CHERRY.

wild cla.ry *noun phrase* (Guyn, Jmca). **CayI, Jmca *scorpion-tail/-weed*; Guyn *white clairie*.** An erect herb with broad, oval-shaped leaves and bearing tiny white or mauve flowers, used to treat coughs and colds as well as other complaints.

wild cof.fee *noun phrase* (Guyn, Jmca, StKt, Trin). **Baha, Jmca, StKt, Trin *stinking-weed*; Bdos *stinking-bush*; Guyn *creole coffee*; Guyn, Jmca *piss-a-bed*; Guyn, Trin *negro coffee*; Jmca *dandelion*; Jmca, Trin *miamol*; StKt, Trin, USVI *jumbie-coffee*; USVI *pissy-bush*.** A shrub with brownish-red stems, long leaves and small, pale, yellow flowers; its seeds are parched and used a COFFEE substitute and it is also used as folk-medicinally.

wild cu.cum.ber *noun phrase* (Bdos, BrVI, Gren, Jmca). **StLu *ti-kokom*.** A pale-green, oval-shaped, prickly fruit borne on a vine whose fruit looks like a small CUCUMBER, and is edible, but the vine is a weed.

wild ed.doe *noun phrase* (Guyn). A low-growing plant resembling the EDDOE, but its leaves and roots are not edible.

wild-ge.ra.ni.um *noun* (Baha). See BAY-GERANIUM.

wild li.quor.ice *noun phrase* (Jmca). See BEAD-VINE BUSH.

wild mi.mo.sa *noun phrase* (Bdos, Berm). See WILD TAMARIND[1].

wild mint[1] *noun phrase* (Trin). A creeping vine with long, thin stems and small purple and white flowers, used as folk-medicine in the form of a tea.

wild mint[2] *noun phrase* (Jmca). A variety of SAGE-BUSH popularly used to treat colds.

wild o.kra *noun phrase* (Gren, USVI). A stout herb with many branches and covered with stiff, yellow hairs, which bears yellow, white or lavender flowers and fruit with small, brown seeds; the leaves and seeds are used folk-medicinally.

wild phy.sic-nut *noun phrase* (Bdos, VIls). See BELLY-ACHE BUSH.

wild pine[1] *noun phrase* (Dmca, Gren, Guyn, Jmca, Trin). A parasite that grows on the branches of trees.

wild pine[2] *noun phrase* (Gren). See SCREW-PINE.

wild pine[3] *noun phrase* (Bdos). See PAIN-KILLER BUSH.

wild plan.tain *noun phrase* (Gren, Guyn, Tbgo). See HELICONIA.

wild poin.set.tia *noun phrase* (Tbgo, Trin). See CHACONIA.

wild sage *noun phrase* (Jmca, Trin). See WHITE SAGE.

wild sen.na *noun phrase* (Jmca, Tbgo, Trin). See CHRISTMAS-CANDLE.

wild spin.ach *noun phrase* (Antg, Bdos, Mrat, StVn). **CarA *calalu*[1]; Dmca *zépina*; Guyn, Trin *bhaji*[1]**. A plant with a soft, reddish stalk and stems, bearing spikes of greenish-white flowers, whose leaves are stewed as part of a meal, much valued by East Indians, and also used as a folk-medicine.

wild ta.ma.rind[1] *noun phrase* (Belz, Grns, Trin, VIls). **Baha, Berm *jumbie-bean*; Baha, Gren *cow-tamarind*; Baha, TkCa *cow-bean, cow-bush*; Bdos *miamossi, river-tamarind, wild mimosa*; Jmca *lead-tree*; Trin *shack-shack*[2], *West-Indian mimosa*; USVI *tantan***. A fast-growing, sturdy shrub with compound leaves, small, mimosa-like flowers and bearing thin dry pods containing small, hard, shiny, brown seeds, sometimes used in ornamental work.

wild ta.ma.rind[2] *noun phrase* (CayI). See WOMAN'S TONGUE.

wild tea *noun phrase* (Guyn). See DITAY-PAYEE.

wild to.bac.co *noun phrase* (Jmca). See CATTLE-TONGUE.

wild yam *noun phrase* (Jmca). A dark-skinned yam with white flesh, which is not really tasty, and borne on a reddish vine which can grow to the tops of trees in some areas and is considered a parasite.

wil.low *noun* (Jmca). See CASUARINA.

wind-break *noun* (StKt). See GLIRICIDIA.

wind-flow.er *noun phrase* (CarA). See AMARYLLIS.

wi.ri-wi.ri pep.per *noun phrase* (Guyn). See CHERRY-PEPPER.

wist (whisk, whist, wis(k)) *noun* (CarA). A tough, parasitic vine or any dry bough which is sliced lengthwise and used especially in basket-making.

wo.man-pi.a.ba *noun* (Bdos, Guyn). **Baha, Jmca *greasy-bush* 1**. A wild herb bearing many small clusters of purplish flowers, whose leaves and bark are used folk-medicinally by some, especially for female complaints.

wo.man('s)-tongue *noun* (CarA). **Baha** ***whistling bean*; Bdos *Barbados ebony*; Bdos, Trin *sha(c)k-sha(c)k*; StLu *lang-fanm*; TkCa *monkey(-fiddle)*; Trin *West Indian ebony;* CayI *wild ta.ma.rind***[2]. A medium-sized tree that bears numerous long, flat, light-brown pods which, when they are dry, chatter continuously in the wind, as the name suggests.

won.der-of-the-world *noun* (Bdos, Gren, Tbgo, Trin). See LEAF-OF-LIFE.

wool.ly py.rol *noun phrase* (Trin). See MUNG-BEAN.

worm-bush/-grass/-weed *noun* (CarA). See SEMI-CONTRACT.

worm.wood 1. *noun* (Bdos, Trin). See BAY-GERANIUM.

worm.wood 2. *noun* (Jmca). See ANGELIN.

yam *noun* (CarA). A root vegetable of which there are many varieties, some edible and some inedible; the edible ones are cooked in many different dishes throughout the Caribbean.

yam-bean *noun* (Jmca). See SAEME.

yanm-a.tou.tan (a.tou.ta(n), yam-a-tout-temps) *noun* (StLu, Trin). See YELLOW-YAM.

yanm-jonn (yam-jaune) *noun* (Dmca). See YELLOW YAM.

yanm-pen *noun* (Dmca). See BREADFRUIT.

yard-bean *noun* (Gren, Guyn, Trin). See BODI (BEAN).

yel.low-bell *noun* (Angu, Antg, Tbgo). See ALLAMANDA.

yel.low-boy *noun* (Bdos). See DWARF-COCONUT.

yel.low-coat plum *noun phrase* (Jmca). See HOG-PLUM[1].

yel.low-dad/dod *noun* (Angu). See LOVE-VINE.

yel.low-dwarf (co.co.nut) *noun (phrase)* (Belz, Jmca, StLu). See DWARF-COCONUT.

yel.low-love *noun* (VIls). See LOVE-VINE.

yel.low-plum *noun* (Belz, CayI, Jmca, Trin). See CHILLI-PLUM.

yel.low pou.i *noun phrase* (ECar). A slow-growing forest tree, usually found on hillsides, which loses all its leaves in the dry season and bears masses of golden-yellow trumpet-shaped flowers that only last a few days. It also yields a highly valuable timber that is used in construction.

Yellow poui

Yellow-yam

yel.low-yam *noun* (CarA). **Dmca** ***yanm-jonn*****; Gren** ***atouta*****; Guyn** ***dye-yam, hard-yam, neroo yam*****; Jmca, Tbgo, Trin** ***afu yam*****; Mrat** ***Ibo yam*****; StLu, Trin** ***yanm-atoutan*****; StVn** ***Dominica yam*****; Tbgo, Trin** ***prickle yam***. A YAM that has a rough skin and pale-yellow flesh which becomes dry and floury when boiled, and is widely eaten throughout the Caribbean.

Z

za.bò.ka (za.bo.ca) *noun* (Dmca, Gren, Mrat, StLu, StVin, Trin). See AVOCADO (-PEAR).

za.bwi.ko *noun* (Dmca, StLu). See MAMMEE-APPLE.

za.ka.cha *noun* (Dmca). See ACACIA.

za.mand (zan.mann) *noun* (Crcu, Dmca, Gren, StLu, Trin). See ALMOND.

zan.na.na (a.na.na) *noun* (Dmca, StLu). See PINE(-APPLE).

zèb-a-fanm[1] **(z'herbe-à-femme)** *noun* (Gren, Trin). **Bdos, BrVI, Jmca, StKt, Tbgo, Trin** ***sweet bar.zey***. A low bush with hairy stems and oval-shaped leves that bears little bunches of mauve flowers; it is said to be effectively used for female complaints.

zèb-a-fanm[2] **(z'herbe-à-femme)** *noun* (Dmca). See CARPET-DAISY.

zèb-a-pik (z'herbe-à-pique) *noun* (Gren, Trin). **Gren** ***bitter-bush***[3]**; Tbgo, Trin** ***zebapip***. A shrub with long, lance-like leaves which make a yellow stain when held, and which bears clusters of tiny, tube-shaped, yellow flowers that are used, together with the leaves, to make a tea for treating fevers and menstrual cramps.

zèb-chat (z'herbe-à-chat) (Dmca, Trin). A large shrub with beavy veined, oval-shaped, velvety leaves and numerous little clusters of whitish flowers; it is used folk-medicinally for female complaints.

zeb-grass (zep-grass, zèb-gwa) *noun* (Dmca, Guyn). See WATER-GRASS.

zé.pi.na *noun* (Dmca). See CALALU[1].

zi.caque *noun* (Dmca, StLu). See ZIKAK.

zi.kak (zi.caque, z'i.caque) (Dmca, StLu). See COCO-PLUM[1].

zi.ri.co.te (si.ri.co.te, zi.ra.co.te, ze.ri. co.te) *noun* (Belz). A forest tree which yields a hard, heavy wood, with black, brown and yellow streaks, highly valued for wood carving.

z'o.range-gros-peau *noun* (StLu). See SOUR ORANGE.

zò.ti (zor.tie) *noun* (StLu). See STINGING-NETTLE.

zou.ti[1] **(zoo.tee, zoo.tie)** *noun* (Dmca, Gren, Trin). The same plant known as ZÒTI in St Lucia.

zou.ti[2] *noun* (Trin). A small, twining vine with oblong leaves and slim stalks bearing tiny flowers; both stems and leaves are covered with stinging hairs.

zo.wanj-gòs.po (z'o.range-gros-peau, zo.wanj-gros-po) *noun* (Dmca, StLu). See SOUR ORANGE.

zoy.si.a-grass *noun* (CarA). A thick grass which grows abundantly, covering the ground like a carpet and much used as a lawn grass.

Z

FOOD

A

a.ca.ra *noun* (Baha). See ACCRA.

ac.cra (ac.kra, ak.wa) *noun* (CarA). **CarA** ***salt-fish cakes*****; Baha** ***acara*****; StLu** ***akwa-lanmowi***. A fritter made of shredded saltfish mixed with seasonings.

ac.cra-and-float *noun* (Trin). See ACCRA.

a.char (a.chaar, aa.tchar, am.char) *noun* (Guyn, Trin). An East Indian sauce made of a mixture of pieces of green mango and other fruit with peppers, ground massala, vinegar and salt in mustard oil; it is usually eaten with CURRY or other East Indian dishes. (Bhojpuri *atchara* from Hindi *achaar* 'pickles'.)

Achar

ac.kee and saltfish *noun phrase* (Jmca). A meal made of ripe ackees, fried up with oil, onions and salted codfish.

Ackee and saltfish

a.gi.di (a.gee.dee. a.gri.di) *noun* (Baha, Gren, Guyn, Jmca). A pudding made of finely ground cormeal or mashed boiled corn, seasoned and wrapped in pieces of plantain or almond leaf. (Probably Yoruba *agidi*, a similar food.)

ak.wa-lan.mo.wi *noun* (StLu). See ACCRA.

a.loo *noun* (Guyn, Trin). The ENGLISH POTATO. (Hindi *aaluu* 'potato'.)

a.loo-pie *noun* (Guyn, Trin). A small pie filled with fried mashed potato and herbs, which is widely popular as a snack.

am.char *noun* (Guyn, Trin). See ACHAR.

A.mer.in.di.an pep.per.pot *noun phrase* (Guyn). A dish of boiled fish and wild meat in boiled juice of the bitter cassava mixed with herbs and spices.

a.ra.pe *noun* (CarA). See AREPA.

a.re.pa (a.ra.pe) (Trin). A fried cornmeal cake with a filling of meat, fish or cheese. (Spanish *arepa* 'a griddle cake made of soaked maize ground into a paste or dough'.)

asham *noun* (Antg, Brbu, Gren, Jmca). **Jmca** ***coction*****; Belz, Gren** ***corn-sham*****; Belz** ***parch-corn*****.** Roasted corn and brown sugar ground together, with grated coconut added in some places. (From Twi *o-siam*, 'parched and ground corn'.)

Asham

at.char (Guyn). See ACHAR.

a.vo.ca.do and car.rot sa.lad *noun phrase* (CarA). Chopped AVOCADO rings and finely shredded carrot seasoned with salt, mayonaaise, tomato, cabbage and lime-juice mixed together and served as a salad.

a.vo.ca.do ice-cream *noun phrase* (CarA). A dessert made of AVOCADOS, evaporated milk, sugar, water and lemon juice, whipped together and frozen.

a.vo.ca.do sa.lad *noun phrase* (CarA). Sliced or cubed AVOCADO seasoned with salt and served as a salad.

B

ba.ba.lé (ba.ba.lait) *noun* (Gren). See SOURSOP DRINK.

ba.bache (ba.bash) *noun* (Trin). See BUSH-RUM.

ba.ca.lao (bac.ca.low) *noun* (CarA). Saltfish, salted codfish. (From Portuguese *bacalhao* 'codfish'.)

bake *noun* (Bdos, Gren, StLu, StVn). **Antg, Jmca** ***fry-dumpling*****; Baha, Jmca, StKt, VIls** ***johnny-cake(s)*****; Guyn** ***soda-bakes*****; StLu** ***salt bakes, sweet bakes*****.** A small, round piece of dough, fried golden-brown in boiling hot oil; several of them are usually served with a meal.

bak.ed chick.en *noun phrase* (CarA). **CarA** ***roast chicken*****.** Chicken cooked in the oven.

bak.ed pork *noun phrase* (CarA). **CarA** ***roast pork*****.** Pork cooked in the oven.

bam-bam *noun* (Crcu, Gren, StVn). See CASSAVA-BREAD.

bam.bu.la *noun* (Antg). See CASSAVA-BREAD.

bam.mie (bam.my) *noun* (Jmca). **CarA** ***cassava bread*****.** A special type of CASSAVA-BREAD that is much thicker than the one normally found in the Eastern Caribbean; it is baked brown in a circular metal pan. (From Gã-Adangme *bami* 'cakes of bread or cassava'.)

Bammy

ba.na.na-bread/cake *noun* (CarA). A dessert made of a mixture of mashed bananas, yeast or baking powder (if it is a cake), sugar, flour, salt, grated nutmeg and eggs into a dough and baked until golden-brown.

Banana bread

ba.na.na-flour *noun* (Jmca). Pounded strips of dried green banana which make a powder that can be used to make porridge or in cooking.

ba.na.na frit.ters *noun phrase* (CarA). A small cake made of mashed BANANAS, flour, sugar, egg, baking powder and vanilla essence, which is then fried and sprinkled with sugar.

ba.na.na-jam/jel.ly *noun* (CarA). A fruit stew made of ripe BANANAS boiled with sugar, water and vanilla essence into a thick mixture which is allowed to cool and then put into bottles.

bang-bang *noun* (USVI). See CASSAVA-BREAD.

bean sa.lad *noun phrase* (CarA). Cooked RED BEANS and STRING BEANS cooled and seasoned with chopped onions, red SWEET PEPPERS, salt and black pepper, then sprinkled with brown sugar and served on lettuce-leaves.

beef balls *noun phrase* (CarA). **(CarA).** ***meatballs.*** A fried ball of seasoned meat mixed with bread cumbs; several are served as a part of a meal.

beef cur.ry *noun phrase* (CarA). See CURRIED BEEF.

beef pat.ties *noun phrase* (CarA). **CarA** ***patties.*** A semicircular piece of pastry folded over seasoned mince meat, commonly served as a snack.

Beef patties

beef soup *noun phrase* (CarA). Soup in which beef is the main ingredient, boiled with various herbs and in some territories, green and root vegetables.

beef stew *noun phrase* (CarA). **Bdos** ***stew, stew beef.*** A dish made of seasoned meat cut into small pieces, which are lightly fried, after which water is added and the beef left to simmer, then vegetables are added.

bev.er.age *noun* (Antg, CayI, Jmca, StKt). See SWANK.

bha.ji (baa.ji. bhaa.gee) *noun* (Guyn, Trin). Any dish made up of mostly edible leaves, and usually prepared by East Indians. (From Hindi *bhaajii* 'vegetable leaves, green or cooked'.)

black beans and rice *noun phrase* (CarA). A dish made up of black beans, rice, cubes of salt meat, chopped onions, green pepper, garlic, salt and black pepper, cooked together after the meat and seasonings have been lightly fried.

black cake *noun phrase* (CarA). **Bdos *great-cake*; Jmca *Christmas pudding, fruit cake*.** A rich, dark cake, like a pudding, made of fruits soaked in rum with burnt brown sugar added to give the cake its dark colour; it is traditionally

Black cake or Christmas pudding

served at Christmas time and at weddings.

black-pep.per *noun* (CarA). A seasoning item made from grinding the whole berries of the black-pepper plant to be used in cooking.

black-pud.ding *noun* (CarA). **CarA *pudding*; Antg *rice-pudding*; Antg, Gren, StLu, Trin *blood-pudding*.** A popular Eastern Caribbean dish made by stuffing cleaned pig's large intestines with well-seasoned boiled rice or mashed SWEET POTATO mixed with cow's blood; the stuffed intestines are then boiled until they look like large sausages. □ Not all territories stuff the potato mixture into pig's intestines, as in Barbados the potato mixture is served by itself and is referred to as PUDDING.

black su.gar *noun* (CarA). See MUSCOVADO SUGAR.

blood-pud.ding *noun* (Antg, Gren, StLu, Trin). See BLACK-PUDDING.

blue-draws (blue-draw.ers) *noun* (Jmca). See DUKUNA.

boil-in[1] *noun* (StVn). **StVn *fish boil-in*.** A thick soup made by boiling together root vegetables, breadfruit, green bananas and dumplings with fish, seasonings and butter.

boil-in[2] *noun* (StVn). A clear broth seasoned with herbs and into which whole fish are put.

boil-up *noun* (Belz). See SANCOCHE.

bo.llos *noun* (Belz). See TAMALES.

bo.yo *noun* (BELZ, JMCA). SEE DUKUNA.

braf *noun* (Dmca). See FISH-BROTH.[1]

bread.fruit cou-cou *noun phrase* (CarA). Boiled BREADFRUIT mashed and mixed into a paste, together with pieces of meat and herbs, and shaped into a round ball.

B

bread.fruit frit.ters *noun phrase* (CarA). A batter made with mashed BREADFRUIT, shaped into small, round balls and fried in hot oil until golden-brown.

bread-kind *noun* (CarA). Any starchy cooked food, such as breadfruit, plantains, root vegetables, dumplings and also bread.

broth[1] *noun* (ECar). See FISH-BROTH[2].

broth[2] *noun* (Dmca). **Dmca *braf*.** A thick vegetable soup mainly flavoured with fish, or sometimes, smoked pork.

bul.jol *noun* (Trin). **StVn *bull-jowl*.** Shredded saltfish sesasoned with hot peppers, onions, tomatoes and olive oil, usually served with breadfruit or another starchy vegetable.

bull-foot soup *noun phrase* (VIls). See COW-HEEL SOUP.

bun-and-cheese *noun* (Jmca). See JAMAICAN BUN.

bush-rum *noun* (Gren, Guyn. Trin). **Trin *babache*; Guyn *bushie*; Nevs, StKt**

hammond; **Gren, Grns, StVn** ***jack-iron***; **Trin** ***mountain-dew***. Very strong home-made rum usually made illegally.

bush-tea *noun* (CarA). Any kind of herbal tea made with dried herbs, including their roots and flowers, considered to be medicinal and used for a variety of complaints, or to maintain good health.

buss-up-shot (buss-up-shirt) *noun* (Trin). See PARAT(H)A-ROTI.

C

ca.beche (ca.viche) *noun* (Guyn). See ESCAVEITCH FISH.

ca.la.lu (cal.(l)al.loo (ou, u), ka(l.) la.loo 2. *noun* (Dmca, StVn, Tbgo, Trin). **Angu, Antg** ***pepperpot***[2]; **Guyn** ***crab-and-calalu***; **Mrat, StVn** ***calalu-soup***. A thick soup, made of CALALU or DASHEEN leaves mixed with other ingredients such OKRAS, root vegetables, crabs and herbs, dumplings, salt meat or ham-bone, all boiled together; it is served as a main meal and is the national dish of Trinidad & Tobago.

ca.la.lu-soup *noun* (Mrat, StVn). See CALALU.

can.died sweet po.ta.toes *noun phrase* (CarA). Slices of SWEET POTATO baked in a mixture of brown sugar, water, a little vinegar, salt and pepper; it is usually served as a side dish with meat.

cane-sy.rup *noun* (CarA). **Bdos, StKt** ***fancy molasses***. A thick, dark-brown syrup, or MOLASSES before the cane-sugar begins to crystallize, sold commercially.

can.kie (can.kee.con.kie, kaan.ki) *noun* (Guyn). See DUKUNA.

ca.ram.bo.la-drink (CarA). **Guyn** ***five-finger drink***. A cooling drink made by either cutting the fruit into small pieces, then soaking them in water for one or two days, and straining and sweetening the juice, or juicing the fruit in a blender and adding sugar and water; it is usually refrigerated and served cold.

ca.ram.bo.la-jam *noun* (CarA). A fruit preserve made by boiling pieces of CARAMBOLA with sugar and water and letting the mixture cook slowly until it thickens; it is then cooled and stored in bottles.

ca.sa.reep (cas.reep, cas.sa.reep, cas.se.ripe) *noun* (CarA). A thick, dark-brown liquid looking like MOLASSES produced by boiling the juice of grated BITTER CASSAVA to extract the poison; it is used to make PEPPERPOT[1].

ca.si.ri (cas.si.ri) *noun* (Guyn). An Amerindian drink made of boiled cassava meal and a little cassava juice, coloured with a potato called 'kashiri' and left to ferment.

cas.sa.va-bake *noun* (Bdos). See CASSAVA-BREAD.

cas.sa.va-bread *noun* (CarA). **Angu** ***choky banjo***; **Antg** ***bambula***; **Jmca** ***bammie***; **Bdos** ***cassava-bake***; **Crcu, Gren, StVn** ***bam-bam***; **USVI** ***bang-bang***. A large, dry, flat, round biscuit made

Cassava-bread

from the meal of the BITTER CASSAVA and prepared in different ways in different territories. In Guyana, it is a thin, brittle, sun-dried mixture, made from a paste of the cassava with salt and water, in Jamaica it is smaller and thicker, made from a more cake-like mixture baked over fire, and in the Bahamas it is a sweet with grated COCONUT, baked in pan.

cas.sa.va-cake *noun* (Belz, Guyn). **Guyn *quinch, sugar-cassava***. A sweet variety of CASSAVA-BREAD, made with sugar, milk, grated coconut and baked; in another version the sweet layer is placed between the dryer layers of CASSAVA.

cas.sa.va-coo.coo *noun* (Tbgo). A dish made from SWEET CASSAVA boiled and pounded in a mortar.

cas.sa.va-fa.rine *noun* (Dmca) See FARINE.

cas.sa.va-flour *noun* (CarA). The dried meal of the grated BITTER CASSAVA from which the poisonous juice has been extracted, and which is used to made CASSAVA BREAD.

cas.sa.va pone *noun phrase* (Bdos, Guyn). **Bdos, Guyn, Trin *pone***. A mixture of grated CASSAVA, grated coconut, currants, butter, sugar and spices, baked and usually served in slices.

chan.na *noun* (Guyn, Trin). Chickpea(s), boiled and seasoned, or fried crisp with salt and sold as a snack.

cha.pat.ti *noun* (Guyn, Trin). A flat, smaller, courser type of ROTI.

cheese bis.cuits *noun phrase* (CarA). A savoury snack made of flour, grated cheese, beaten eggs, salt, pepper and shortening mixed together, and shaped into rounds or squares and baked.

cheese-cut.ter *noun* (Bdos). See CUTTER.

cheese-sauce *noun* (CarA). A sauce made of grated cheese, milk, flour, salt, pepper and finely minced onios mixed together and put to simmer until the mixture is smooth and creamy; it is often served with fish.

cheese-straws *noun* (Guyn). A snack that is made from the same mixture as that for CHEESE BISCUITS, but the dough is rolled out and either passed through a biscuit cutter or cut into strips which are then baked until they are crisp and golden-brown.

chip-chip su.gar-cake *noun phrase* (Gren, Trin). See SUGAR-CAKE².

cho.co.late *noun* (Guyn). A heavy mixture of finely ground cocoa-beans and hot water which is rolled into finger-length sticks used for making CHOCOLATE-TEA.

cho.co.late lumps *noun phrase* (TkCa). A breakfast item made by dropping a dough made of flour, sugar, eggs and cream into boiling cocoa, producing lumps which are then stored to make a sweetened hot drink.

cho.co.late-tea *noun* (ECar). **Trin *creole cocoa*; Jmca *country-chocolate***. A hot breakfast drink made from boiling either chocolate-sticks or lumps to which milk and sugar are added.

coag *noun* (Guyn). A thick, milky drink made of beaten eggs in milk with sugar and sometimes rum is added. (Probably Irish dialect.)

co.co.nut-bake *noun* (Tbgo, Trin). A dough similar to that made for ROAST BAKE mixed with grated coconut or with COCONUT-MILK.

co.co.nut-boil-in *noun* (StVn). **Gren *oil-down***. A meal made up of fish or pork, CALALU, BREADFRUIT and/or GROUND PROVISIONS boiled to a heavy, soup-like mixture in COCONUT MILK, and served as one dish.

co.co.nut-bread *noun* (Bdos, Jmca). **CarA *sweet bread***. A heavy bread made by baking together flour, spices, vanilla essence, grated COCONUT, raisins and eggs.

C

co.co.nut-bun(s) *noun (plural)* (CarA). Small cakes which have grated COCONUT as the main ingredient, dropped on a flat pan and baked.

co.co.nut-cake[1] *noun* (CarA). A cake chiefly flavoured by COCONUT.

co.co.nut-cake[2] *noun* (Baha). See SUGAR-CAKE[2].

co.co.nut-cream *noun* (CarA). A type of sauce made by pouring milk over grated COCONUT, chilled and used in different ways.

co.co.nut-drop(s) *noun (plural)* (Jmca). See SUGAR-CAKE[2].

co.co.nut-fudge *noun* (CarA). A sweet made by boiling milk, sugar, essence and COCONUT together into a thick mixture which is then cut into squares and put to cool.

C

co.co.nut-jam *noun* (CarA). A jam made with grated or chipped coconut as its main ingredient.

co.co.nut-jel.ly *noun* (CarA). The soft, white, jelly-like lining of the young coconut.

co.co.nut-juice *noun* (Gren). See COCONUT-MILK.

co.co.nut-milk *noun* (CarA). The sweet, white, milky liquid sqeezed from grated dry coconut and widely used in Caribbean cuisine.

co.co.nut-pie *noun* (CarA). A baked dessert made with grated coconut and other ingredients, usually baked in a pastry shell.

co.co.nut-pud.ding *noun* (CarA). A baked sweetened pudding made chiefly with grated coconut and butter.

co.co.nut-wa.ter *noun* (CarA). The clear liquid found in the young coconut, which is much used as a refreshing drink.

coc.tion *noun* (Jmca). See ASHAM.

com.press *noun* (Guyn). See SNOW-CONE.

con.ga.tay (co.go.tay, con.kan.tay, con. quin.tay) *noun* (Guyn, Tbgo, Trin). **Jmca** ***plantain-porridge***. A porridge made by pounding together sun-dried slices of plantains or green bananas, used especially for feeding infants. (Probably from Gã-Adangme *kokonté* 'cassada dried in the sun and then made into a flour'.)

con.kie (can.kie, kaan.ki. kon.kee) *noun* (Angu, Bdos, Guyn, StKt, Tbgo). See DUKUNA.

cook-up (rice) *noun (phrase)* (CarA). **Antg, Jmca** ***seasoned rice***. A dish made of peas or beans and rice boiled in COCONUT-MILK and flavoured with salt meat.

cool-drink *noun* (CarA). **(CarA)** ***aerated drink /water, sweet drink.*** Any bottled, fizzy beverage sold commercially; (AmE) soda.

corn-cou-cou/coo-coo *noun* (BrVI, StVn, Tbgo). See COU-COU.

corn-dump.ling *noun* (StKt). See DUKUNA.

corn-flour *noun* (Bdos, Guyn). See CORN-MEAL.

corn-meal *noun* (CarA). The golden-yellow, grainy flour made by grinding corn and widely used in Caribbean cooking.

corn-pone[1] *noun* (Bdos, Guyn, Jmca, Tbgo). **Antg, Brbu** ***cornmeal pudding***. A heavy, baked, sweet pudding made of cornmeal and grated coconut.

corn-pone[2] *noun* (Jmca). See DUKUNA.

cou-cou (coo-coo) *noun* (CarA). **Angu, Antg, Brbu, Nevs, StKt, StVn, VIls** ***fungee***; **BrVI, Guyn, StVn, Tbgo** ***corn(meal)/corn-flour cou-cou***; **Jmca** ***turn-corn-meal***; ***turn-meal***; **Nevs, StKt** ***turn-corn***. A dish made by boiling a mixture of CORNMEAL, OKRAS, and butter until it is firm enough to be shaped into a ball. (Compare Twi ŋkuku 'a species of yam', also Twi *kuku* 'cook'.)

coun.try-cho.co.late *noun* (Jmca). See CHOCOLATE-TEA.

cow-foot soup *noun phrase* (Baha, Belz, Jmca). See COW-HEEL SOUP.

co.ver.ty po-chanm *noun* (Dmca). See KOUVÈTI-PÒT-CHANM.

cow-heel soup, *noun phrase* (Gren, Guyn, StVn, Tbgo, Trin). **Baha, Belz, Jmca *cow-foot soup,* VIls *bull-foot soup*.** A thick soup made from the ankle and hoof of the cow boiled to a soft, jelly-like substance with vegetables and seasonings added.

crab-and-ca.lalu *noun* (Guyn). See CALALU.

crab-back(s) *noun (plural)* (CarA). The cleaned shell of the crab that is stuffed with seasoned, cooked crabmeat, sprinkled on top with breadcrumbs, then baked; it is considered a delicacy.

cre.ole cocoa *noun phrase* (Trin). See CHOCOLATE-TEA.

crush-ice *noun* (Guyn). See SNOW-CONE.

cur.ried beef (beef cur.ry, cur.ry beef) *noun phrase* (CarA). A dish made of beef, sometimes with vegetables included, cooked in a sauce made from curry powder.

cur.ried chick.en (chick.en cur.ry, cur.ry chick.en) *noun phrase* (CarA). A dish consisting of pieces of chicken, well seasoned and cooked with curry powder and sometimes coconut milk into a tasty stew, usually eaten with ROTI or rice, and widely used in the Caribbean.

cur.ried goat (cur.ry goat) *noun phrase* (CarA). Seasoned goat meat cooked with curry powder into a stew.

cush-cush (cuss-cuss, kus(s)-kus(s)) *noun* (Angu, Guyn). Meal made from grated cassava or coconut after the liquid has been squeezed and washed out of it, and sugar added; it is used as a sweet.

cut.ter[1] (cheese cut.ter) *noun* (Bdos). **Trin *hops*.** A snack made of a small bread roll cut in half with a piece of ham, cheese or fish in between; it is used to 'cut' hunger hence the name.

cut.ter[2] *noun* (Gren, Guyn). Salty dish of pickled snacks served at parties, used to 'cut' the effects of alcohol, hence the name.

daal (dahl, dal, dhal, dholl) *noun* (Guyn, Trin). Ground yellow split peas put into a type of ROTI, or made into a thick soup-like mixture. (A Bhojpuri word from Hindi *daal* meaning 'pulse'.)

daal pu.ri *noun phrase* (Guyn, Trin). A type of ROTI made with a filling of DAAL, traditionally served at Hindu weddings, but also a hugely popular item in Caribbean cuisine.

da.ru *noun* (CarA). Rum, or any strong liquor that can make a person drunk.

dip-and-fall-back (dip-and-run-down) *noun* (Jmca). **CayI, Jmca *run-down*.** A dish made of mackerel or salt-fish boiled in COCONUT-MILK until it is oily and grey; root vegetables, breadfruit or dumplings are dipped into the mixture and eaten.

dou.bles *noun* (Trin). A type of sandwich made of two East Indian patties with a filling of CHANNA, widely popular as a snack.

dough-boy[1] *noun* (Baha, Jmca, TkCa). A type of tough dumpling boiled in soup.

dough-boy[2] *noun* (Guyn, StVn). **Jmca *dough-bread*.** A small, hard, homemade sweetbread.

dove peas *noun phrase* (Bdos, Guyn, Jmca). PIGEON-PEAS boiled slowly and sometimes with meat, and allowed to simmer until the peas (and meat, if added) are tender.

dry-food[1] *noun* (Bdos, Trin). A meal consisting mainly of GROUND PROVISIONS.

dry-food[2] *noun* (Guyn, Tbgo). A meal mainly of root vegetables boiled together with little meat or fish.

dry-peas *noun* (CarA). Dried PIGEON-PEAS.

duff *noun* (Guyn). A tough dumpling made of cornflour and usually put in METAGEE.

du.ku.na *noun* (Antg, BrVI, Mrat, StVn). **Angu, Bdos, StKt** ***conkie*****; Bdos, StVn** ***stew-dumpling*****; Belz, Jmca** ***boyo, dokonu*****; Guyn** ***cankie*****; Jmca** ***blue-drawe(r)s, pone***[1], ***corn-pone***[2]; **StKt** ***corn-dumpling.*** A small pudding made of mixtures of gated sweet-potatoes, cornmeal, grated coconut, plantain-flour, raisins, spices, sugar and essence, wrapped either in a piece of banana or plantain leaf and steamed. (Akan, Gã-Adangme *doko na* 'sweeten (verb) mouth'.)

Dukuna

E

ed.doe-soup *noun* (CarA). A soup made mostly of EDDOES, herbs and meat or fish.

egg nog *noun phrase* (CarA). See PONCHE DE CRÈME,

em.pa.na.das (em.pa.na.des, em.pe.na.da) *noun (usually) plural* (Belz). **Belz** ***panades.*** A type of large PATTY made of a fried tortilla folded over, filled with fish, usually served with onion and vinegar. (From Spanish *empañada* from *pan* 'bread', the name of this food.) □ The plural form is used as the singular in Belize, largely in writing, but *panades* is the form used in speech.

es.ca.be.che *noun* (Belz) A dish made of sliced onions soaked in vinegar and combined with red pepper and other seasonings and poured over a boiled chicken, removed from the mixture, cut up and browned to be served. (Spanish *escabeche* 1. 'pickle, brine' 2. 'soused fish'.)

es.ca.veitch.(ed) fish (es.co.veitch(ed) fish) *noun phrase* (Jmca). **Guyn** ***cabeche*****; Jmca** ***scaveeched fish*****.** A dish made of fish that has been deep fried, drained and pickled in a mixture of vinegar and oil, red pepper, spices, sliced CHOCHO, etc. (See ESCABECHE.)

Escaveitch fish

F

fa.ler.num (Bdos). An alcoholic syrup made of rum and lime juice, used either as a liqueur or as a base for drinks mixed with rum.

fan.cy-mo.las.ses *noun* (Bdos, StKt). See CANE SYRUP.

fa.rine (fa.win) *noun* (Angu, Dmca, Gren, Guyn, StLu, StVn, Tbgo). A coarse-grained meal made from the grated remains of BITTER CASSAVA (having extracted the poisonous juice). (From French *farine* 'flour'.)

fes.ti.val *noun* (Jmca). A fritter made of flour, cornmeal, sugar, salt, baking powder, allspice, milk and vanilla, deep fried until golden-brown.

fish-boil-in *noun* (StVn). See BOIL-IN.

fish-broth[1] *noun* (Dmca, Gren, StLu, Tbgo, Trin). **Antg *man-soup*; Belz, Jmca, StVn, Tbgo, Trin *fish-tea*; Dmca, StLu *braf, broth***. A thick, grey, seasoned soup, made largely of fish and vegetables, or a thinner broth made using fish-head or whole JACKS.

fish-broth[2] *noun* (Gren). A soup using RED SNAPPER to which is added either ketchup or fresh tomatoes.

fish-cakes *noun plural* (CarA). Small deep-fried fritters made from cooked fish, flour and mashed potatoes mixed with seasonings.

fish-tea *noun* (Belz, Jmca, StVn, Tbgo, TkCa, Trin). A FISH-BROTH[1] served steaming hot in a cup.

float *noun* (Bdos, Guyn, Tbgo, Trin). A type of BAKE, made with flour, baking powder or yeast, fried in hot oil until it puffs out, becomes brown and rises to the top of the oil.

food *noun* (CarA). See DRY FOOD[2], HARD-FOOD.

foo-foo[1] *noun* (Baha, Belz, Guyn, Jmca, Tbgo). See FUFU[1].

foo-foo[2] *noun* (Antg, Tbgo). See FUNGEE[2].

fres.co (fres.ko) *noun* (Belz). See SNOW-CONE.

fried-cake(s) *noun plural* (TkCa). See BAKE(S).

fried fish (fry fish) *noun phrase* (CarA). Whole small fish or fish steaks seasoned with onion, garlic, herbs, salt and pepper cooked in hot oil and usually served as a main meal or part of it.

fried plan.tain (fry plan.tain) *noun phrase* (CarA). Ripe plantains cut into portions lengthwise and fried in hot oil. □ This term is used in Caribbean cuisine to refer to plantains that are ripe, as opposed to plantains that are not, although green plantains are also fried in Guyanese cooking.

fried rice (fry rice) *noun phrase* (CarA). A dish made of cooked rice lightly sauted and mixed with seasonings, vegetables, and meat (chicken, pork, beef) or shrimp.

fruit cake *noun phrase* (Jmca). See BLACK CAKE.

fruit punch *noun phrase* (CarA). A drink made from a combination of tropical fruit juices, including PINEAPPLE, orange, GRAPEFRUIT, GUAVA, etc., served chilled.

fruit sa.lad *noun* (CarA). A dessert made from a mixture of tropical fruit, BANANAS, oranges, PAPAW, cherries, etc., cut into small pieces, put into a light syrup and served chilled.

fry-dump.lin(g) *noun* (Antg, Jmca). See BAKE(S).

F

fudge *noun* (CarA). A sweet made by boiling together milk, sugar and essence with or without cocoa powder until thick. It is beaten, poured into a greased tin or tray and cut into squares when cool.

fu-fu (foo-foo) *noun* (Baha, Belz, Guyn, Jmca, Tbgo). Boiled green plantains pounded together in a wooden mortar into a dough, which is then divided into small balls usually served with soup. (From Twi *fufuu* with the same meaning.)

fun.gee[1] (foon.gee, fun.ji) *noun* (Angu, Antg, Brbu, Jmca, Nevs, StKt, VIls). See COU-COU.

fun.gee[2] (foon.gee, fun.ji) *noun* (Antg, Tbgo). See FUFU.

gee.ra *noun* (Guyn, Trin). A small greyish grain ground as an ingredient of curry powder; cumin. (From Hindi *jiraa* 'cumin seed'.)

gin.ger-beer *noun* (CarA). A sweet, spicy, non-alcoholic drink made from boiling grated ginger and mixing it wth lime-juice and spices, served chilled.

giz.za.da *noun* (Jmca). A small, open, round tart, with a filling of grated and sweetened coconut. (From Spanish *guisado* 'prepared, cooked, stewed'.)

glass.ie (glass.y) *noun* (Bdos). See NUT-CAKE.

goat-head soup *noun phrase* (Jmca, Tbgo, Trin). **Jmca *mannish-water*.** A well seasoned, often peppery soup, in which the head of a goat is the main ingredient, widely popular and served on festive occasions.

goat-wa.ter *noun* (Antg, Mrat, Nevs, StKt). A thick, tasty soup made by boiling chunks of goat meat, including bones and parts of the entrails with spices, peppers, vegetables, sometimes with liquor added, extremely popular at weddings and parties.

gold.en-ap.ple jam *noun phrase* (CarA). A jam made of sliced GOLDEN-APPLES boiled with sugar, water and spices; the item is also referred to as golden-apple stew or stew(ed) golden-apple.

gra.ter cake *noun phrase* (Jmca). See SUGAR-CAKE[1].

great cake *noun phrase* (Bdos). See BLACK CAKE.

ground-food(s) *noun* (Belz, USVI). See GROUND-PROVISIONS.

ground-pro.vi.sions *noun plural* (CarA) **Belz, USVI *ground-foods*.** A collective name for all starchy vegetables grown locally on lands or GROUND, once set on or near sugar plantations to feed slaves, and later on, to provide labourers with daily food; these include the following: breadfruit, cassava, dasheen, sweet potatoes, yams, and so on.

gua.va-cheese *noun* (CarA). A sweet made by boiling a mixture of ripe GUAVAS and sugar until it is of a firm, cheese-like consistency, which is then cut into chunks.

gua.va ice-cream *noun phrase* (CarA). A dessert made by boiling a number of GUAVAS in water to make a juice, which is then strained, sweetened, thickened and left to cool; it is then mixed with milk and put to freeze.

gua.va-stew (stew.ed gua.va) *noun (phrase)* (CarA). The peeled skins of seeded GUAVAS, boiled with a quantity of sugar.

gui.nea-corn flour *noun* (CarA). The

flour used in a variety of foods and made from any one of a number of varieties of small-grained corn of different colours, borne on tall, sturdy stalks that resemble maize. (Called Guinea because it is mostly cultivated in Africa.)

ham-cut.ter *noun* (Bdos). **Trin *hops-and-ham.*** A small loaf of bread rolled, sliced horizontally in half with a slice of ham and some lettuce in between, usually sold as a snack.

ham.mond *noun* (Nevs, StKt). See BUSH-RUM.

hard-dough bread *noun phrase* (Jmca). A dense, white loaf, very popular with labourers and rural folk.

hard-food *noun* (Bdos, Jmca, StVn). **Jmca *food*[3]**. Cooked GROUND PROVISIONS as the substantial part of a meal.

herb-tea *noun* (CarA). See BUSH-TEA.

hops(-bread) *noun* (Trin). A small, crisp, light roll of white bread.

hot sauce *noun phrase* (CarA). See PEPPER-SAUCE.

I

ice-block *noun* (Dmca, Gren, Guyn). A cube, made of egg custard, frozen in an ice-tray and popular with schoolchildren in some Caribbean territories.

ital *noun, adjective* (CarA). Natural food as opposed to fish or animal flesh. Vegetable or fruit. (From *vital* without the 'v', a term used by the Rastafarians to mean that the food is completely wholesome because it is natural.)

jack-i.ron *noun* (Gren, Grns, StVn). See BUSH-RUM.

Ja.mai.can bun *noun phrase* (CarA). **Jmca *bun and cheese***. A rich, dark, heavy, sweet loaf, made with raisins, candied peel and spices. It is served with cheese as a snack.

Ja.mai.can pat.ty *noun phrase* (CarA). **Jmca *patty***. A semicircular pastry filled with seasoned minced meat and usually served as a snack.

jerk[1] *noun* (Jmca). The meat or fish barbecued with a typical Jamaican combination of salt, pepper and PIMENTO.

jerk[2] *transitive verb* (Jmca). To barbecue meat or fish with a typical Jamaican combination of seasonings.

jerk-chick.en *noun* (Jmca). Pieces of chicken, seasoned with a typically Jamaican mix of herbs, barbecued on an outdoor fire, chopped into pieces when done and served with JERK SAUCE.

jerk-pork *noun* (Jmca). Pieces of pork shoulder seasoned with the same mixture of spices as JERK-CHICKEN.

jerk sauce *noun phrase* (Jmca). The spicy sauce in which the chicken or pork is soaked before cooking.

john.ny-bake *noun* (Trin). See BAKE(s).

john.ny-cake(s) *noun* (Baha, Jmca, StKt). See BAKE(s).

jub-jub *noun* (Gren, Guyn, Trin). A soft, sticky, coloured sweet that can be chewed or sucked.

jug (jug-jug) *noun* (Bdos). A heavy, well-seasoned dish made from minced beef, pork, boiled PIGEON-PEAS, herbs, butter and GUINEA-CORN FLOUR mixed into a paste, and usually served at Christmas.

K

kaan.ki *noun* (Guyn). See CONKIE.

ka.chow.ri *noun* (Guyn, Trin). A small, fried, East Indian patty, made from ground split peas, flour, ghee and seasoning.

ka(l).la.loo (ca.la.lu) *noun* (Dmca, StVn, Tbgo, Trin). See CALALU.

kill-dev.il *noun* (CarA). Pure alchol; rum.

kou.vè.ti-pòt-chanm (co.ver.ty po-chanm) *noun* (Dmca, Trin). A crisp, thin, sweet ginger-flavoured biscuit, baked light-brown and popular with older people at Easter. (French Creole from French *couvert de pot-de-chambre* because of its shape like that of a chamber-pot cover, an item used in the past.)

lam.bie (lan.bi) *noun* (Dmca, Gren, StLu). The seasoned and cooked meat of the CONCH which is considered a delicacy.

lead-pipe *noun* (Bdos). A small, oblong sweet and heavy bread very popular with schoolchildren and workmen.

len.til soup *noun phrase* (CarA). A seasoned soup of boiled lentils.

ma.ca.ro.ni pie *noun phrase* (Bdos). **CarA *macaroni cheese*.** A thick pie, the main ingredients of which are macaroni and grated cheese.

man.go chut.ney *noun phrase* (CarA). A sauce made of dried or crushed green MANGOES, pepper, garlic, salt and other spices, eaten with vegetables, meat and snacks.

mau.by (mau.bie) *noun* (CarA). A slightly bitter-tasting drink made by boiling MAUBY-BARK and other spices in water, sweetening the mixture and leaving it to ferment. (From Carib *mabi* 'potato whose root is good to eat'.)

meat balls *noun phrase* (CarA). See BEEF BALL.

me.ta.gee (me.tem, me.tem.gee) *noun* (Guyn). See SANCOCHE.

mi.thai (me.thai) *noun* (Guyn, Trin). A finger-shaped East Indian snack made with flour and water, coated with sugar and fried. (Bhojpuri from Hindi *miṭhaaii* 'sweetness, sweetmeat'.)

Mithai

moun.tain-dew *noun* (Trin). See BUSH-RUM.

mus.co.va.do (su.gar) *noun (phrase)* (CarA). **CarA *black sugar*.** A damp, dark sugar, usually caked together, that is produced just after the crystallization of molasses, and sold to sweeten coffee. (From Portuguese *mascavado* 'unrefined, impure'.)

N

no.ni juice *noun phrase* (CarA). The juice made from the fruit of the PAIN-KILLER BUSH, and used folk medicinally to treat a number of complaints.

Noni juice

nut-cake *noun* (Bdos, Guyn, Trin). **Bdos *glassie*; Jmca *pindar-cake*.** A square, flat, brittle sweet made of thickly candied peanuts.

O

oil-down *noun* (Gren, Tbgo, Trin). See COCONUT BOIL-IN.

o.vers *noun plural* (Dmca, Gren, Trin). Left-over items of food.

ox.tail stew *noun phrase* (CarA). A stew in which seasoned pieces of oxtail are the major ingredient.

P

pa.lo(w).rie (balls) *noun (phrase)* (Guyn). See PHULOURIE.

pa.na.des (pe.na.da) *noun (usually) plural* (Belz). See EMPANADAS.

pa.ra.t(h)a-ro.ti *noun* (Guyn, Trin). Trin ***bus-up-shot***. A light, flaky, pastry-like ROTI, valued for its fine texture. (Hindi *paratha* 'a pancake-like roti fried in ghee'.)

pas.telle *noun* (Tbgo, Trin). A small pudding made of minced and seasoned beef and pork, together with raisins and olives, enclosed in a layer of cornmeal batter, wrapped in a banana leaf and boiled. (From Spanish *pastel* 'cake, pie'. The spelling *-elle* is probably influenced by French in Trinidad, where the item was most popular.)

pat.ty *noun* (Jmca). **1.** See JAMAICAN PATTY. **2.** (Guyn) A small, round, pastry filled with beef or chicken and with a crimped edge, often used as a cocktail appetizer.

peas and rice; rice and peas *noun phrases* (CarA). A dish of rice boiled with a large quantity of PIGEON-PEAS; it is a regular main dish of Caribbean meals. □ In Jamaica, this dish is generally made with red kidney beans.

pe.lau (peleau, pi.lao, pi.lau) *noun* (CarA). A one-pot dish made of rice boiled with pieces of different meats to which PIGEON-PEAS and other vegetables are added; it is sometimes cooked with COCONUT-MILK. (An Indic word, Urdu *pilao*.)

pep.per.pot[1] *noun* (Bdos, Gren, Guyn). A dark-brown stew in which are boiled together pieces of meat (usually beef, pork, cow-heel or oxtail) with CASAREEP, red pepper and other herbs, sugar and spices for several hours; it can be kept on the stove and boiled every day, or in the refrigerator.

pep.per.pot[2] (pep.per.pot soup) *noun phrase* (Angu, Antg, Jmca). See CALALU[2].

pep.per-sauce *noun* (CarA). **CarA *hot sauce*.** A hot condiment made from the pulp, juice and seeds of ground red or yellow peppers, mixed with chopped onions, vinegar and mustard.

phu.lou.ri(e) (pa.lo(w).rie (balls) *noun (phrase)* (Guyn, Trin). Small round balls made from a well seasoned mixture of ground split-peas and flour, fried in deep fat. (From Hindi *phulauri* 'gram flour'.)

pic.kled bread.fruit *noun phrase* (Bdos). A side dish made by cutting boiled BREADFRUIT into chunks, which are placed in a pickle made of lime juice, salt, cucumbers and red or sweet pepper.

P

pin.da (pin.dar, pin.der) *noun* (Belz, Jmca, USVI). Peanuts.

pin.dar-cake *noun* (Jmca). See See NUT-CAKE.

pine-drink *noun* (CarA). A refreshing drink made from soaking the peelings of a ripe PINEAPPLE in hot water with cloves and orange peel and leaving the contents to soak for two or three days, after which it is strained and sweetened.

pine-tart *noun* (CarA). A pastry filled with stewed PINEAPPLE.

plan.tain-flour *noun* (Guyn). Meal obtained by pounding slices of green PLANTAINS, dried in the sun to make a nutritious porridge, especially for infants. See CONGATAY.

plan.tain-por.ridge *noun* (Jmca). See CONGATAY.

ponche de crème (pon.cha cream, punch au crème, punch de crème) *noun phrase* (ECar). **CarA *egg nog*.** A thick, creamy, alcoholic drink made of eggs, rum and spices beaten up together in milk, and used traditionally as a Christmas drink in some places. (From French ponche 'punch' + crème 'cream, 'milk punch'.)

pone *noun* (Bdos, Guyn Trin). See CASSAVA-PONE.

press *noun* (Gren, Trin). See SNOW-CONE.

pud.ding *noun* (Bdos) **1.** Any kind of cake, apart from GREAT-CAKE. **2.** See BLACK-PUDDING.

pu.ri *noun* (Guyn, Trin). See DAAL PURI.

quinch *noun* (Guyn). See CASSAVA-CAKE.

re.lle.no *noun* (Belz). A rich, festive, Belizean dish, consisting of a chicken stuffed with highly seasoned, fried, minced pork, boiled eggs, mixed fruit and peppers; the whole item is then boiled in a broth coloured with a herb seasoning known as 'black ricardo'.

rice and peas *noun phrase* (CarA). See PEAS AND RICE.

rice-pud.ding *noun* (Antg, Brbu, StKt). See BLACK-PUDDING.

ro.ti *noun* (CarA). A type of bread made of flour, water and salt mixed together into a soft dough, which is cut into smaller pieces and rolled into flat discs, each baked separately on a greased baking-iron; it is usually served with CURRY. (From Hindi *roti* 'bread'.)

rum cake *noun phrase* (CayI, USVI). See TORTUGA RUM CAKE.

S

salt-bake(s) *noun (plural)* (StLu). See BAKE(S).

salt-bread *noun* (Bdos, Guyn). A fairly large white roll of bread.

salt-fish(salt.fish) *noun* (CarA). **Trin *bacalao*.** Dried, salted cod, imported from Canada and used as an ingredient in many dishes.

salt-fish cakes/frit.ters *noun phrase* (CarA). See ACCRA.

salt food *noun phrase* (Gren, Guyn). **Jmca, USVI *salting*.** A cooked meal of meat or fish with vegetables.

salt-meat *noun* (CarA). Pieces of salt-beef or salt-pork used to flavour food in Caribbean cooking.

salt-pork *noun* (CarA). Pieces of pickled pork on the bone, used to flavour food in cooking.

san.coche *noun* (Dmca, Gren, Jmca, Trin). **Belz *boil-up*; Guyn *metagee*.** A solid meal consisting of several boiled root vegetables, breadfruit, green bananas or plantains, together with cornflour dumplings, SALT-FISH and pigtail in COCONUT-MILK, until the milk boils down to a thick, grey sauce. (From South American Spanish *sancocho* 'stew made of meat, yucca, etc.'.)

sca.veech.ed fish *noun phrase* (Jmca). See ESCAVEITCHED FISH.

sea.son.ed rice *noun phrase* (Antg, Jmca). See COOK-UP (RICE).

shave-ice *noun* (Guyn, Jmca, StVn, Trin). See SNOW-CONE.

sky-juice *noun* (Jmca). See SNOW-CONE.

smoke-her.ring *noun* (CarA). Smoke-dried herring which is widely imported into the Caribbean, and much used in cooking.

snow-ball *noun* (Bdos, Gren, Jmca, Trin). See SNOW-CONE.

sno(w)-cone *noun* (CarA). **Bdos, Gren, Jmca, Trin *snow-ball*; Belz *fresco*; Gren, Trin *press*; Guyn, Jmca, StVn, Trin *shave-ice*; Guyn, Trin *compress*, *crush-ice*.** Crushed ice packed tightly into a paper cone or plastic cup on which different flavours of syrup are poured, sold in the street.

so.da-bake(s) *noun* (Guyn). See BAKE(S).

sor.rel(-drink) *noun* (CarA). A cooling drink made of the fruit of the SORREL, cut up and put to set in boiling water and cloves for about 24 hours.

So.lo.mon Gun.dy *noun phrase* (Jmca). A salty, brown seasoned paste, made of shredded SMOKE-HERRING, often used on crackers as a snack.

Solomon gundy on crackers

sour.sop-drink *noun* (CarA). **Gren *babalé*, *babalait*.** A drink made of the mashed pulp of a SOURSOP, added to the amount of water required.

sour.sop ice-cream *noun phrase* (CarA). A dessert made of the mashed pulp of a SOURSOP mixed with milk, sugar and cornstarch, then frozen.

souse *noun* (CarA). A cold dish made of boiled pig's trotters, face and ears, served in a pickle consisting of lime juice and vinegar, slices of onions and cucumber.

spice-bun *noun* (Jmca). See JAMAICAN BUN.

spi.nach-soup *noun* (CarA). A soup made by boiling together finely chopped SPINACH with English potatoes, onion, salt, pepper, water or stock, butter, flour and milk.

spin.ners *noun* (Jmca). Tiny flour dumplings usually found in soup.

stamp-and-go *noun* (Jmca). A small SALTFISH fritter.

stew-dump.ling *noun* (Bdos, StVn). See DUKUNA.

su.gar-cake[1] *noun* (CarA). **Jmca *grater-cake***. A sweet made from boiling a quantity of grated COCONUT with a large amount of brown sugar and water and then dropping it on a flat surface to cool.

T

sugar-cake[2] *noun* (CarA). **Baha *coconut-cake*[2]; Dmca, StLu *tablèt*; Gren, Trin *chip-chip sugar-cake*; Jmca *coconut-drops***. A sweet made of chipped pieces of dried COCONUT boiled in heavy syrup and dropped in spoonfuls on a flat surface to cool.

su.gar-wa.ter *noun* (CarA). A sweet drink of sugar and water, used widely in the Caribbean, originally as a morning drink and still so used by poorer rural dwellers.

swank *noun* (Bdos, Guyn, StKt, StVn). **Antg, CayI, Jmca, StKt *beverage*; Baha, TkCa *switcher*; Jmca *wash***. A sweet drink made with lime juice, water and plenty of brown sugar; lemonade.

sweet bakes *noun phrase* (StLu). See BAKE(S).

sweet.bread *noun* (CarA). **Bdos *coconut-bread***. A sweet loaf made of a mixture of flour, sugar, margarine or butter, spices, essence, eggs and usually grated coconut.

sweet drink *noun phrase* (CarA). See COOL DRINK.

sweet-po.ta.to pie *noun phrase* (CarA). **Jmca *sweet-potato pudding***. A pie made of grated SWEET POTATO mixed with sugar and spices.

sweet-po.ta.to pone *noun phrase* (Jmca, Tbgo). **Jmca *sweet-potato pudding***. A heavy pudding made of grated SWEET POTATO mixed with sugar, butter, and spices with a little rum or sherry added.

sweet-po.ta.to pud.ding *noun phrase* (Jmca). See SWEET-POTATO PIE.

switch.er *noun* (Baha, TkCa,). See SWANK.

swiz.zle *noun* (CarA). A Caribbean drink made by adding rum or another alcoholic substance to a sweet milky mixture flavoured with grated nutmeg, and stirred vigorously with a SWIZZLE-STICK until it foams.

T

tab.lèt (ta.blette) *noun* (Dmca, StLu). See SUGAR-CAKE. (French Creole from French *tablette* 'cake, slab (of chocolate)'.)

ta.ma.les *noun plural* (Belz). **Belz *bollos***. A dish made from Indian corn, chicken, or other meat, seasoned with herbs and peppers, wrapped in plantain leaves and then boiled. (From Nahuatl *tamalli* 'dough made of maize flour and mixed with meat and chilli pepper wrapped in corn leaves'.)

ta.ma.rind balls *noun phrase plural* (CarA). Small sweets made from the stewed pulp of the TAMARIND and still with the seeds in, shaped into rounds and rolled in sugar.

ta.ma.rind drink *noun phrase* (CarA). **Angu** ***tamon bug*****; StKt** ***tamarind punch, tamarind sizzle*****; StLu** ***tamarind juice*****.** A drink made from the pulp of the TAMARIND.

Tamarind drink

ta.ma.rind jam *noun phrase* (CarA). A jam made by boiling the pulp of the TAMARIND.

ta.ma.rind juice *noun phrase* (StLu). See TAMARIND DRINK.

ta.ma.rind punch *noun phrase* (StKt). See TAMARIND DRINK.

ta.ma.rind siz.zle *noun phrase* (StKt). See TAMARIND DRINK.

ta.mon bug (Angu). See TAMARIND DRINK.

ti.ti.ri-cake (tri-tri cake) *noun phrase* (Gren). A fritter made of seasoned TITIRI batter which is then fried. (*Titiri* Carib meaning 'little fish'.)

to.ma.to sa.lad *noun phrase* (CarA). A salad made with diced or sliced tomatoes.

Tor.tu.ga rum cake *noun phrase* (CayI). **CayI, USVI** ***rum cake*****.** A cake made with the usual ingredients, to which are added walnuts and Tortuga gold rum, thereby giving it a special flavour and soft texture.

to.ta (to.to) *noun* (Jmca). A sweet snack made of a batter of grated coconut that is cut into squares when cooled. (From Spanish *torta* 'cake, tart'.)

tri-tri cake *noun* (Gren). See TITIRI-CAKE.

wa.rap *noun* (Trin). Fermented sugar-cane juice used as a cheap liquor in the past. (From Spanish American Spanish *guarapo* 'sugar-cane liquor'.)

wash *noun* (Jmca). See SWANK.

wet su.gar *noun phrase* (CarA). Raw, dark sugar in the first stage of crystallization, and used to made sweets or other items.

white pud.ding *noun phrase* (Bdos). A sausage type dish made of the same mixture of SWEET POTATO and herbs used for BLACK PUDDING, but without blood being added.

white rum *noun phrase* (Bdos). Clear, colourless, blended, uncured rum which is quite strong, usually utilized for mixing punches and quite widely exported.

white su.gar *noun phrase* (CarA). Sugar refined in Britain from which all the molasses has been extracted, hence the colour.

yam frit.ters *noun phrase* (CarA). A fritter made of boiled mashed YAMS fried by the teaspoonful in hot oil.

MUSIC, MUSICAL INSTRUMENTS, AND DANCE

A

a.beng (horn) *noun (phrase)* (Jmca). A bull's horn, historically used as a signal by the Maroons or as a musical instrument. (From Twi *abɛŋ* 'horn of animals; flute, whistle, musical instrument, wind-instrument.)

Abeng horn

al.to pans *noun phrase* (Trin). See DOUBLE-SECONDS.

a.ro.po *noun* (Trin). A dance of Spanish origin performed in parts of Trinidad.

Auouh.sah (Awou.sah) *noun phrase* (Crcu). A NATION-DANCE of Carricou.

B

bam.boo-band *noun* (Trin). A TAMBOO-BAMBOO band.

bam.bou.la *noun phrase* (Tbgo, Trin, USVI). A lively, African street-dance done to singing and drumming; the singing is often led by a BAMBOULA QUEEN (in the USVI), and usually deals with social scandal; the drum is large, often mounted on a cart and played by two men.

band *noun* (Trin). **1**. A group of STICK-FIGHTERS who fight with rival groups in neighbourhood contests, especially during festive seasons. **2.** (ECar). [At CARNIVAL time, (*Tbgo, Trin*) or during KADOOMENT (*Bdos*)] A group of hundreds of masqueraders in bright decorative costumes illustrating a particular theme, that jump up through the streets to the music of a STEELBAND or CALYPSO MUSIC, finally parading on stage to be judged against other groups for the prize of BAND OF THE YEAR.

ban.ja *noun* (Bdos). A song or music for dancing that apparently used to be accompanied by a banjo.

bash.ment soca *noun phrase* (CarA). A type of SOCA music indigenous to Barbados, but its roots lie in older Jamaican reggae and dancehall rhythms which are recreated in a fast tempo and sung in Barbadian dialect.

base-gui.tar.ist *noun* (CarA). See BASSMAN.

bass.man *noun* (CarA). **1.** (CarA) **CarA *bass-guitarist*.** The player of the base electric guitar in a combo. **2.** (ECar) The player of the BASS-PAN in a STEELBAND.

bass-pan *noun* (ECar). **ECar *boom-pan*.** One of four to six whole steel drums with one end cut out, and the other beaten and grooved into large sections to produce three or four bass notes, in order for the set of pans to provide the entire range of bass notes that their player, the BASS-MAN needs.

bel.air (bel.aire, bel.lair, bel.laire) *noun* (Dmca, Gren, StLu, Tbgo, Trin). See BÈLÈ.

bè.lè (bel-air, bel.aire, bel.lair, bel.laire) *noun* (Dmca, Gren, StLu, Tbgo, Trin) **1.** (Traditionally) a vigorous, outdoor group dance performed by women, signalling to the male drummers by their body movements the change of beat they want. **2.** (Dmca, Gren, StLu) A carnival folk dance led by a female solo singer or CHANTRELLE who dances backwards and gives the time to the drummer. (French Creole from French *bel air*, but probably West African in origin.)

big-drum *noun* (Crcu). One of the group of three drums, made from a small barrel over which goat-skin is stretched, tightened and tuned at one end, so that the centre or 'mother' drum produces a higher note than the others; the drums, whose loud rhythmic beat can be heard a great distance away, are used for ceremonial occasions.

big-drum dance *noun phrase* (Crcu). **Crcu *nation-dance*.** A set of dances organized to celebrate a festive occasion or for a spiritual purpose, beginning with the particular NATION-DANCE of the celebrant and followed by others; the dance is performed by two couples who set the pattern, rhythm, and length of each dance, within a circle of people termed the BIG-DRUM dance-ring.

bon.go *noun phrase* (Dmca, Tbgo, Trin). **Tbgo, Trin *bongo-dance/-dancing*.** A dance performed at wakes by different pairs of men to honour the dead, to drumming and singing by persons in a ring.

B

boom-pan *noun* (ECar). See BASS-PAN.

bram[1] **1.** *noun* (CarA). **Jmca *breakdown*** **2.** ***bruckins*; Belz *brukdown*; ECar *wash-foot-and-come*.** **1.** A noisy, usually disorderly party open to anyone. **2. Belz** A type of folk music with communal singing, especially related to BRAM[2].

bram[2] *intransitive verb* (Belz). To tramp, dance noisily in the streets as members of a CARNIVAL or MASQUERANDE-BAND.

break.down *noun* (Jmca). **Belz *brukdown*.** **1.** A vigorous, hip-swinging dance with much bending of the body, and WINING. **2.** A noisy, informal FETE with plenty of food, drink and loud music.

bruck.ins *noun* (Jmca). See BRAM[1].

bruk.down *noun* (Belz). See BRAM[1].

ca.dence (ka.dans) *noun* (Dmca). **1**. A popular Dominican type of dance music which is a blend of the Guadeloupean French MERENGUE with the beat of the CALYPSO and sometimes that of Jamaican REGGAE. **2**. The dance corresponding to this music, which involves much hip and body movement, but allows for individual variation in the movement. (From French *cadence* 'rhythm'.)

ca.dence-lyp.so *noun* (Dmca). Cadence Lypso is a popular genre from the 1970s in the Caribbean islands (particularly Dominica, Guadeloupe and Martinique). The genre is a unique Caribbean creation that combines elements from Haitian's cadence rampa and compas with Trinidad's calypso. See https://rateyourmusic.com/genre/Cadence+Lypso/.

ca.dence ram.pa *noun phrase* (Hait). A Haitian genre of dance music that emerged in Haiti in the 1960s, but is strongly influenced by Cuban rhythms; it spread throughout the French islands of Guadeloupe, Martinique and Dominica, and is the precursor to ZOUK.

ca.len.da (ca.lin.da) *noun* (ECar). See KALINDA.

ca.lyp.so *noun* (CarA). **ECar** ***kaiso***. **1.** A popular, often satirical song, usually in rhyming verses, that is traditionally associated with Trinidad, and that comments on any recognized figure or aspect of social life. **2.** The type of tune or music with a beat that is typical of this composition, and the spontaneous BREAKAWAY dancing related to this type of music.

Ca.lyp.so King/Queen *noun phrase* (ECar). The winner of the CALYPSO contest in a national CARNIVAL.

ca.lyp.so.ni.an *noun* (ECar). **ECar** ***kaisoman***. A professional and competitive CALYPSO singer.

ca.lyp.so tent *noun phrase* (ECar). The building (in earlier years an actual tent, from which it gets the name) associated with a particular team of CALYPSONIANS who stage CALYPSO shows throughout the CARNIVAL (CROPOVER in Barbados) season.

cel.lo-pans *noun* (Trin). A joined set of three pans for one player, made from oil drums and cut to two-thirds or three-quarters their length, with a sunken surface a little less than that of the bass pans, but made in segments that will yield five or six notes each. They are usually found in the middle of a STEELBAND.

chant.wèl (chant.relle) *noun* (Crcu, Dmca, StLu, Trin). **1.** The female lead singer and dancer in BELAIR (BÈLÈ) dancing. **2.** The name formerly given to a male calypsonian. (French Creole from French *chanterelle* 'the treble in singing' hence a female singer.)

chig.(g)oe-foot dance *noun phrase* (Bdos). A dance done by Blacks and performed on the heels rather than the toes which were often infected with CHIGOES.

chow.tal *noun* (Guyn). A special type of song sung by a group during the PHAGWA festival.

chut.ney so.ca *noun phrase* (CarA). A fusion of popular East Indian music and musical instruments with the catchy rhythm of SOCA to form a new Caribbean musical form.

com.fa-dance (cum.fa-dance) *noun* (Guyn). A vigorous dance performed by one or two women to the beating of big drums, intended to produce spirit possession.

cua.tro *noun* (Gren, StLu, StVn, Trin). A small folk-guitar with four strings, which produces high-pitched notes; it is an instrument that is crucial to the accompaniment of PARANG songs or other types of folk-music. (Spanish *cuatro* 'four' because of the strings, and the Latin American origin of the instrument.)

Cuatro

cua.trist *noun* (ECar). A skilled or professional CUATRO player. (CUATR(O) + ist as in pianist, pannist, etc.)

D

dancehall *noun phrase* (Jmca). A type of REGGAE music which is strongly influenced by pop-music themes, but maintains the REGGAE beat and is usually played in dancehalls, thus giving the music its name.

dou.ble-se.conds *noun* (Trin). **Trin *alto pans*.** The second line of pans representing the lower treble notes of a piano in the arrangement of a STEELBAND; there are four pairs of pans, each of which has one player, the surface of each divided into 10 segments representing the lower treble notes of a piano.

dub; dub-music *noun* (CarA). **1.** A rhythm with two beats provided mainly by bass and drums without an actual tune, originally derived from REGGAE, and usually recorded on the flip side of a record. **2. (i)** (CarA) A type of dancing in which partners keep their bodies extremely close to each other. **(ii)** A public dance at which only DUB-MUSIC is played.

F

fête[1] *noun* (ECar). A party or celebration with music and dancing. (From French *fête* 'festival, festival-holiday').

fête[2] *intransitive verb* (ECar). To dance, eat, drink and have a good time.

G

gui.tar pan(s) *noun phrase (plural)* (Trin). A pair of STEEL PANS joined together for one player, made out of half length oil drums and sectioned into about seven or eight notes each, which are the third in line in the arrangement of pans in a STEELBAND.

H

heel-and-toe (dance/pol.ka) *noun phrase* (CarA). A dance popularly performed in earlier times in which two partners would step together, first on their heels then on their toes.

I

i.wer *noun* (Trin). A type of dance in which the legs are lifted high on the same spot, similar to SOCA, and named after the Trinidadian calypsonian Iwer George.

J

jump-up *noun* (ECar). Open-air dancing by a crowd, usually to to CALYPSO music.

K

ka.dans *noun* (Dmca). See CADENCE.

ka.lin.da (ca.len.da. ca.lin.da, ka.len. da) *noun* (ECar). **1.** (Dmca, Gren). A strongly suggestive group dance, surviving from slavery. **2.** (Trin) A stick-fight dance which involves drumming to a special rhythm and call-and-response singing accompanying the stick-fight. **3.** (Dmca, Trin) [Also KALINDA MUSIC, KALINDA SONG] The call-and-response narrative song and music accompanying the stick-fight.

ket.tle(-drum) (kit.tle(-drum)) *noun* **1.** ***rattle-drum, title-drum*** (Jmca) (ECar). A small, double-headed drum about 15 in. in diameter, which produces a rattling, metallic sound; it is slung at the player's side, played with two sticks and is one of the main instruments in Caribbean masquerade and street bands.

L

last-lap (jump-up) *noun (phrase)* **1.** (Trin) The vigorous dancing and reveling in the streets before midnight on the Tuesday before Lent which ends the carnival celebrations. **2.** (CarA) Any final dancing in the last hour or so of any public festivities or private dance.

lead-pan *noun* (Trin). **Trin *ping-pong, tenor-pan*.** One of the set of six leading PANS in a STEELBAND, each cut about 6 in. deep from an oil-drum; its surface is sunk deepest of all the PANS and made to provide up to 32 notes of the highest pitch; it provides the melody of the music being played.

lim.bo (CarA). A solo dance in which the dancer displays the supple condition of their body from the neck to the ankles, by bending backwards to pass under a stick set horizontally very low to the ground. (Probably from the Caribbean English adjective *limber* with a change of grammatical function to a verb.)

mash-po.ta.to *noun phrase* (CarA). A dance in which both feet are moved outwards and sideways, looking as though the dancer is crushing or mashing potatoes.

mas.que.rade-band *noun* (CarA). **Guyn *santapee-band;* Bdos *tuk-band*.** A folk band consisting usually of one bass-drum, one KETTLE, a flute, fife, iron-triangle and rattle, which goes through the streets in festive seasons, playing music with a rhythm dominated by a drum beat, and accompanied by one or more masquerade dancers.

men.to *noun* (Jmca) A type of rural Jamaican folk-music with a dominant rhythm which encourages dancers to swing their hips, and is usually accompanied by a song with a couple of spicy verses, related to some popular event. The music is now usually only played in organized competitions. (Originally from Cuban Spanish.)

me.ren.gue (ma.ren.ga, ma.rin.ga) *noun* (CarA). A lively dance extremely popular throughout the Caribbean and Latin America. (Puerto Rican name for this dance.)

N

na.tion-dance *noun* (Crcu). See BIG-DRUM DANCE.

Ny.a.bin.gi sing.ing/drum.ming *noun phrase* (Jmca). The festive celebration of NYABINGI religious rites carried out with drumming and singing which generally lasts throughout the night.

P

pan *noun* (CarA). **1. CarA *steel-pan*.** A musical instrument made from the bottom end of a steel oil-drum hammered into sections tuned to produce different notes; the end is cut off at varying lengths to create different pitches, from soprano to bass-pan; the full range of groups of pans that together make up a STEELBAND. **2.** The music of the STEELBAND. **3.** The STEELBAND movement as a whole.

Steel-pans

pan.man.ship *noun* (Tbgo, Trin) Skill in playing a PAN.

pan-mu.sic *noun* (CarA) STEELBAND music.

pan.nist *noun* (Trin). A highly accomplished STEEL-PAN player who gives professional solo performances.

pan.o.lo.gy *noun* (Tbgo, Trin). The study and art of STEELBAND music and playing.

pan-tu.ner *noun* (Tbgo, Trin) A man who is skilled in creating the note sections and obtaining the right pitch of a STEELBAND PAN by beating and hammering the drum used.

pa.rang *noun* (Tbgo, Trin). **1.** House-to-house serenading by groups singing carols (AGUINALDOS) in Spanish, originally brought from Venezuela, especially at Christmas and also at Easter in rural areas; the music is accompanied by CUATROS, mandolins and other instruments, and also involves Spanish folk dancing. **2.** Competitions organized nationally to recognize the festival of PARANG, and which involve the crowning of a queen. **3.** Hispanic folk music for dancing associated with a PARANG. (From Spanish *parranda* 'a spree, a binge'.)

par.ty-song *noun* (Trin). A song that is sung during CARNIVAL, but is composed primarily for entertainment, rather than to address any social, national or political issue.

passa-passa *noun* (Jmca). Suggestive, rowdy, open-air dancing, especially at night parties.

pi.cong *noun* (ECar). A spontaneous verbal battle usually in rhyme, between two or more competing CALYSONIANS, which is generally very witty and indicates who is a superior performer. (From Caribbean Spanish *picón* 'mocking' from Spanish verb *picar* 'to pick, prick, peck at'.)

P

ping-pong *noun* (Trin). See LEAD-PAN.

pun.ta *noun* (Belz). A vigorous group dance accompanied by drumming and singing, performed by the GARIFUNA people of Belize.

qua.drille *noun* (CarA). An old-fashioned, now rural dance, for groups of couples and consisting of five figures, the rhythm of each getting faster and faster until the finale. (A French word meaning a square dance.)

queh-queh *noun* (Guyn). Lively singing and dancing by women to drumming performed for a few days before a wedding and reaching a climax on the night before the wedding.

quel.be *noun* (StVn, Tbgo). Songs, drum-rhythms and dances performed by females and believed to have originated in the Congo.

rag.ga rag.ga *noun phrase* (Bdos). A type of dance music originating in the 1990s from a popular calypso of the same name, sung by the Barbadian calypsonian Red Plastic Bag.

rag.ga so.ca *noun phrase* (Bdos). Dance music combining RAGGA RAGGA and SOCA.

rap.so *noun* (CarA). A genre of dance music fusing 'rapping' with SOCA.

reg.gae *noun* (CarA). **1.** A type of dance-music with a steady heartbeat rhythm, usually played on an electric bass-guitar and a drum, accompanied by singing that reflects Jamaican folk-life and is associated with RASTAFARIAN culture. **2.** The dance to this music, usually performed individually and characterized by shoulder and body movements and bent knees. (Compare Yoruba *ręgę-ręgę* 'rough, roughly', Jamaica *rege-rege* 'ragged clothes' and Tobago adjective *rege-rege* 'rough, uncultured'.)

reg.gae.ton *noun* (CarA). A type of Spanish-language dance music which became popular in Puerto Rico in the 1990s and fuses Latin rhythms, dancehall, and hip-hop or rap.

rhum.ba *noun* (CarA). A rhythmic dance, combining African and Spanish elements, originating in Cuba as far back as the middle of the 19th century.

road-march *noun* (ECar). The street-parade of a fully costumed CARNIVAL band, accompanied formerly by a STEELBAND, now more commonly by a truck full of several DJs and all the necessary electronic musical equipment, and usually followed by a large crowd who tramp to the music.

rock stead.y *noun phrase* (CarA). Dance music with a steady and slow rhythm with an offbeat, developed in Jamaica between the SKA and REGGAE and combining elements of both.

S

sam.ba *noun* (CarA). **1.** A popular and catchy type of music, with African roots originating in Brazil in the early 1900s which has come to be known as the national music of Brazil, from where it spread to the rest of the world and also became immensely popular in the Caribbean, especially in the 1940s through the 1960s.

shan.to *noun* (Guyn). A ballad-type song which tells a story, peculiar to Guyana. (From Standard English *shanty,* referring to the river boatmen's and pork-knockers' work songs.)

ska *noun* (CarA). **1.** Jamaican dance music with a quick, lively drum beat and folk lyrics, originating among poor Jamaican folk and widely popular in the 1960s; the forerunner of ROCK STEADY and REGGAE. **2.** The actual dance to this music. (Probably from Black American *scat* in the 1920s made popular by Louis Armstrong who, when he forgot the words of a song would make up syllables sounding like musical instruments. This music was first brought to Jamaica by a band called the Skatalites, so SKA may have originated from that name.)

Ska

skank (scank) *noun* (Jmca). An individual dance with a partner, to DUB or REGGAE music.

so.ca *noun* (ECar). Music accompanied by song and combining Black soul music with Trinidadian calypso, starting with the 1978 CARNIVAL. (A combination of Black American soul + CALYPSO.)

so.pra.no pan *noun phrase* (Trin). An earlier name for the LEAD PAN in a STEELBAND.

spouge *noun* (CarA). **1.** A typically Barbadian dance rhythm with lyrics and a quick beat combining something of REGGAE and CALYPSO, and created by the late singer Jackie Opel in the late 1970s. **2.** The actual dance to this music, usually with a partner.

steel.band *noun* (CarA). A percussion band made up of a set of STEEL-PANS tuned to cover an entire range of musical notes, keys and pitches. The PANS are of different depths and are mounted on stands and played with rubber-tipped sticks. The bands originally developed through the Trinidad CARNIVAL are played throughout the Caribbean to provide festive open-air music.

steel-pan *noun phrase* (CarA). See PAN.

T

tas.sa *noun* (Guyn, Trin). **Guyn, Trin *tassa drum***. A type of drum beaten at Hindu ceremonies and festivals, especially weddings.

tas.sa drum.ming *noun phrase* (Guyn, Trin). The art of beating the tassa drum.

ten.or-bass *noun* (ECar). A set of four linked PANS in a STEELBAND sunk to a less shallow depth than the BASS-PANS and grooved to provide a range of notes above the bass, but lower than the CELLO-PANS.

ten.or-pan *noun* (Trin). See LEAD-PAN.

took *noun* (Bdos). See TUK-BAND.

tuk-band (took(-band), tuck-band) *noun* (Bdos). See MASQUERADE BAND.

RELIGION

A

Ar.ya.sa.ma.jist (Ar.ya.sa.ma.ji(st)) *noun* (Guyn, Trin). A follower of the Arya Samaj, a Hindu religious order, founded in India late in the 19th century and brought to Guyana and Trinidad in 1910.

B

Bap.tist *noun* (Bdos, Jmca, Trin). See SPIRITUAL BAPTIST.

Bha.ga.vat (Bha.ga.wad, Bhag.wat Jag) *noun* (Guyn, Trin). A set of Hindu prayer-meetings continuing over seven nights, based on ceremonial readings from the Bhagwat Gita, one of the Hindu gospels, and organized as a sacrificial offering.

bha.jan *noun* (Guyn, Trin). Hindu religious singing, or the ceremonial song itself.

C

Com.fa *noun* (Guyn). A folk religion practised in Guyana which combines Christianity, Hinduism, and Islam with African elements and which reflects the cultures of the different ethnic groups in Guyana.

Eid *noun* (Guyn, Trin). A Muslim religious festival.

Eid-ul-Azah *noun* (Guyn, Trin). The Muslim religious festival held in the twelfth month of the Muslim calendar, celebrating Abraham's obedience to God when he was told to sacrifice his son, Ishmael (Isaac). The festival is marked by the ceremonial sacrifice of a sheep, cow or goat, to provide food for the family and for the poor.

Eid-ul-Fitr *noun* (Bdos, Guyn, Trin). The Muslim religious festival celebrated at the end of Ramadan, the month of fasting and the ninth month of the Muslim calendar; it is marked by feasting and charitable acts.

Ho.li *noun* (Guyn, Trin). **Guyn, Trin** ***Phagwa***. The main Hindu religious festival celebrated every year in March or April and illustrating the triumph of good over evil.

Ho.sein; Ho.say *noun* (Trin). A Muslim religious festival held every year to commemorate the martyrdom of Hassan and Hosein, grandsons of the prophet Muhammad; it is celebrated in late February or early March and during the festival there are processions as well as drumming and dancing.

Hosein

K

Ku.mi.na (Jmca). A folk religious festival of singing, drumming and dancing, held to pay respect to the spirits of the ancestors at births, deaths and other occasions that form part of family life. (Probably from Cambinda, a Kongo nation.)

Kumina

M

my.al (ma.yal) *noun* (Jmca). A folk religion which invokes spirits of the dead to solve problems or drive away evil; it makes use of herbal medicines of baths, drumming and dancing, and other ceremonial rites. (From Hausa *maye* (masculine), *mayye* (feminine) 'sorcerer, sorceress', also *maye* (verb) 'to relieve'.)

my.al.ism (ma.yal.ism) *noun* (Jmca). The practice of MYAL beliefs and rites. (From MYAL + the Standard English suffix *-ism* 'organized belief system'.)

my.al.ist (ma.yal.ist, ma.yal-man/wo.man, my.al-man/wo.man) *noun* (Jmca). The man or woman who leads MYAL ceremonies. (From MYAL + Standard English suffix *-ist*, 'organizer of MYAL ceremonies'.)

N

Ny.a.bin.ghi *noun* (CarA). A belief system involving spiritual resistance to foreign control, introduced into Jamaica from East Central Africa, and which has become the faith of a major group of RASTAFARIANS.

P

Phagwa *proper noun* (Guyn, Trin). See HOLI.

Po.co.ma.ni.a *proper noun* (Jmca). A religious practice in which there is singing, spiritual dancing, spirit possession, speaking in tongues and acts of healing; it combines both African and Christian beliefs and is mainly practised by black people in urban Jamaica. (Probably a combination of Spanish *poco* 'little' + English *mania*.)

pu.ja *noun* (Guyn, Trin). The act of praying to and worshipping a Hindu god/goddess, either individually or collectively in a special ceremony. (From Hindi *puujaa* 'worship'.)

R

Ras.ta.far.i.ans *noun plural* (CarA). People who believe that the Emperor Haile Selassie is divine, and who practise these beliefs, following Old Testament principles which include refusing to cut their hair, being vegetarians and smoking ganja.

A Rastafarian man

Ras.ta.far.i.an.ism; Ras.ta.far.ism *noun* (CarA). The beliefs and lifestyle of RASTAFARIANS. □ Although this term is generally used, the preferred term used among Rastafarians when discussing their religion and philosophy of life is Rastafari.

re.vi.val.ism *noun* (Jmca). A religious system that believes in and promotes Afro-Christian religious practices, having links with KUMINA and MYALISM.

S

shak.er.ism *noun* (StVn). The organization and practice of religious worship observed by the SHAKERS.

Sha.kers *noun* (CarA). Any one of several black religious groups, whose form of worship promotes the vigorous shaking of the body and spirit possession.

Shan.go *noun* (Gren, Guyn, Tbgo, Trin). **1.** The Yoruba god of thunder and thunderbolts, who punishes wrongdoers and rewards those who worship him. **2.** A religious sect in which Yoruba gods are worshipped and whose practices are largely related to the god SHANGO, a West African deity, brought to the Caribbean by enslaved people.

Shout.ers *proper noun* (ECar). A religious group who claim to be spiritually descended from John the Baptist.

Spir.i.tu.al Bap.tist *proper noun* (Bdos, Gren, Guyn, StVn, Trin); **Bdos, Jmca, Trin *Baptist***. A member of a Christian religious group which originated in St Vincent sometime in the 19th century; the religion manifests West African spiritual characteristics, baptism by immersion, spirit possession, wearing of robes and headties and is organized similarly to the British Protestant church and headed by archbishops.

FESTIVALS

A

Au.gust bank ho.li.day *noun phrase* (CarA). See EMANCIPATION DAY.

C

Can.na.bal Day *noun phrase* (Belz). Carnival Day in Belize (formerly occurring on Ash Wednesday, but is no longer celebrated on that day).

CARIFESTA *acronym noun* (CarA). The Caribbean Festival of Creative Arts.

Car.ni.val *noun* (CarA). The national festival of competitive costumed bands, continuous street-dancing and CALYPSO singing usually held in the last four days before Ash Wednesday in Trinidad & Tobago, but shifted to other festive times of the year in some territories, such as Antigua, St Kitts, St Vincent and Jamaica.

chaa.ti *noun* (Guyn, Trin). See NINE-DAY.

Chi.nese New Year *noun phrase* (CarA). A holiday celebrated by the Chinese usually between 21 January and 20 February. It is also known as Spring Festival and is celebrated by Chinese living in the Caribbean.

Cor.pus Chris.ti *noun phrase* (Tbgo, Trin). A Christian festival, originating in the Catholic Church to celebrate the Last Supper of Christ when He gave communion to His disciples the day before the Crucifixion; it is a national holiday in Trinidad & Tobago.

Cre.ole Day *noun phrase* (Dmca). The last Friday in October, called by this name from 1980, in recognition of all aspects of Dominican French creole culture.

Crop-O.ver *noun* (CarA). The national festival held during July in Barbados to celebrate the end of the sugar-cane harvest, ending with a national holiday for KADOOMENT, a day of carnival-type celebrations, which normally takes place on the first Monday of August.

Crop-Over

D

Deep.val.li *proper noun* (Guyn, Trin). See DIVALI.

Di.manche Gras *noun phrase* (Tbgo, Trin). The national festivities promoted to celebrate the climax of the CARNIVAL season on the last Sunday night before the beginning of Lent, including the CALYPSO KING competition, King and Queen of Carnival costume competitions and so on. (French Dimanche Gras 'meat Sunday' the last Sunday before Lent when Christians can eat meat.)

Di.va.li (De.va.li, Deep.val.li, Dip.va.li, Di.wa.li) *noun* (Guyn, Trin). The annual Hindu festival of lights which occurs on the appearance of the October/November new moon, to honour Lakshmi, the Hindu goddess of light, by the lighting of small lamps in deep clay saucers placed along driveways, fences, staircases, windows, etc. indicating the triumph of good over evil. (From Hindi *dipak* 'light' + *vali* 'line', hence 'line of light'.)

di.ya *noun* (Guyn, Trin). A lamp in the form of a small deep clay saucer, filled with oil or ghee and with a cotton wick; hundreds of them are lit and placed along railings of houses or in yards as a display of light for the celebration of the Hindu festival DIVALI. (From Hindi *diyaa* 'lamp'.)

Divali

E

Eid *noun* (Guyn, Trin). A Muslim religious festival.

Eid-ul-A.zah *noun* (Guyn, Trin). The Muslim religious festival celebrated in the twelfth month of the Muslim calendar. (See the section on religion.)

Eid-ul-Fitr *noun* (Bdos, Guyn, Trin). The Muslim religious festival held on the first day after the end of Ramadan the month of religious fasting and the, ninth month of the calendar. (See the section on religion.)

E.man.ci.pa.tion Day *noun phrase* (CarA). **CarA *August bank holiday*.** The holiday on 1 August, in memory of the actual date of emancipation from slavery, which was 1 August 1834.

F

Fête la Mar.guerite (Fèt La Ma.gwit) *noun phrase* (StLu). See LA MARGUERITE.

Fête La Rose (Fèt La Woz, Fèt la Wòz) *noun phrase* (StLu). See LA ROSE.

H

Ho.li *proper noun* (Guyn, Trin). **Guyn, Trin *Phagwah*.** The main Hindu religious festival, usually celebrated every year in March or April, representing the triumph of good over evil; it is the sacred aspect of the festival.

Ho.sein; Ho.say *noun* (Trin). See the section on religion.

J

Jou.vé (jou.vay, jou.vert, j'ou.vert, jour ou.vert) *noun* (Dmca, StLu, Tbgo, Trin). **1.** The beginning of the CARNIVAL celebrations before dawn on the Monday of the beginning of the week in which Lent begins, characterized by street-dancing to STEELBANDS, and people 'playing mas'. **2.** The first day of CARNIVAL, including parades and competitions throughout the day. (French Creole from French *jour ouvert* 'open day', which is misleading and does not reflect the meaning of this festival.)

Jun.ka.noo (John Ca.noe) *noun (phrase)* (Baha, Jmca). The joyful festival of street-dancing and parading led by the chief male street-masquerader, called JUNKANOO and a band of traditional characters in costume, the Devil, or related to some popular topic; the festival now takes place largely during the Christmas season.

K

Ka.doo.ment *noun* (Bdos). The annual CARNIVAL-style, one-day festival which features a parade of competing costumed bands and is the culmination of the CROP-OVER festival. (Probably from dialectal English *looka* + *doment, dooment* 'a commotion, disturbance, merry-making'.)

Ka.li Mai Pu.ja/Poo.jay *noun phrase* (Guyn). A three-day celebration held usually from Friday to Sunday in honour of the Hindu goddess Kali, to overcome the forces of evil; it is characterized by the sacrifice of a goat and the flogging of those devoted to the goddess. (From Hindi *Kali Mai* 'Black Mother' + *puja* 'worship'.)

Kid.dies Car.ni.val *noun phrase* (ECar). A mini-carnival in which children are dressed in elaborate costumes, usually held on the Saturday afternoon of the week before the actual CARNIVAL weekend.

Junkanoo

L

La.bour Day *noun phrase* (CarA). The first of May on which there is a national parade of workers of various categories, in recognition of their contribution to their country.

La.ma.gwit (La Mar.gue.rite) *noun (phrase)* (StLu). **StLu *Marguerite Festival*.** A flower festival which has as its main symbol the BACHELOR'S BUTTON, 'la marguerite'; it is held on 17 October in honour of St Margaret Mary Alacoque. (French Creole from French *la marguerite* 'bachelor's button'.)

La.wõz (La Rose) *noun (phrase)* (StLu). A flower festival centered around the rose 'la rose' French, dedicated to St Rose of Lima and usually celebrated on 31 August. (French Creole from French *la rose* 'rose'.)

M

Mar.gue.rite Fes.ti.val (La Ma.gwit) *noun phrase* (StLu). See LAMAGWIT.

Mash.ra.ma.ni *noun* (Guyn). A week of annual national festivities celebrating Republic Day, 23 February. (An Arawak word *masaramani* 'voluntary work done cooperatively'.)

Mashramani

N

nine-day *noun* (Gren, Guyn, Jmca, StVn). **1.** The period of mourning after the death of a person, during which wakes, the burial, and other organized activities take place. **2. Guyn, Trin *chaati*.** The ninth-day celebration held to observe the birth of a baby.

Nine Morn.ings *noun phrase plural* (StVn). A period of festivities and celebrations held on the nine mornings before Christmas just before dawn.

nine-night *noun* (CarA). **1.** Organized festive singing, dancing, eating, drinking and speech-making held every night for nine nights after the burial of a dead person, together with rituals performed to ensure that the spirit of the person rests in peace. **2.** Celebrations held on the ninth night only, or as the climax of nine nights of festivities after someone's death.

O

Ole-Mas (Old-Mas') *noun* (Dmca, Gren, StLu, Tbgo, Trin). The opening festival of the CARNIVAL during which there is masquerading early on JOUVERT morning, characterized by the wearing of last year's masquerade costumes (the old), making fun of public figures or issues by caricature costumes and humorous placards, and general comic representation of individual phrases or slogans, etc.

P

Phag.wa(h) *noun* (Guyn, Trin). **Guyn, Trin** ***Holi***. The public aspect of the Hindu religious celebrations of HOLI, well known for the splashing of abir, a red liquid representing the blood of martyrs, on participants in the celebrations.

R

Ram Nau.mi *noun phrase* (Guyn). A Hindu religious celebration, held to observe the birthday of Lord Rama, usually held early in April and marked by fasting and prayers.

T

tad.jah (ta.ja, ta.zia) *noun (plural)* (Guyn, Trin). [Indic] **Trin *Hosay* 2.** Replicas of the tombs of Hassan and Hosein, Muslim martyrs, paraded through the streets in celebration during the HOSAY/HOSEIN festival. (From Hindi *taagiyaa/taaziyaa* 'replica' of the shrines of Hassan and Hosein taken out in procession on the occasion of 'Muharram'.) See HOSAY.

Y

You.man Na.bi (Y(a)oum.un Na.bi) *noun phrase* (Guyn, Trin). The Muslim festival celebrating the birth and death of the prophet Muhammad on the twelfth day of the third month of the Islamic calendar; a national holiday.

Phagwa

FOLKLORE

A

a.jab.lès *noun* (Dmca). See DJABLÈS.

B

bac.coo (ba.cou, bac(k).oo, bak.(k)oo) *noun* (Bdos, Crcu, Gren, Guyn, Trin). **Dmca *mons*.** A wicked spirit, said to be in the shape of a small, living, partly human being, which must be kept in a bottle and fed bananas; it is believed to make its owner very wealthy or to do harm or evil to others.

bad-eye *noun* (Belz, Guyn). **Gren, StVn, Tbgo, Trin *maldjo, ole-yard* Guyn, StVn**. An evil spell believed to be caused by one person looking at somebody or something with malice or envy in their heart, especially a baby or a flowering plant; the power to cause harm or evil.

black-heart man *noun phrase* (Jmca). An evil man who entices young children away from their homes.

bush dai-dai *noun phrase* (Guyn). A small and hideous Amerindian jungle spirit, somewhat like a BACCOO.

C

ca.nai.ma *noun* (Guyn). See KANAIMA.

chic.char.nie *noun* (Baha). A well-known mischievous figure, which is said to have three legs, and to be half bird, half human, to live in SILK-COTTON trees where it is found and to be seriously harmful to humans, especially if laughed at.

D

diab.lesse (Dmca, StKt, StLu, Tbgo, Trin). See DJABLÈS.

djab.lès (diab.lesse. jab.lesse) *noun* (Dmca, StKt, StLu, Tbgo, Trin). **Dmca *adjablès*; Crcu, Gren, StLu, Tbgo, Trin *ladjablès*.** An evil creature that usually appears on lonely roads in moonlight, looking like an exceedingly pretty, well-dressed young woman, so as to lure men into a wooded or bushy place, then revealing her true self as a hideous old woman with cloven hoofs; this sight causes the man to go mad or die.

dup.py (dup.pie) *noun* (Baha, Bdos, Belz, CayI, Jmca). **Baha, ECar *jumbie*.** An invisible evil spirit of a dead person.

dwenn (du.enne) *noun* (Trin). A tiny creature, believed to be the spirit of an infant who died before being baptized, and which now wanders in the forest, with its feet turned backwards; it wears a big hat shaped like a mushroom so its face is not seen, and leads children and hunters astray in the forest. (French Creole from Spanish *duende* 'goblin, mischievous child'.)

F

fair-maid *noun* (Guyn). **Tbgo** ***fairy-maid*****, Dmca, Gren, StLu, Trin** ***mama-glo*****; Jmca** ***river-mumma*****; Guyn** ***water-mama***. A mermaid-like creature with a beautiful face and long hair which she is seen combing on moonlight nights; the comb, if taken up by somebody, is an instrument used to lure persons and can either lead to great fortune, death, or disappearance of a young person, particularly a young man.

fire-hag *noun* (Bdos). See SOUKOUYAN.

G

gu.zu(m) (gu.zung) *noun* (Belz, Jmca). **1.** Evil caused to another person by an act or wish that causes a supernatural bad influence to affect that person or something they want to do. **2.** A charm worn to protect somebody against evil.

hag (heg, higue) *noun* **1.** (Baha, Belz, StVn). See SOUKOUYAN.

heart-man *noun* (Bdos). An evil being believed to collect the hearts of young boys for devil-worship.

ka.nai.ma (ca.nai.ma, ke.nai.ma) *noun* (Guyn). An evil being, who may be a real man or a spirit, invisible or dwelling in a bird, reptile, or animal, and responsible for the sickness or death of somebody, as an act of vengeance.

la.djab.lès *noun* (Crcu, Gren, StLu, Tbgo, Trin). See DJABLÈS.

lou.ga.wou (la.ga.hou, li.ga.ru, li.ga.wu, lu.ga(r). hoo) *noun* (Dmca, Gren, Grns, StLu, Trin). **1.** A well-known evil figure that can change into a vicious beast or a ball of fire (after shedding and moving his skin); he is known to suck the blood of his victims. **2.** A figure resembling an animal that can be heard passing in the night, with clanking chains, going to do some evil act. **3.** A frightening old man, living alone, feared for being able to lay curses on people, but also known to cure illnesses with folk-medicine. (From French *loup-garou* 'werewolf'.)

mal.djo (mal.jo, mal.joe, mal-yeux) *noun* (Gren, StVn, Tbgo, Trin). See BAD-EYE.

ma.ma-do-good *noun* (Gren). See OBEAH-MAN/WOMAN.

ma.ma-glo *noun* (Dmca, Gren, StLu, Trin). See FAIR-MAID.

ma.ma-ma.la.die *noun* (Gren). The restless spirit or crying of a woman who has died in childbirth and who has been buried with the unborn child inside her; her cries are said to be heard up to nine nights after her death, as her spirit moves between the house where she died and the graveyard in which she is buried. (French Creole from French *maman* 'mother' + *maladie* 'sickness'.)

ma.sa.ku.ru.man (ma(s).sa.cu.ra.man) *noun phrase* (Guyn). A huge, hairy, male river monster, known to be active at nights when it destroys boats and consumes travellers.

mons *noun* (Dmca). See BACCOO. (French Creole from French *monstre* 'monster'.)

o.be.ah-man/-wo.man *noun* (CarA). **Gren** ***mama-do-good; papa-do-good;*** **Guyn, Gren, Jmca, Nevs** ***scientist.*** A man or woman who learns and secretly carries out the practices of OBEAH for which he or she is paid by their clients.

old heg; old higue (ole higue) *noun phrase* (Guyn, Jmca). See SOUKOUYAN.

old-suck *noun* (Jmca). See SOUKOUYAN.

ole-yard *noun* (Guyn, StVn). See BAD-EYE.

P

Pa.pa Bois (Pa.pa-bwa) *noun (phrase)* (StLu, Trin). A supernatural creature in the shape of a sturdy, ragged old man with a beard, a very hairy body and cloven hoofs; he is protector of the trees and animals of the forests and can change into an animal, leading a hunter to get lost; the male counterpart to LADJABLÈS. (French Creole from French *papa* 'father + *bois* 'wood'.)

pa.pa-do-good *noun* (Gren). See OBEAH-MAN.

pe.ai.man (pi.ai.man) *noun* (Guyn). A male folk healer who is said to relieve or remove sickness, evil or fear (especially of the KANAIMA) in members of his community, using ritual methods. (From the Macusi language *piai* 'medicine man'.)

R

ri.ver-mumma *noun* (Jmca). See FAIR-MAID.

rol.ling calf (roar.ing calf) *noun phrase* (Belz, CayI, Jmca). A supernatural being in the form of a calf with flaming eyes that roams the street at night, making a sound like the clanking or dragging of chains and causing panic when it is around; the spirit of a wicked, deceased person.

sci.en.tist *noun* (Guyn). See OBEAH-MAN/WOMAN.

see-far man/wo.man *noun phrase* (Guyn). **BrVI, Gren, Trin** ***seer-man/woman.*** A person said to be able to see into somebody's troubles or future and to give advice on remedies; an OBEAH-MAN/WOMAN.

sou.kou.yan (sou.cou.yant, su.co.yan) *noun* (Dmca, Gren, StLu, Tbgo, Trin). **Bdos *fire-hag*, 1; Baha, StVn *old heg*; Guyn, Jmca *old-higue*; Jmca *old-suck*.** An evil, wrinkled old woman, who sheds her skin which she hides in a jar at night, then turns into a ball of fire going in search of sleeping victims, especially babies, whose blood she sucks before going back into her skin. (French Creole from Soninke *sukunya* 'man-eating sorcerer' and also *soukougnan* in Guadeloupe and probably with a wide number of comparative creatures in West Africa.)

steel-don.key *noun phrase* (Bdos). A supernatural creature who suddenly appears, followed by jangling or metallic sounds and causes fear and panic in neighbourhoods where it is reported to be.

stone-feast (tombstone-feast) *noun* (Crcu). A feast held in the day-time and specially prepared at the home of a deceased person, usually about a year or two after the person has died, to mark the setting up of a tombstone at the person's grave.

wa.ter-ma.ma *noun* (Guyn). See FAIRMAID.

ARCHITECTURE

A

a.do.be *noun* (Belz). **Dmca *ajoupa, mud-house*.** A hut-like dwelling using the earth, rammed and smooth, as floor, with thickly clay-coated walls and a roof of thatched palm leaves.

a.jou.pa *noun* (Dmca, StLu, Tbgo, Trin). **Belz *adobe, cabbage-house*.** An Amerindian-type hut usually with wattle-and-daub walls and a thatched roof.

B

back.house *noun* **1.** (Bdos). The rear section of a house (as opposed to the FRONT HOUSE) and usually in older buildings comprising the dining room and kitchen. **2.** (CayI). An outdoor toilet built at some distance away from the house; a latrine.

back.yard *noun* (CarA). Situated in or belonging to the area behind a house; [by extension] unsophisticated; of low standard.

Adobe hut

bay-house *noun* (Bdos). A seaside house, usually far from town, used or rented by the month, as a family resort.

block-house *noun* (Antg). See WALL-HOUSE.

board-and-shin.gle house *noun* (Guyn). See CHATTEL-HOUSE.

bot.tom-house *noun* (Guyn). **1.** (Belz) ***house-bottom***. **2.** [By extension]. The ground (often with a concrete surfacing) under the house used as an area for domestic service or playing. **3.** A lower or ground-floor dwelling providing additional living space by constructing walls.

Bottom-house

Boucan barn

bou.can *noun* **1.** (Dmca, Gren). **Dmca, Trin *cocoa-house***. A construction for drying cocoa-beans consisting of a tray-like floor and gable shed, one of which moves on wheels to protect the drying beans from rain. **2.** (Gren) A huge barn or shed on the floor of which cocoa-beans are laid out to dry.

cab.bage-house *noun* (Belz). See AJOUPA.

ca.boose *noun* (TkCa). See SHED-ROOF.

chat.tel-house *noun* (Bdos). **Bdos, Guyn *board-and-shingle house***. A single-roofed board-and-shingle house, or one

Chattel-house

of about the same size (about 20 ft × 10 ft × 8 ft) with a galvanized-sheet roof (originally), sitting on a groundsel of loose stones so that it can be removed wholly by its owner from leased land.

clo.set *noun* (CarA). An outside wooden latrine with a pit.

Closet

co.coa-house *noun* (Trin). See BOUCAN. **1.**

D

dwell.ing-house *noun* (CarA). A building erected for people to live in (usually a small and simple kind); (Standard English) a dwelling.

drop-shed *noun* (Antg, Nevs, StKt). See SHED-ROOF.

dry-wall *noun* (Baha, Mrat, Nevs, StKt, TkCa). See GROUNDSEL.

F

front-house *noun* **1.** (Baha, Bdos, Jmca, Nevs, StKt). **Baha, Bdos, Jmca, Nevs, StKt *front-room***. The living-room area of a dwelling, especially such as the gable-ended chattel-house part, often including the bedroom. **2.** (Guyn) The house that faces the road, usually the first of two or three buildings on a single lot.

G

ground.sel (ground.sill) *noun* (Bdos). **Baha, Mrat, Nevs, StKt, TkCa *dry-wall*; Angu *rubble-stone foundation***. The foundation for a small, wooden house, such as a CHATTEL-HOUSE, made by stacking large pieces of stone to fit closely together without mortar.

P

pal.ing *noun* (Bdos, Guyn). A property fence made of galvanized sheeting.

S

shed-roof *noun* (Bdos, Mrat). **TkCa *caboose*; Antg, Nevs, StKt *drop-shed***. A small addition to a chattel-house, with a flat, sloping roof; its main use is to add dining and kitchen space at the back end, and sometimes to provide an entrance ensuring the privacy of the main house.

T

ta.pi.a *noun* (Trin). A thatched or mud wall or roof; a wattle-and-daub wall or roof.

ten.ant.ry *noun* (Bdos) A group of CHATTEL-HOUSES owned by people who worked on sugar plantations and who were legally allowed tenancy of the land on which their houses stood; [by extension] such a set of houses owned, on leased land, by the descendants of the original owners.

two-by-two/-three/-four *noun* (CarA). A very small dwelling; a one-room house.

up.stairs house; up.stairs and down. stairs house *noun phrases* (CarA). A two-storeyed house.

wall-building/wall-house/ wall-property *noun phrase* (ECar). **Antg** ***block-house***. A dwelling-house with walls of coral stone or concrete blocks (as opposed to wood).

wood-and-wall house *noun phrase* (Bdos). A house, a part of which (the lower storey or the back section) is constructed in stone or concrete blocks, and the rest in wood.

Tapia

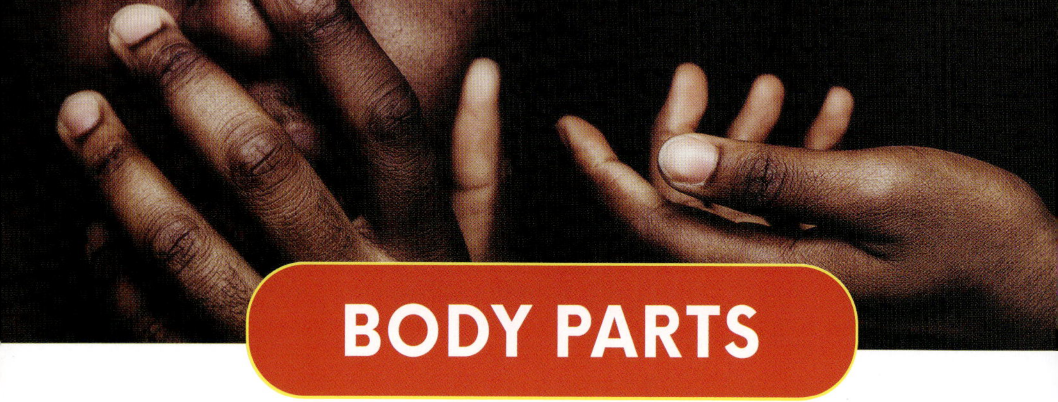

BODY PARTS

B

bel.ly *noun* (CarA). A general word used for the inside of the human body from about mid-chest downwards, abdomen, bowels, guts, womb etc.

B

F

foot *noun* (CarA). The whole or any part of the leg from the thigh down to the toes.

foot-bottom *noun* (Bdos, Guyn, Jmca). The sole of the foot.

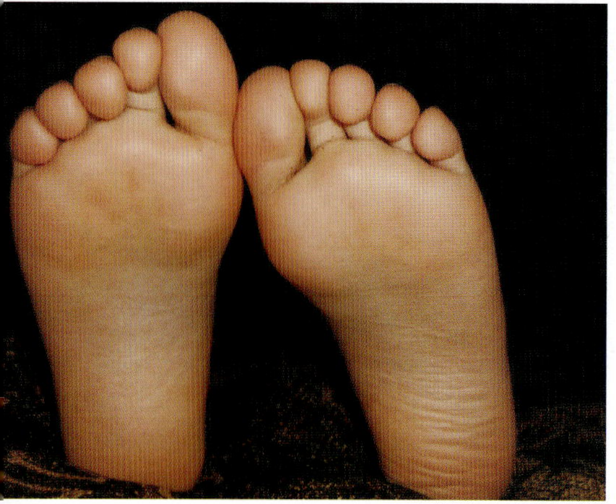

Foot-bottom

H

half-a-foot *adj* (Bdos, Dmca, Guyn, Jmca, Tbgo, StVn). Having lost part or the whole of one leg (whether using a crutch or having a wooden leg).

hand *noun* (CarA). The whole arm, from the shoulder to the fingers, of the human body; any part of the whole limb (upper arm, forearm or hand).

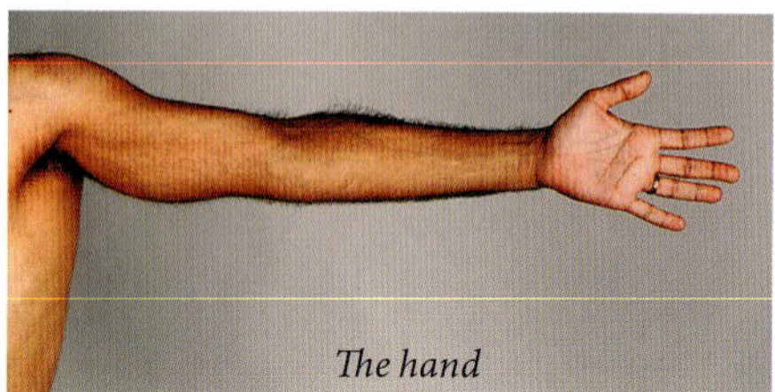

The hand

hand-middle *noun* (Belz, Guyn, Jmca). The palm of the hand.

N

neck-back *noun* (Guyn, Jmca). The nape of the neck.

S

sto.mach *noun* (CarA). The chest and abdomen, but often the upper part of the human body.

swal.low-pipe *noun* (Bdos). The wind-pipe; [by extension] the throat.

CLOTHING

B

bag.gie *noun* (Jmca). Knickers (underpants) for a baby or little girl.

blou *noun* (ECar). A blouse.

blouse *noun* (ECar). A man's jacket (as well as a women's upper garment).

bu.gas *noun plural* (Jmca). See CREPESOLES.

C

can-can *noun* (ECar). Petticoat. An underskirt of stiff material used to give the outer skirt more body.

che.mise *noun* **1.** (CarA). A long white dress, with low, round neck, long sleeves, and tied at the waist, worn by household enslaved women; chimmy. **2.** (USVI) A woman's white short-sleeved bodice. **Antg, Guyn, Trin *chimie*; Guyn, StKt *shimmy*.** A baby's loose-fitting garment.

crepe.soles *noun plural* (Guyn, Jmca, Tbgo, Trin). **Jmca *bugas, crepes, gym-shoes*; Bdos *half-cuts*; Antg, Mrat *hoppers*; Bdos *pumps*; Crcu, Gren *punkasal*; Jmca *puss(-boots)*; BrVI, StKt *rubbers*; StVn *soft-mash*; Bdos, Gren, StLu *soft-shoes*; Angu, Mrat *soft-walkers*; Tbgo, Trin *washicongs*; Guyn, Jmca *yachtings, yachting-shoes*.** Rubber-soled canvas shoes that are usually laced. (American English ***sneakers***.)

D

dan.dan *noun* (CarA). **1.** A child's pretty dress. **2.** [By extension] New and pretty clothes worn by a woman.

da.shi.ki *noun* (Trin). A man's short-sleeved upper garment that is fairly loose-fitting, without collar or buttons, V-necked, and usually of plain material brightly embroidered around the neck and borders.

Dashiki

dho.ti *noun* (Guyn, Trin). An East Indian man's white loincloth consisting of a single piece of cloth wrapped around the waist, folded over and passed loosely between the legs.

F

fou.lard *noun* (Dmca, StLu). A shawl or large neckerchief of decorative material partly covering the bodice of a dress so that its ends tuck into the belt; it is worn as part of the national costume.

G

gan.sey *noun* (Bdos). **Bdos *vest-shirt*.** A jersey or T-shirt, usually a coloured one; a pullover.

gym-shoes *noun plural* (Bdos). See CREPESOLES.

H

half-cuts *noun plural* (Bdos). See CREPESOLES.

head.tie *noun* (CarA). A cloth of either pure white or ornately coloured cotton, worn by a woman, tied around the head, covering the forehead, and knotted at the back or side with two ends sticking out in different patterms; in Dominica, and St Lucia, it is used as part of the national costume.

hop.pers *noun plural* (Antg, Mrat). See CREPESOLES.

hot-shirt *noun* (CarA). A man's shirt made of material with brightly contrasting colours and usually worn outside the pants; it is considered suitable for festive wear.

K

kur.ta *noun* (Guyn, Trin). [Indic] A loose, light-fitting upper garment, usually high-necked, long-sleeved, and reaching below the waist; it is traditionally a man's formal garment, made of plain white cotton and worn with a DHOTI, but embroidered variations are now also fashionable women's wear.

Kurta

M

me.ri.no *noun* (CarA). **Angu, Belz, Dmca, StVn *marina, merina*; Guyn *singlet*; Antg, Bdos, Guyn *vest*.** A man's white low-necked, sleeveless undershirt (formerly made of merino wool and cotton, hence the original name).

P

pumps *noun plural* (Bdos). See CREPESOLES.

pun.ka.sal *noun* (Crcu, Gren). See CREPESOLES.

puss(-boots) *noun (plural)* (Jmca). See CREPESOLES.

R

rub.bers *noun* (BrVi, StKt). See CREPESOLES.

S

sa.ri *noun* (Guyn, Trin). A female garment consisting of a single length of light, colourful cloth which is wrapped about the body so that the entire body is elegantly covered, with one end draped over the shoulder.

Sari

shirt-jac(k) *noun* (CarA). A man's loose-fitting, shirt-like garment, designed like a bush-jacket without a belt, usually with short sleeves and made of light shirting material; it is worn outside the trousers.

sin.glet *noun* (Guyn). See MERINO.

soft-mash *noun* (StVn). See CREPESOLES.

soft-shoes *noun plural* (Bdos, Gren, StLu). See CREPESOLES.

soft-walkers *noun plural* (Angu, Mrat). See CREPESOLES.

T

tam *noun* (CarA). **Guyn *tamashanta,* Gren *tam-hat.*** A knitted woolen cap, often in rings of red, yellow, black, green, (and sometimes with a peak); it is popular Rastafarian headwear made spacious enough to bag the dreadlocks.

vest *noun* (Antg, Bdos, Guyn). See MERINO.

vest-shirt *noun* (Bdos). **1. Bdos** GANSEY. **2.** A coloured, sleeveless vest sometimes worn by men outdoors as the only upper garment.

wa.shi.congs (wat.che.kongs) *noun plural* (Gren, Trin). See CREPSOLES.

yacht.ings, yachting-shoes *noun* (Guyn, Jmca). See CREPESOLES.

CHILDREN'S GAMES

A

Ab.ner. Bab.ner, La.dy's knee *noun phrase* (Guyn). **USVI *aka baka*; Bdos *Hobner, Bobner, Lady's knee*.** First line of a children's rhyme used to eliminate players in any game; the last one left is usually chosen as the one to play first in whatever game the children are about to begin.

B

baby-pot *noun* (Guyn). **Antg, Gren, Nevs, StVn *dolly-pot*.** A child's make-believe game, in which various items, such as mud and wild fruit are used to prepare dishes.

black girl in the ring *noun phrase* (Antg, Brbu). See BROWN GIRL.

blind man *noun phrase* (Bdos, Trin). A game in which the participants' eyes are covered as they try to catch the person nearest to them.

boo boo catch.er *noun phrase* (Bdos). A game in which the participants have to run as fast as they can in order not to get caught; if they're caught, they're out.

brown girl *noun phrase* (CarA). **Angu, Brbu *black girl/yellow girl in the ring*.** A children's ring game in which the players stand in a circle singing the song of the game, with one girl in the circle. 'There's a brown (black/yellow) girl in the ring, tra la la la la / Show me your motion / Tra la la la la / Run to your partner / Tra la la la la / He/she is sweeter than sugar and plum.' The dancer's place is then taken by another girl, each girl dancing with a hip-swinging motion.

C

cache-cache ma balle/-belle *noun phrase* (Dmca). See KACH-KACH-MA(N)-BAL.

cat-and-mouse *noun* (StVn). **Belz, BrVI, Dmca, Guyn, StLu *cat-and-rat*.** A ring game in which two children representing cat and mouse are left out of the ring; the cat chases the mouse out of the ring and when the mouse is caught, two fresh players are chosen and the game continues.

catch.er (ECar). **Guyn *catcher-coop*; Baha *catchers*; StVn, USVI *coop*; ECar *hoop*.** A children's game of hide-and-seek played in several different ways, but in which the person being chased is usually caught by somebody touching them and the person touched then becomes the chaser.

catch.er-coop *noun* (Guyn). **Baha *catch.ers***. See CATCHER.

Child.ren! Child.ren! *noun phrase* (Guyn). A group game of call and response in which one player is chosen as the mother who calls out, 'Children! Children!' and the other players represent the children who answer their mother's call, saying, 'Yes, Mama!', followed by several questions put by the mother; after the last question, 'Who is the dog?', and the children's answer 'You', the mother runs after the children and whoever she catches becomes the next mother.

chinks *noun plural* (StVn). A ring game of marbles, in which players try to tip or knock out a marble or marbles in the ring.

cock.fight[1] *noun* (Antg, StVn). Children use the flowers of the FLAMBOYANT TREE to play this game, and the winner is the one who manages to pull all the stamens off the flower.

cock.fight[2] *noun* (Trin). A rough game played by children, competing in pairs as one carries his partner on his back (as a jockey) and each jockey attempts to throw off the other.

coop *noun* (StVn, USVI). See CATCHER.

D

dol.ly house *noun* (Antg, Gren, Nevs, StVn). A game in which several children assume the role of various family members, mother, father, uncle, aunt, godfather, godmother and children; after a make-believe wedding, the mother and father, then called husband and wife, will pretend that they have a baby and after having the baby 'christened' at church, they return to their home, made of bushes, branches etc., and participate in a ceremony including dancing and eating.

dol.ly-pot *noun* (Antg, StVn). See BABY-POT.

ducks and drakes *noun phrase* (Guyn). A game which consists of children throwing a piece of flat stone, a seed or other object several times to skim the water of a pond or trench.

F

farm.er in the den *noun phrase* (Guyn). A ring game played by both boys and girls in which the child chosen as the farmer stands in the middle of the ring and the children forming the ring sing and clap their hands, going through several lines and taking into the ring the person whom they are talking about. The game ends with someone pretending to be a piece of cheese and that person becomes the new farmer, as the game starts again.

firms *noun plural* (Bdos). See OUT-FOR-PLAY.

freeze *noun* (Baha, Dmca, Gren, StLu). A children's game in which any member of the group is required to stay frozen in one position as the song is played; that person can move only if someone else touches them or says 'Melt'.

fol.low-the-cap.tain *noun* (Bdos). A game between parents and children in which the parent acts out an instruction and the child has to obey it.

H

hid.dy-biddy *noun* (Bdos). **Bdos *hit.ty-bit.ty*.** The same as the game KACH-KACH-MAN-BAL (Dmca) except that the player says to each girl seated in the ring, 'Hiddy-biddy, hold fast! Shut up your lap tight, tight.'

Hob.ber, Bob.ner, La.dy's knee *noun phrase* (Bdos). See ABNER, BABNER, LADY'S KNEE.

hoop *noun* (ECar). See CATCHER.

K

kach-kach-ma(n)-bal/ma-bèl *noun* (Dmca). **Bdos *hiddy-biddy*.** A girls' moonlight game in which they sit in a circle with knees closed, while a player, holding a seed or a small marble hidden in her hand, goes from person to person saying 'cache-cache, ma belle' and sneakily leaves the seed/marble in one girl's lap; that player calls on one of them to say who has the seed; if the chosen player correctly identifies the 'lap' then the first player is out; if wrong, the chosen player is out.

L

lit.ti(e) *noun* (Guyn). See PICK-UPS.

leaps *noun* (Bdos). A game in which a child leapfrogs over their parent and vice versa.

O

O'Gra.dy says *noun phrase* (Guyn). A group game, in which a leader is selected who is 'O'Grady' and who gives various commands to the other players; the command must be preceded by the words 'O'Grady says', if not the players following the incomplete command are eliminated; the winner then becomes the next leader.

out-for-play *noun phrase* (Guyn). **Bdos *firms*.** An improvised game of cricket without runs, played by schoolboys in which any member of his small group (called a firm in Barbados) earns the right to bat by catching or bowling out the batsman.

P

pick-ups *noun plural* (Bdos, Dmca, Mrat, Nevs StLu, Trin). **Guyn *litti(e)*; Gren *stones*; StLu *tikitok*; Trin *trié*.** A children's game similar to the game called 'jacks' in International English, played with pebbles, seeds or small marbles.

R

ring o' ring o' ros.es *noun* (Bdos, Guyn). A game in which players hold hands in a circle and sing 'Ring o' ring o' roses / Bucket full o' posies / A tishoo, a tishoo / All fall down', and at the end of this chant, all the players fall down.

S

sad.dle *noun* (Bdos). In this game, a parent imitates any animal and the child rides on top.

sift-n-spell *noun* (Bdos). A game in which letters are placed in a sand-box and the child has to find the appropriate letter to make the word that matches a picture which is in the possession of the other person(s) playing the game.

stones *noun plural* (Gren). See PICK-UPS.

sto.ry tell.er *noun phrase* (Bdos). A game in which someone starts a story and the other players build on it and finish it.

T

ti.ki.tok (ti.ki.toc) *noun* (StLu). See PICK-UPS.

tri.é (t(h)ree-A, tree.ay) *noun* (Trin). See PICK-UPS.

touch-and-feel *noun* (Bdos). A game in which a parent puts an item into a box and the child has to guess what the item is by using their hands only.

war.ri (wa.ri. war.rie, wah.ree) *noun* (Antg, Bdos, Jmca, StLu, Trin, USVI). A board game played with 48 seeds on a rectangular board divided into 12 'houses' or receptacles arranged in 6 pairs along the boards; two players sit with the board placed between them and by the end of the game the winner is the one who has been able to capture the most seeds in the 12 'houses'.

x-and-o; x's and noughts *noun* (Bdos, Guyn, Trin). A game usually played on paper by two people who try to get a group of either X's or O's in a row drawn on the paper, either straight across or diagonally.

Warri board

ORGANIZATIONAL ABBREVIATIONS AND ACRONYMS

B

BADMC *abbreviation* (Bdos). Barbados Agricultural Development and Marketing Corporation

BAMC *abbreviation* (Bdos). Barbados Agricultural Management Company Limited

BAMP *acronym* (Bdos). Barbados Association of Medical Practitioners

BAPE *abbreviation* (Bdos). Barbados Association of Professional Engineers

BBC *abbreviation* (Bdos). Barbados Bottling Company

BCA *abbreviation* (Bdos). Barbados Cricket Association

BEC *abbreviation* (Bdos). Barbados Employers Confederation

BHTA *abbreviation* (Bdos). Barbados Hotel and Tourism Association

BNOC *abbreviation* (Bdos). Barbados National Oil Company

BOA *abbreviation* (Bdos). Barbados Olympic Association

BSTU *abbreviation* (Bdos). Barbados Secondary Teachers Union

BUT *abbreviation* (Bdos). Barbados Union of Teachers

BWA *abbreviation* (Bdos). Barbados Water Authority

BWIA *acronym* (CarA). British West Indian Airways, the abbreviation used formerly to identify the airline, now known as Caribbean Airlines, the headquarters being in Trinidad & Tobago.

C

CAREC *acronym* (CarA). Caribbean Epidemiology Centre; it provides laboratory reference and epidemiology services to a number of countries, including all CARICOM states, Bermuda and the Netherland Antilles; it was instituted in 1975 and has its headquarters in Port of Spain.

CARICOM *acronym* (CarA). The CARIBBEAN COMMUNITY, originally an organization of 15 Caribbean nations established in 1973, all of whom are full members, namely, Antigua & Barbuda, the Bahamas, Barbados, Belize,

Dominica, Grenada, Guyana, Haiti, Jamaica, Montserrat, St Kitts & Nevis, St Lucia, St Vincent & the Grenadines, Suriname, Trinidad & Tobago; their main purposes are to promote economic integration and cooperation among members, to ensure that the benefits of integration are equitably shared, and to coordinate foreign policy.

CARIFESTA *acronym* (CarA). Caribbean Festival of Creative Arts (originally established in Guyana in 1972).

CARIFTA *acronym* (CarA). Caribbean Free Trade Association, consisting originally of Heads of Government of Antigua, Barbados and Guyana, who agreed to form this body in 1965; it was later expanded to include Dominica, Grenada, Jamaica, Montserrat, St Kitts-Nevis, St Lucia, St Vincent, Trinidad & Tobago, and in 1971, Belize; also known as the Caribbean Free Trade Area.

CBI *acronym* (CarA). The Caribbean Basin Initiative is vital to the good relations between the United States and its neighbours in Central America and the Caribbean; launched in 1983, through the Caribbean Basin Economic Recovery Act (CBERA), it consists of 24 beneficiary countries (all the CARICOM territories + 10 Latin American countries), and currently provides them with duty-free access for most goods from the US market.

CBU *abbreviation* (CarA). Caribbean Broadcasting Union.

CCA *abbreviation* (CarA). Caribbean Conservation Association.

CCJ *acronym* (CarA). Caribbean Court of Justice.

CD *abbreviation* (Jmca). Commander of the Order of Distinction, a Jamaican national order awarded for distinguished service to Jamaica; the letters are placed after the awardee's name.

CDB *abbreviation* (CarA). Caribbean Development Bank (1970–); its headquarters are in Barbados.

C

Caribbean Development Bank headquarters, Barbados

CDERA *acronym* (CarA). The Caribbean Disaster Emergency Response Agency is a regional inter-governmental agency, established in 1991 by a CARICOM Heads Agreement to be responsible for assisting with any disastrous event in any of the participating states, once that assistance is requested.

CHB *abbreviation* (Bdos). Companion of Honour of Barbados, a national honour awarded for distinguished national achievement; it is the second highest national honour in Barbados and the letters are placed after the recipient's name.

CONCACAF *acronym* (CarA). Confederation of North Central American and Caribbean Football Associations (the continental federal grouping of Federal International Football Associations consisting of Antigua & Barbuda, Bahamas, Barbados, Belize, Bermuda, Grenada, Guyana, Jamaica, and Trinidad &Tobago. Its headquarters are in Guatemala.

CSME *acronym* (CarA). Caribbean Single Market and Economy; a single economic system including all CARICOM states, fully inaugurated in 2007, and allowing for free movement of persons, goods and services, as well as having a common external policy, within a unified legal framework, throughout the member states.

CTO *acronym* (CarA). Caribbean Tourism Organization (combining the former Caribbean Research Tourism (and Development) Centre, representing 28 English-, French-, Spanish- and Dutch-speaking territories across the region and based in Barbados, and the former Caribbean Tourism Association in New York City) with headquarters in Bridgetown, Barbados.

CTRC *abbreviation* (CarA). Caribbean Research and Tourism Development Centre (see CTO).

CUT *abbreviation* (CarA). Caribbean Union of Teachers, including the teachers' unions of 14 English-speaking Caribbean territories and Bermuda, formed in the 1970s out of the older Caribbean Confederation of Teachers, and having its secretariat sited in whichever territory the elected secretary is.

CXC *abbreviation* (CarA). Caribbean Examinations Council, the official body responsible for organizing and overseeing secondary school-leavers' examinations for most of the English-speaking Caribbean. (X is the abbreviation used for examinations.)

D

DA *abbreviation* (Bdos). Dame of St Andrew of the order of Barbados, it is one of the two highest national honours awarded for outstanding and excellent service to Barbados or to humanity in general; the recipient is addressed as Dame and the letters are written after her name.

DAH *abbreviation* (Dmca). The Dominica Award of Honour, the highest national award of the Commonwealth of Dominica; the letters are written after the name of the awardee.

E

ECCB *abbreviation* (ECar). Eastern Caribbean Central Bank, established in 1983 to provide a central banking system for seven Eastern Caribbean States: Antigua & Barbuda, Dominica, Grenada, Montserrat, St Kitts & Nevis, St Lucia, St Vincent & the Grenadines; the bank issues its own currency for those states, the EC dollar.

ECLAC *acronym* (CarA). Economic Commission for Latin America and the Caribbean, an intergovernmental organization founded in 1948 by the United Nations Economic and Social Council in order to develop cooperation, regional economic growth and external trade so as to benefit all its members which include all CARICOM states.

GCM *abbreviation* (Bdos). Gold Crown of Merit of the Order of Barbados, a national honour awarded for highly meritorious service or achievement in the arts, science, literature, sport, civic duties or any other endeavour worthy of national recognition; the letters are placed after the recipient's name.

GCSL *abbreviation* (StLu). Grand Cross of the Order of St Lucia; it is the highest rank of the Order and is awarded only to the governor general of St Lucia, enabling that person to use the title 'His/Her Excellency' for life.

GIS *abbreviation* (CarA). Government Information Service.

HBM *abbreviation* (Trin & Tbgo). The Hummingbird Medal of the Order of the Trinity, a gold, silver or bronze medal awarded as a national honour for outstanding loyal and devoted service that has brought benefit and prestige to Trinidad & Tobago in the person's field of endeavour; the letters are placed after the recipient's name.

ICTA *acronym* (CarA). Imperial College of Tropical Agriculture, founded at St Augustine, Trinidad in 1921 and incorporated into the University of the West Indies in 1963.

ISER *abbreviation* (CarA). The Institute of Social and Economic Research of the University of the West Indies.

KA *abbreviation* (Bdos). Knight of St Andrew of the Order of Barbados, the highest national honour awarded for extraordinary and outstanding achievement and excellence in service to Barbados or humanity in general; the letters are placed after the recipient's name.

LDCs *abbreviation* (CarA). Less-developed countries, a term applied to less economically developed CARICOM countries, such as Anguilla, Antigua & Barbuda, Belize, Dominica, Grenada, Montserrat, St Kitts & Nevis, St Lucia, St Vincent & the Grenadines.

LIAT *acronym* (ECar). Leeward Islands Air Transport, an Eastern Caribbean airline.

MDCs *abbreviation* (CarA). More-developed countries, namely, the group of original CARICOM member-states comprising Barbados, Guyana, Jamaica, and Trinidad & Tobago, which have larger populations and more economic development than the other 8 of the original 12.

MSA *abbreviation* (Dmca). The Meritorious Service Award, the third highest national honour of the Commonwealth of Dominica.

NSC *abbreviation* (StLu). The National Service Cross, a national honour awarded to a senior member of the police, fire service, or prison officer for loyal and dedicated service to St Lucia; the letters are placed after the recipient's name.

OD *abbreviation* **1.** (Antg, Brbu) The Order of Distinction, of the Order of Antigua & Barbuda, a national honour awarded to any individual who has rendered outstanding and meritorious service to the state; the letters may be placed after the recipient's name. **2.** (Jmca) Officer of the Order of Distinction, a national honour awarded for distinguished service to Jamaica; the letters are placed after the recipient's name.

OE *abbreviation* (Guyn). The Order of Excellence of Guyana, the highest national honour awarded to a citizen for national or international eminence in the field of human endeavour; the letters O.E. are placed after the recipient's name.

OECS *abbreviation* (CarA). Organization of Eastern Caribbean States, an international organization established in 1981 and made up of the seven member states of the Eastern Caribbean Common Market, Antigua & Barbuda, Dominica, Grenada, Montserrat, St Kitts & Nevis, St Lucia, St Vincent & the Grenadines; St Martin and Martinique are overseas territories with observer status.

OH *abbreviation* (Antg, Brbu). The Order of Honour of Antigua & Barbuda, conferred on any person who has rendered outstanding and beneficial service in any field of human endeavour or for bravery or any other humane action; the letters are placed after the recipient's name.

OJ *abbreviation* (Jmca) The Order of Jamaica, the highest national honour awarded to a person of the highest distinction; the recipient is addressed as 'Honourable' and the letters are placed after the person's name.

ON *abbreviation* **1.** (Antg, Brbu) The Order of the Nation, a national honour awarded to any person for heroic service to the state; the letters are placed after the person's name. **2.** (Jmca) The Order of the Nation, a national honour conferred on a person who has been appointed governor-general; the person is addressed as 'the Most Honourable' and the letters O.N. are placed after the person's name.

OR *abbreviation* (Guyn). The Order of Roraima of Guyana, an award made to a person who has performed most outstanding service to Guyana; it is the second highest award of the state and the letters are placed after the recipient's name.

OTN *abbreviation* (CarA) Office of Trade Negotiations. See the RNM.

R

RNM *abbreviation* (CarA). The Caribbean Regional Negotiating Machinery was set up on 1 April 1997 by CARICOM governments with a view to developing and executing a unified negotiating strategy for trade negotiations in which the region is involved; its headquarters are in Jamaica, with a sub-office in Barbados. □ This organization is now known as the OTN, the Office of Trade Negotiations.

S

SCM *abbreviation* (Bdos). Silver Crown of Merit of the Order of Barbados, a national honour awarded for distinguished service or achievement in the sciences, the arts, literature, sport, civic duties, or any other endeavour worthy of national recognition; the letters are placed after the recipient's name.

T

TC *abbreviation* (Trin & Tbgo). The Trinity Cross Medal of the Order of the Trinity, a gold medal awarded as a national honour for outstanding service to Trinidad & Tobago, or for gallantry beyond the call of duty; it is the highest national award and the letters are placed after the recipient's name.

WIGUT *acronym* (CarA). West Indies Group of University Teachers, the trade union of the academic staff of the University of the West Indies, with independent branches in each of the campus territories, Barbados, Jamaica, Trinidad & Tobago, and Five Islands; the academic staff of the Open Campus would also be included in this group.

GENERAL VOCABULARY

A

a.bove[1] *adverb, preposition* (CarA). **StKt, Tbgo *upperside*.** Beyond; (often) to the east (or windward) side.

a.bove[2] *adjective* (Bdos). East; further.

ab.stract[1] *noun* (Belz). Any pendant worn on a necklace. (Probably from designs that remind one of abstract art.)

ab.stract[2] *adjective* (Belz). Odd, extremely unusual, strange.

a.buse *verb* (CarA). **ECar *buse*.** To use very loud, foul and threatening language to somebody.

act; act up *verb* (Bdos, Guyn, Jmca). To behave in a strange manner, as though mentally disturbed.

ad.vi.ces *noun plural* (Bdos). Pieces of advice.

af.ro *noun* (CarA). A hairstyle, round in shape which emphasizes the natural thickness of the hair of both male and female persons of African descent.

af.ro beads *noun plural* (CarA). Necklaces made of small, coloured beads, shells, and small seeds worn by both men and women, considered to be part of African fashion.

af.ro comb *noun phrase* (CarA). **CarA *afro pick*.** A type of comb with a handle shaped like a head and neck, and long prongs of metal, wood or hard plastic, used to produce the afro hairstyle.

af.ro puff *noun phrase* (CarA). A girl's hairstyle in a soft, round mass of hair produced by teasing and shaping the tied off ends.

af.ter-cul.ti.va.tion *noun* (CarA). Any process of soil culture, which involves loosening, forking, etc., applied between the planting of the crop and its reaping.

a.gain *adverb* **1.** (Belz, Gren, Trin). More, still, in adition. **2.** (CarA) (Not) any longer, anymore.

age.a.ble *adjective* (Bdos, Belz, Tbgo). Aged, advanced in years.

age-pa.per *noun* (Belz, Jmca). **CarA *birth-paper*, Guyn *born-paper*.** Birth certificate.

a.gree (gree) *verb* (CarA). To dwell in peace and harmony with each other; to have no ill feelings towards each other.

a.gro-cli.mac.tic *adjective* (CarA). Relating to climate, particularly as it affects agriculture.

a.larm *verb* (CarA). [Of a clock] To make a ringing or other sound in order to wake somebody up.

all-age school *noun phrase* (CarA). **Bdos** ***composite school***. A school which children of all ages between 5 and 16 can attend.

all is one *idiomatic phrase* (Bdos, Guyn). **ECar** ***all (is) (the) same khaki pants***. It makes no difference; they're alike.

all-you; you-all *pronoun* (CarA). **Bdos** ***wunna, all o[f] wunna***. You (plural); all of you.

a.long with *prepositional phrase* (CarA). Together with, side by side with.

A.mer.in.di.an Cap.tain *noun phrase* (Guyn). **Guyn** ***Touchau***. The officially recognized leader of an Amerindian village in Guyana.

an.wa.jé *adjective* (StLu). See VEX[1]. (French Creole from French *enragé* 1.'angry'.)

arm.chair *noun* (Guyn). See BERBICE-CHAIR.

a.round *preposition* (CarA) **1.** About, approximately at/in (a stated time). **2.** In the same place; in the area of.

a.su(e) *noun* (Baha). See SUSU[1].

ba.bache (ba.bash) *noun* (Trin). See BUSH-RUM.

Ba.by.lon (CarA) **1.** [According to the Rastafarians] Any Western government or its supporters, particularly in the Caribbean. **2.** The police; a policeman; a fireman or any agent employed in protective services of any Caribbean society.

back-ans.wer[1] *noun* (CarA). **CarA** ***back-talk*; StVn** ***high-cheeks*; Guyna** ***hot-mouth***. A rude reply; immediate and embarrassing reply from a young person or a subordinate.

back-ans.wer[2] *verb* (CarA). **CarA** ***back-talk***[2]**; StVn** ***give (somebody) high-cheek*; Guyn** ***give (somebody) hot-mouth***. To make a quick and rude reply to a superior.

back-foot *noun* (CarA). **1.** The hind leg (of an animal). **2.** [In cricket] The batsman's leg placed behind the crease.

back-pock.et *noun* (CarA). The hip pocket; pocket at the back of a pair of trousers.

back.ra (bac.cra, bak.ra, buck.ra) *noun, adjective* (CarA). **Guyn** ***backra-man*; Dmca, Gren** ***béké*; StLu** ***bétjé***. **1.** A white person, especially a white man. (From Efik *mbakara* < plural prefix *mba* 'all, whole' + verb *kara* 'to encompass, master, understand'.) **2.** A person, who is in a position of great authority, or an important person (of any race), who is feared, white or non-white. **3.** BACKRA-NIGGER (Tbgo) A person whose physical appearance is more nearly white than black, especially one who despises black people; a quadroon, or an octoroon. **4.** (Especially in the phrase POOR-BACKRA) A white Barbadian indentured plantation servant in the 17th century; in the present, a white peasant or low-level worker who is the descendant of the 17th-century indentured servants.

back.ra-man *noun* (CarA). See BACKRA.

back.ra-miss.sy *noun phrase* (CarA). The daughter of a sugar planter.

back.ra-john.ny *noun* (Trin). **Dmca, Gren** béké-nèg**; CarA** ***red nigger***. A mulatto; a light-skinned person of mixed black and white ancestry who is despised.

back.ra pick.ney *noun phrase* (CarA). Any white child; [by extension] any light-skinned child.

back-step *noun* (Gren, Guyn, Tbgo, Trin). A stairway outside and leading to the back entrance or kitchen door of a house; backstairs.

back.store *noun* (CarA). The rear section of the building housing a supermarket or department store, which is shut off from the main store and in which goods are prepared for display and sale.

back-talk[1] *noun* (CarA). See BACK-ANSWER[1].

back-talk[2] *verb phrase* (CarA). See BACK-ANSWER[2].

bad-be.hav.ed *adjective* (CarA). **StLu *bad-mannered*; Dmca *malkasé*; Bdos, Guyn, Jmca *outlawed*.** Unruly, ill-mannered and noisy, grossly misconducting yourself.

B

bad-be.ha.viour *noun* (CarA). Noisy misconduct, especially among young persons.

bad-bel.ly; bad bow.els *noun* (CarA). **CarA *belly-work(s), belly-working*; Guyn, StVn, Trin *belly-working*; ECar, TkCa *the belly*; Antg, Baha, Tbgo *the runnings*.** Diarrhoea, running of the bowels, especially in babies over several days.

bad-man.ner.ed *adjective* (StLu). See BAD-BEHAVED.

bad-mouth[1] *noun* (CarA). **1.** A supposed ability or tendency to cause misfortune or bad luck by talking about it. **2.** (Guyn). See BAD-TALK[1].

bad-mouth[2] *transitive verb* (Baha). See BAD-TALK[2].

bad-talk[1] *noun* **1.** (CarA). **Guyn *bad-mouth*[1] 2. USVI *bad-tongue*[1]; StLu, Tbgo, Trin *mové-lang*.** Malicious gossip. **2.** (Jmca, StVn) Carelessly spoken English, with many Creole features; sub-standard spoken English.

bad-talk[2] *intransitive verb* (CarA). **Baha *bad-mouth*[2]; Tbgo *ill-speak*; Dmca, StLu *malpalé*; StLu, Tbgo, Trin *mové-lang*[3]; Guyn, Tbgo *pound somebody's name*; CarA *talk bad about somebody*.** **1.** To speak maliciously (usually in private conversation, about a person, place or thing) intending to cause harm, disadvantage or discredit. **2.** To openly condemn a public figure, a place or a country.

bag *noun* (CarA). See CROCUS-BAG.

bak.ing-pot *noun* (Belz). See THREE-FOOT POT.

bak.ing-i.ron *noun* (Trin). **Antg, Tbgo, Trin *baking-stone*; Belz *comal*; Gren, StVn, Tbgo, Trin *platin(e)*; Guyn, Trin *tawa*.** A flat, circular or rectangular piece of iron, used for baking or roasting ROTI or CASSAVA-BREAD.

bak.ing-stone *noun* (Antg, Tbgo, Trin). See TAWA, BAKING-IRON.

bak.sis (back.sheesh, back.sis) *noun* (Guyn). See BRAATA(s).

ballahoo *noun* (Belz). See KONMÉS.

Bar.ba.dos leg *noun* (CarA). See BIG FOOT.

bark *noun* (CarA). See BUSH-BATH.

bark.ing-down *noun* (CarA). See BUSH-BATH.

base out; bas.ing out *verb phrase* (Belz). See LIME[1]; LIMING.

bath *noun* (CarA). See BUSH-BATH.

bed.room-dress.er *noun* (Guyn). See DRESSER **1**.

bé.ké-nèg *noun* (Dmca, Gren). See BACKRA-JOHNNY.

be.low[1] *adverb, preposition* (Angu, Antg, Bdos, StLu, StVn). Beyond, to the left of, to the west of, to the leeward side of.

be.low[2] *adjective* (Bdos). To the west or to the left.

bem.be *noun* (Belz). A big, strong, somewhat arrogant person; a male or female bully. (Probably from *Bemba*, a Central African people'. Also Spanish *bemba* 'Negro's thick lips'.)

Ber.bice-chair *noun* (Bdos, Dmca, Guyn, Jmca). **Guyn *arm-chair*.** A reclining chair about 7 ft in length, usually covered from the back to the bottom with canvas or carpet, and arms that extend about 2 ft beyond the chair; in some designs, the extension folds in to provide a leg-rest.

bick.le (bit.tle) *noun* (Bdos, Belz, Guyn Jmca). Cooked food; a meal served at the table.

big-able *adjective* (Bdos, Guyn, Trin). Enormous; huge; massive.

big-eye *adjective* (CarA). **Gren, Jmca *craven*; Bdos *cravichous-minded*, *cravishing*; Baha, Belz, Jmca *gravalicious*; Dmca, StLu *g(w)ozyé*; Bdos, Guyn, StVn *lickerish*.** Shamelessly greedy; ready to choose the largest share, especially of food. (Probably a loan-translation from West African languages, Igbo and also Yoruba.)

big-foot *noun* (CarA). **CarA *Barbados leg*; Guyn *filaria*, *swell foot*.** A severe swelling of the leg caused by the bite of a mosquito which deposits a parasitic worm into the flesh, which multiplies in the body, especially the legs; elephantiasis.

Big Four *noun phrase* (CarA). The four CARICOM territories that have the largest populations: Jamaica, Trinidad & Tobago, Guyana, and Barbados.

big.gi.tive *adjective* (BrVI, Guyn). **Antg, BrVI *nuff*; BrVI, Guyn *upstarted*.** Showing off, wanting to be noticed and respected by others.

big-talk (big talk) *noun (phrase)* (CarA). Big, empty promises.

big-time *adjective* (CarA). **1.** Important, successful or famous [referring to persons]. **2.** Important-looking, considerable, expensive-looking [referring to things].

big-up[1] *noun* (Bdos). An important person.

big-up[2] *adjective* (Bdos). In a top position, socially highly placed.

big-up[3] *verb* (Bdos). To flatter, praise somebody highly.

bil.ly-boat *noun* (Grns, StVn). See MOSES.

bit.ter-cup *noun* (Guyn, Jmca). A cup made of the wood of the lignum vitae tree in Guyana or the bitter-wood tree in Jamaica, which, if water is placed overnight in it draws out the bitterness of the wood, and this water is then used as a folk medicine against fevers or poor appetite.

blue-soap *noun* (CarA). A very hard, blue, cheap kitchen soap that is also used on laundry.

blue-vex *adjective phrase* (CarA). Furious.

Bo.bo-Johnny *noun* (StKt). See COUNTRY-BOOKIE.

bo.bol *noun* (ECar). Organized fraud or corrupt practices by senior persons in a company or in government administration.

bo.bol.ise *verb* (Tbgo, Trin). To steal a company's public funds or property by fraud, together with others.

bo.bo.list *noun* (ECar). One who steals the public's or a company's funds.

bold-face *adjective* (ECar). See FACETY.

bossman *noun* (CarA). The man in charge; the top man; the winner; Sir (a form of address used by one man to another).

B

bot.tle-flam.beau *noun* (StVn, Trin). **Gren, Guyn, StKt** ***bottle-lamp*****; Gren, Guyn** ***bottle-torch*****; Dmca** ***bouzay*****; Bdos** ***slut-lamp, smut-lamp*****; CayI, Dmca, Gren, Trin, USVI** ***torch***. A bottle half-filled with kerosene and stuffed with a cloth wick, used as a home-made lamp out of doors, and also for catching crabs at night. (From *bottle* + *flambeau* (French 'flame').)

bot.tle-lamp *noun* (Gren, Guyn, StKt). See BOTTLE-FLAMBEAU.

bot.tle-torch *noun* (Gren, Guyn). See BOTTLE-FLAMBEAU.

bot.tom *noun* (Angu, Bdos). A low-lying piece of land that is, or can be cultivated, sometime surrounded by sloping ground (as in Anguilla).

B

bouch-kabwit *noun* (Dmca). See GOAT-MOUTH.

bou.zay *noun* (Dmca). See BOTTLE-FLAMBEAU.

box *noun* (Guyn). See SUSU.

box-hand *noun* (Guyn). See SUSU-HAND.

box-o.ven *noun* (Guyn). **Bdos** ***Dutch oven*** **1**. A portable, wooden, structure resembling a cupboard about 5 ft high, 4 ft wide and 3 ft deep with a closed door; it is fully lined on the inside with tin or aluminium sheets and its two or three shelves are also lined; a lighted COAL-POT on its floor supplies the heat used for baking.

braa.ta(s) (bra.ta, broth.a, brought.a) *noun* (Antg, Belz, Jmca, Mrat, Tbgo, USVI). **Guyn** ***baksis, braatas*****; Tbgo, Trin** ***lanyap*****; Guyn** ***overs*****; Gren** ***pwayen***. **1.** An extra bit of something purchased or some other small gift added by a seller, especially in the marketplace, to encourage the buyer to return. **2.** Any unexpected extra gain, advantage or some welcome feature.

break.away *noun* (ECar). Music for dancing and having a good time.

break.away *adjective* (ECar). Rhythmic beat of music that would make people dance without restraint.

break.er *noun* (TkCa). See GABION (-BASKET).

bring-and-car.ry[1] *intransitive verb* (StVn). To carry news; bear tales.

bring-and-car.ry[2] *noun* (StVn). **Angu, Bdos, StVn** ***busy lickum*****; Jmca, StVn** ***carry-go-bring-come*****; Bdos** ***lick-mouth***. A gossip; a news-carrier; a tale-bearer.

Bro.ken Tri.dent, The *noun phrase* (Bdos). The name of the national flag of Barbados.

brought.up.sy *noun* (Antg, Bdos, Gren, Trin). Good manners; appropriate behaviour that shows a well-trained upbringing. (From *(well) brought up* + *sy* as in 'courtesy'.)

brown-skin *adjective, noun* (CarA). **Bdos, Guyn** ***cob***. A person whose skin is less than quite black, of light or dark brown skin; a COB.

buck.et-a-drop *adverb* (Gren, Guyn, Tbgo). **1.** [Of rain or tears] In large amounts. **2.** PHRASES **2.1 cry bucket-a-drop** *verb phrase* (Tbgo). See CRY LONG WATER (CarA). **2.2 rain falling bucket-a-drop** *idiomatic phrase* (Gren, Guyn). It is raining heavily.

bull *noun* (Bdos, Guyn). A semicircular piece of paper attached to a kite to make a humming sound as it flies.

bum-drum *noun* (Bdos). A large bass drum (played on both ends with hands and drumstick in a TUK-BAND). (So called because of the booming sound it makes.)

bush-bath *noun* (CarA). **CarA** ***bark, barking-down, bath*****; Mrat, StKt** ***wash-down***[2]**; TkCa** ***washing-down***. A herbal bath prepared from a combination of various medicinal herbs and pieces of the bark of particular trees, intended to heal a persistent sickness or to drive away evil spirits from the body.

bush.ie *noun* (Guyn). See BUSH-RUM.

bush-rum *noun* (Gren, Guyn, Trin). **Trin *babash*; Guyn *bushie*, Gren, Grns, StVn *jack-iron*; Trin *mountain-dew*.** Unlicensed (very strong) rum distilled in secret from a mixture (called a ***wash***) of molasses, ammonia, lemons, in a home-made vessel.

bush-tea *noun* (CarA). Any infusion of dried herbs or 'weeds' that are thought to be medicinal, and sometimes their roots and flowers, used to treat some bodily ailment, or used by older folk to maintain good health.

bu.sy-lick.um *noun* (Angu, Bdos, StVn). See BRING-AND-CARRY.

buss a lime *verb phrase* (Trin). See LIME[1].

butt and bound (on) *verb phrase* (Bdos, StVn). [Of property] To have a common boundary with (another piece of land, a road, etc.). (From Standard English *abut* meaning 'to fix or mark out the limits of (land, etc.) lengthwise'.)

bwa *noun* (Dmca, Gren, Tbgo, Trin). See FIGHTING-STICK, STICK-FIGHTING.

bwa-bwa dancer *noun phrase* (StVn). See STILT-MAN.

bwa-man *noun* (Dmca, Gren, StLu, Tbgo, Trin). See STICKFIGHTER.

ca.cique *noun* (CarA). An Arawakan chief often referred to as 'king' of an island or of a large area of land. (From Arawak *kashikwali* 'male head of a household'.)

ca.doo.ment *noun* (Bdos). See KADOOMENT.

can.dle-grease *noun* (Bdos). See SOFT-CANDLE.

cane-piece *noun* (CarA). A small landowner's piece of land on which sugar-cane is cultivated on contract to the nearest factory.

ca.reen.age *noun* (Bdos). See CARENAGE.

ca.re.nage *noun* (Gren, Trin, USVI). **Bdos *careenage*.** An inner harbour or shallow draft where small vessels especially schooners, were careened or turned on their sides for repairs.

Ca.rib *adjective, noun* (CarA). **1.** (Of or belonging to) any member of an ethnic group of warlike people, native to the northwestern regions of South America, including the Guyanas, and the East Caribbean islands, especially Trinidad, St Vincent and Dominica (also refers to their language). (From Spanish *Caribe* which originally came from Arawak *karifidu* 'Carib'.) **2.** (Dmca) (Of or belonging to) any of the mixed Creole descendants of ISLAND CARIBS who inhabit the central east coast of Dominica and speak French Creole. **3.** (Belz) (Of or belonging to) any of the BLACK CARIBS or GARIFUNA; (also of) their language.

Ca.rib.be.an *adjective* **1.** Of or belonging to the chain of islands from Trinidad to Cuba, but also including the South and Central American rimlands of Guyana and Belize. **2.** [In a general sense] WEST INDIAN (referring to the English-speaking territories of the region, including the Bahamas). **3.** [Referring to all peoples of the area] Antillean.

Ca.rib.be.an *noun* **1.** The Caribbean; the WEST INDIAN islands as a geographical unit. **2.** The Caribbean Sea. **3.** The peoples of the entire area as a cultural group.

Ca.rib.be.an Com.mon Mar.ket *noun phrase* (CarA). A trading arrangement between the 12 member-states of CARIFTA, established through the Treaty of Chaguramas in Trinidad (1973) to create industrial programming within the Association, and common negotiating positions in relation to external trading.

Ca.rib.be.an Com.mu.ni.ty *noun phrase* (CarA). **CarA *CARICOM*.** A legal international grouping, first established by the GEORGETOWN ACCORD (1973) and then expanded in 1974 to include the 12 member-states of the CARIBBEAN COMMON MARKET and the Bahamas, in order to promote cooperation in all essential fields of national economic development and to coordinate foreign policies.

C

Ca.rib.be.an.iza.tion *noun* (CarA). The act or process of Caribbeanizing.

Ca.rib.be.an.ize *verb* (CarA). To make something (such as an institution or festival etc.) CARIBBEAN in staffing, composition or appearance.

cas.cade *verb* (Baha). **1.** To vomit. **2.** (Jmca) To have a heavy menstrual period.

cat-boil *noun* (CarA). **Antg, Gren, StVn, Tbgo, Trin *cattle-boil*.** A swelling on the eye thought to be a penalty for taking back something that was freely given away.

cat.sprad.dle *verb* (Bdos, Trin). **1.** To fall headlong and sprawl on the ground. **2.** *transitive verb* (Bdos) ***maulsprig*.** To beat someone to the ground with heavy blows. (Probably refers to a cat falling from a height on its outstretched paws + *spraddle* 'to sprawl'.)

cat.tle-boil *noun* (Antg, Gren, StVn, Tbgo, Trin). See CAT-BOIL.

Cay.man Brac.er *noun phrase* (CayI). An inhabitant of Cayman Brac, the second largest of the Cayman Islands. Usage: The /-k/ sound of the place name is kept in the noun of nationality.

cen.tri.fu.gal; cen.tri.fu.gal bas.ket, cen.tri.fuge *noun (phrase)* (CarA). [Sugar industry] A machine that separates sugar crystals from molasses, which has the form of a large cylindrical metal basket, vertically mounted with many tiny holes, through which the liquid molasses is expelled as the basket rotates at very high speed, leaving the sugar crystals trapped inside it.

cha.ben *noun* (Dmca); **cha.bin (e) (sha. been)** (StLu, Trin). **StVn *raggay* 1.** A person of mixed African and European descent with a pale brown skin, coarse reddish hair, sometimes freckles, and greyish eyes. (French Creole from French *chabins* 'the sheep of Berry with very thick wool, as long as goats' hair'. In France this type of animal was thought to be a cross between a sheep and a goat, and this sense was transferred from the animal to this particular type of black half-breed.)

cheups[1] (chupse, chupes) *exclamation, noun* (Dmca, Gren, Tbgo, Trin). See SUCK-TEETH. See also STEUPS, a frequent alternative spelling and compare SUCK-TEETH.

cheups[2] (cheup, chupse, chupes) *intransitive verb* (Dmca, Gren, Tbgo, Trin). See SUCK YOUR TEETH.

chi.cle.ro *noun* (Belz). A man employed to tap or 'bleed' the gum of the SAPODILLA-TREE for export. (A Spanish loanword.)

chick.en-wire *noun* (BrVI). See WIRE-MESH.

chil.dren-property *noun* (Guyn). See FAMILY-LAND.

chi.na.man *noun* (CarA). [Cricket] A left-arm bowler's ball spun from the wrist and turning into the right-handed batsman. (Refers to Ellis 'Puss' Achong, a Chinese West Indian test cricketer who first bowled that kind of ball at Manchester, England, in 1933 and dismissed an English batsman, who remarked, 'Fancy being bowled by a bloody Chinaman!')

Chi.nee-cre.ole *noun* (Trin). **Guyn *Chinee-dougla*; Jmca *Chinee-royal*.** A person who has one Chinese parent and one African or East Indian parent. (*Chinee* (from *Chinese*) + *creole* 'a black or light-complexioned person born in the West Indies.)

Chi.nee roy.al *noun* (Jmca). See CHINEE-CREOLE.

Cho! *exclamation* (Jmca). **1.** Exclamation of mild disgust, impatience or annoyance. (Compare Twi *twô* 'Surely! Also Ewe *tsoo* 'exclamation of surprise'.). **2.** Exclamation of disbelief.

Christ.mas bank; Christ.mas bank ho.li.day *noun phrase* (Bdos). Boxing Day; 26 December.

clean-skin(ned) *adjective* (CarA). **1.** Having a dark, smooth face and flawless skin. **2.** See CLEAR-SKIN(NED).

clear-skin(ned) *adjective* (CarA). **CarA *clean-skin(ned), clear, fair*[1], *fair-skin(ned), light-skin(ned)*.** Having a very light or light-brown complexion and soft hair.

clear su.gar *noun phrase* (Bdos). The lightest brown, straw-coloured sugar, with extremely fine crystals from which most of the molasses has been extracted, so it is less sweet, but preferred at table. See DARK SUGAR, WHITE-SUGAR, YELLOW-CRYSTAL SUGAR.

clo.set *noun* (CarA). An outside wooden pit toilet. (Probably from English 'water-closet', but the Caribbean English closet does not flush.)

cob (caub, cawb) *noun* (Bdos, Guyn). **CarA *brown-skin*; Bdos *cob(b)-skin(ned)*; Guyn *cobre*.** A person with brown skin; also used to describe any person who is not quite dark. (Probably from Portuguese *cobre* 'copper' or *caboclo* 'copper-coloured, red-skinned', both of which forms might have produced loanwords. Compare also Twi *kɔbere* 'copper', Ewe *kɔba* 'copper coin', Yoruba *kobo* from English copper).

co.bre *noun* (Guyn). See COB.

co.lour.ed *adjective* (CarA). [Of persons] Having a brown, light-brown or CLEAR skin, being of mixed black and white races; not East Indian and not dark-skinned; racially mixed as seen from the person's skin and hair.

C

co.mal *noun* (Belz). See BAKING-IRON. (Central American Spanish *comal* from Aztec *comalli* 'thin earthenware dish for baking tortillas'.)

com.(m)es *noun* (Gren, Tbgo, Trin, USVI). See KONMÈS.

cook-shop *noun* (Guyn). See EATERY.

cool.er *noun* **1.** (Guyn). See DEMERARA-WINDOW. (So called because of the design which keeps out the sun, but allows air to enter through the closed, wooden, louvred window; also in earlier times, a block of ice was placed there to cool the intake of air). **2.** (StKt, TkCa) A DUTCH-JAR (especially one used in the process of distilling rum).

coo.noo-moo.noo. cu.nu-mu.nu *noun* (CarA). See KUNU-MUNU.

corn-jar *noun* (Bdos). **Antg *England-jar*.** A sturdy earthenware wide-mouthed jar about 2½ ft high, wide at the shoulders and tapering towards the base, formerly used for importing salt-pork from England for labourers.

cotch[1] *noun* (Jmca). See SCOTCH.

cotch[2] *transitive verb* (Jmca). **1.** To squeeze somebody or something into a narrow space. **2.** *intransitive verb* To share uncomfortable or inconvenient lodgings with somebody.

co.tay-ci co.tay-la (co.té-ci co.té-la) *noun phrase* (Dmca, Tbgo, Trin). See KOTÉ-SI, KOTÉ-LA.

coun.try-book.ie *noun* (ECar). **StKt *Bobo-johnny*, BrVI, Guyn, Mrat Nevs, StKt, Tbgo *country-booboo*; Bdos *country-buck*.** An unrefined person, especially one from the country come to town; a person who is easily fooled. (From *country* + *bookie,* perhaps = *buckie.* Compare English *buckie* 'a perverse person' perhaps also influenced by BUCK.)

C

cra.ven *adjective* (Gren, Jmca, Nevs, StVn, Tbgo, Trin). See BIG-EYE[1].

crav.en.ous *adjective* (StVn). See BIG-EYE[1].

crav.i.chous-mind.ed (crav.ish.ing, crav.i.cious) *adjective* (Bdos, Trin). See BIG-EYE[1].

cre.ole *noun* (CarA). [Referring to people] **1.** A person whether of European or African origin born in the New World, particularly the Caribbean. (From Spanish *criollo* adapted from Portuguese *crioulo*). **2.** [Referring to animals] (Bdos, Trin) A race-horse bred in the island. **3.** [Usually with a capital C, referring to language] **(i) StKt *bad-talk*; Guyn *creolese*; Jmca *patois*.** The name used, mostly at university level, for any one of a family of languages developed in Caribbean territories out of the contact of the languages of enslaved Africans with one or more European languages, namely, English, French, Spanish, Portuguese or Dutch, used as a first language for later generations, and surviving in many places today as a common language among their descendants. **(ii) Dmca, Gren, StLu, Trin *French Creole, Kwéyòl*; CarA *Patwa*.** A modified (and sometimes systematically written) French-based form of such language current in the Caribbean.

cre.ole *adjective* (CarA). **1.** [Of persons] Born in and [of animals] bred in the Caribbean. **2.** Of, belonging to, or typical of the lifestyle and culture of today's black West Indians from which come many compounds, such as ***creole cooking/food, creole culture, dance, music,*** etc.

cre.ol.i.za.tion *noun* (CarA). The process or stages of being CREOLIZED. Usage: This term is now usually applied to language(s).

cre.o.lize *verb* (CarA). **(i)** To develop marked Caribbean characteristics. **(ii)** To cause something that was originally foreign to become Caribbean in character.

cro.cus-bag/sack (cruck.uss, kro.kos-bag, ku.kus-bag) *noun* (CarA). **CarA *bag, sugar-bag*.** A sack about 2 ft wide and 4 ft deep, made of brown, coarse-woven jute, normally used for the selling of rice, or sugar. (Originally from the shortened form of the botanical name of the plant that yields the fibre *jute*, namely *Corchorus*, that gradually changed for ease of pronunciation and became *crocus*, among the folk.)

crop-o.ver *noun, adjective* (CarA). [Sugar industry] **1.** (CarA) The end of the sugar-cane harvest and activities related to this period. **2. Bdos *Crop-Over*.** National festivities (originally observed since the

1970s) during July to mark the end of the sugar-cane harvest, ending with a national holiday for KADOOMENT.

crop-season (crop-time) *noun* (CarA). [Sugar industry] The period for the reaping of the sugar-cane harvest; it usually occurs during the early months of the year in the Eastern Caribbean, hence the idea of a season. However, in places like Guyana, where there were two crops per year, there were two ***crop-times***.

crown land *noun phrase* (CarA). All land in a British Caribbean territory that is not privately or commercially owned, including foreshore, river-beds, forest-lands and mountains. (Owned by the British crown.)

cu.nu-mu.nu *noun* (CarA). See KUNU-MUNU.

daa.da (da.da) *noun* **1.** (Dmca, Guyn). A term of respect for an old black woman (usually poor and often also a child's guardian or nurse). (Compare Ewe *dada* 'mother', Fante *dada* 'old'.) **2.** (Guyn, Trin) [Indic] Paternal grandfather; also a term of respect for the eldest brother in the family. (Hindi *daadaa* 'paternal grandfather'.)

dam *noun* (Guyn). **1.** Any embankment of packed mud built to enclose a cane-field or rice-field and control their irrigation, also used as a footpath by labourers. **2.** Any country road or path surfaced with mud.

dark eyes *noun phrase* **1.** (CarA) Dimness of sight. **2.** (Bdos, Guyn) Dizziness associated with BAD FEELINGS.

dash *transiive verb* (CarA). To toss, throw, or pitch (not necessarily violently). PHRASE **dash a lash in (somebody/something)** To strike somebody or something violently with a whip.

daugh.ter *noun* (CarA) [Rastafarian] Any young female black member of the RASTAFARIAN sect.

day *noun* PHRASES **1. for days** (ECar) Very or extremely (good). **2. in all my born days** *adverb phrase* (CarA) In all my life. **3. see your days** *verb phrase* (Guyn) CATCH HELL.

day-boat *noun* (Bdos). A small fishing-boat, powered by an engine, but with no refrigeration capacity, meaning that it can only make one-day fishing trips.

day-clean *noun* (CarA). Dawn; the brigheness of daybreak before sunrise. (Probably translated directly from West African langauges.)

dead[1] *verbal adjective* (CarA). Be dead, has, have died.

dead[2] *noun* **1.** (CarA) A corpse. **2.** (Bdos, Guyn) Trouble or some problem that is entirely your own. (A shift in meaning from the general sense of the word in Standard English to a specific person.)

dead-house *noun* (Bdos, Belz, Guyn, Tbgo). The house where a deceased person lived.

dead-wa.ter *noun* (CarA). The water in which a corpse has been washed and which some people believe has supernatural properties.

deal *intransitive verb* (Belz, Dmca, Gren, Guyn, Tbgo, Trin). To practise witchcraft in such a way as to involve trading living souls or 'dealing' with the devil.

deal.er *noun* (Bdos, Guyn). A person, usually a man, who DEALS.

dear-aunt *noun* (Bdos, Guyn). A term of address for a great-aunt or an aunt much older than your parents.

Demerara-shutter

De.me.ra.ra-shut.ter/-win.dow *noun* (CarA). **Guyn *cooler* 1.** A wooden, close-louvred window, about 2 ft wide and 4 ft long, with a hinge at the top, and held open by a stick attached to its base. (From DEMERARA which is the place where it was originally designed, to keep out the heat of the sun as well as the rain.)

De.me.ra.ri.an *noun* (Guyn). A native of British Guiana (now Guyana). (Some older folk in the Caribbean still use this name for a Guyanese.)

de.por.tee *noun* (Jmca). See RECON.

dirt-box *noun* (Belz). A wooden garbage box, with a lid and a door, often built on to a house.

dis.course[1] *noun* (Belz, Guyn). An informative or enlightening exchange of gossip. (Tends to be used more by rural or older speakers.)

dis.course[2] *intransitive verb* (Belz, Guyn). To have an intelligent discussion or speak carefully on a serious subject. (Found in English dialectal usage 'to talk, hold conversation with'.)

dix.ie (dix.y) *adverb* (Bdos). PHRASES **1. behave/get on dixie** *verb phrase* (Bdos). To quarrel noisily with somebody; to make a big fuss. **2. do dixie** *verb phrase* (Bdos). To make a huge success of whatever is being done; to make things go the way you want to. (Refers to American Dixieland jazz music which caused quite a stir in ballroom dancing in the 1930s.)

djan.mèt (ja.met(te)) *noun* (Dmca, StLu, Tbgo, Trin). People of a low and disreputatble class; belonging to the slums. (French Creole from French *diamètre*, 'diameter', referring to a line dividing the upper from the lower half of the social circle, but usually regarded as referring to a woman of loose character.)

doc.tor-shop *noun* (CarA). A pharmacy; a chemist's shop; a drugstore. (Formerly widely used in the Caribbean and probably spread by English people. Now only used by older folk in rural areas, and generally replaced by DRUG-STORE.)

do-flick.y (doo.flick.y) *noun* (Bdos). **1.** General name for any gadget or tool, etc. **2.** Any organized event during a folk-festival season such as CROP-OVER.

Do.min.i.can *adjective, noun* (CarA). A person (or thing) native or belonging to the island of Dominica in the Lesser Antilles. □ Distinguished from the similarly written ***Dominican*** which refers to a native of the Dominican Republic in the Greater Antilles by the fact that the stress for the native of the island of the Lesser Antilles falls on the third syllable, whereas the stress of the island of the Greater Antilles falls on the second syllable.

dou-dou (doo.doo) *noun* (Dmca, Gren, StLu, Tbgo, Trin). A term of endearment; Darling; my little sweetheart. (French Creole from French *doux* 'sweet' which is reduplicated). □ Used most popularly in Trinidad, but copied through calypsos by many in the Eastern Caribbean.

down-is.land *adjective* (USVI). Of or belonging to one of the lesser developed islands to the south and east of the US Virgin Islands.

dray; dray-cart *noun* **1.** (Bdos) A four-wheeled, V-shaped cart, about 10 to 15 ft long, with high-sides and drawn by a mule, used especially in the past for transporting cut canes from the field to the factory. **2.** (Guyn) A flat, open-sided four-wheeled cart about 16 ft long, usually drawn by two donkeys, and used especially in former times for transporting domestic goods over long distances.

Dray-cart

dread[1] *noun;* **dread bro.ther, dread. locks-man** *noun phrases* (CarA). **1.** [Usually plural] A black male member of the RASTAFARIAN movement, who wears his hair uncut and falling in long, plaited, often matted locks over his shoulders. **2.** Any person who adopts a similar hairstyle and appearance.

dread[2] *adjective* (CarA). RASTAFARIAN; belonging to or associated with the DREADS.

dread-lock.ed *adjective* (CarA). [Of a man or boy] Having your hair in DREADLOCKS.

dread.locks (dread-locks, dread locks) *noun (phrase) plural* (CarA). **CarA *locks*.** The hairstyle of a black person, adopted as characteristic of a RASTAFARIAN, the hair remaining uncut and falling in plaited or matted locks over the shoulders.

dread-talk *noun* (CarA). **CarA *Rasta talk*.** The RASTAFARIAN group dialect of English, in which the vocabularly of creolized English is imaginatively recreated and the personal pronoun system is used to represent the believer's view of the world.

dress.er *noun* **1.** (Bdos, Jmca). **Guyn *bedroom-dresser, dressing-case/-table, vanity*.** A lady's dressing-table, as a piece of bedroom furniture with a mirror, and drawers in which clothes are kept. **2.** (Dmca, Guyn, StLu) **Angu, Bdos, Jmca, Trin, USVI *press*. (i)** A wardrobe; a clothes closet. **(ii)** A cupboard. **3.** (Bdos, CayI, Guyn). **(i) Guyn *kitchen-dresser*.** A kitchen counter or table, on which food is prepared (meat dressed, etc.) and sometimes washed WARES put to drain. **(ii) Bdos, Guyn** (Used loosely) **Bdos** WAGON. (Compare general dialectal use in England, Scotland and Ireland 1. 'a long kitchen sideboard, sometimes fixed to the wall, on which crockery, etc. is placed'. Also in Irish English; *Dresser* 'a set of shelves and drawers in a frame in a kitchen for holding plates, knives, etc.' – *English as We Speak It in Ireland*, 251.)

driv.er *noun* (CarA). [Sugar industry] **1.** [Hist] **CarA *slave-driver*.** A trusted enslaved male in charge of a labour gang of enslaved people, whom he controlled with a whip. **2.** [In post-slavery times] The male assistant of an overseer, put in charge of a small work-force.

drop-cord *noun* (CarA). **CayI *expansion-cord*.** An extension electric cord usually fitted with a bulb at one end; an extension cord for any power-tool.

drug-store *noun* (CarA). See DOCTOR-SHOP.

dup.py[1] **(dup.pie)** *noun* (Baha, Bdos, Belz, CayI, Jmca). **Baha, ECar *jumbie*.** A harmful, invisible supernatural being, believed to be raised from the dead; an evil spirit.

dup.py[2] *adjective* (Baha, Bdos, Belz, CayI, Jmca). **ECar *jumbie*[2].** False; misleading; comical; of low status.

Dutch jar *noun phrase* (Guyn). **Bdos *corn-jar*; Antg *England-jar*.** A large wide-mouthed earthenware jar sometimes as deep as 4 or 5 ft, used mostly for keeping drinking water cool in rural areas.

Dutch ov.en *noun phrase* **1.** (Bdos). See BOX-OVEN.

Dutch pot *noun phrase* **1.** (Baha, CayI). **Bdos** THREE-FOOT POT. **2. Jmca *dutchy*.** A heavy, deep pot (of cast iron or thick aluminium) with a rounded bottom, handles and lid, used for baking or roasting.

Dutch oven

E

ease up[1] *verb phrase* (ECar). **1.** To stop teasing or harassing somebody. **2.** To help somebody out of a difficult situation.

ease-up[2] *noun* (ECar). Help given to or received by somebody in a difficult situation.

eat.er.y *noun* (Bdos, Guyn, StVn). **Guyn *cook-shop*.** An inexpensive eating-place, usually with its door open to the street, that sells cooked food.

Eatery

eck.y-beck.y *noun* (Bdos). See POOR-WHITE.

E.leu.the.ran *noun, adjective* (Baha). (A person or thing) native or belonging to the island of Eleuthera in the Bahamas.

em.pol.der[1] *transitive verb* (Guyn). To enclose a great area of low-lying land by connected dams in order to allow the area to be drained for cultivation or land development. (English *em* from *en* (as in *enclose*) + Dutch *polder* 'reclaimed bog land'.)

em.pol.der[2] *noun* (Guyn). **1.** The area of land that has been EMPOLDERED. **2.** One or all the connected dams empoldering an area of land.

Eng.land-jar *noun* (Antg). See CORN-JAR.

Eng.lish Church *noun phrase* (CarA). The Anglican Chuch or Church of England.

e.nough[1] *pronoun* (CarA). **CarA** ***nuff***. Plenty; a great amount; a lot.

e.nough[2] *adjective* (CarA). [With special emphasis] Very much; a great many.

e.nough[3] *adverb* (CarA). **1.** So very. **2.** [With an adjective that is understood, but not stated] Overwhelming, oppressive, etc.

es.tate *noun* (CarA). A plantation, whether sugar, cocoa, coconut, etc., including the fields, factory and all living quarters.

ex.pan.sion-cord *noun* (CayI). See DROP-CORD.

ex.pense your.self *reflexive verb phrase* (Bdos, Guyn, Tbgo, Trin). Put yourself to undue expense.

eye-turn *noun* (Guyn, StVn). Dizziness or faintness (from excessive hunger); vertigo.

eye-wa.ter *noun* (CarA). Tears. (A direct translation from several African languages, for example, Yoruba, *omi l'oju* (*water from eye(s)*) 'tears'. Igbo *anya mmili* (*eye water*) 'tears', etc., French Creole (Dmca) *glo-zyé* (*water-eye*) 'tears' etc.)

F

face *noun* (CarA). PHRASES **1. make up your face** *verb phrase* (CarA). **Bdos, Nevs, StKt** ***push up your face*** **2.** (ECar) **skin up your face (i)** To grimace disapprovingly (at food, at somebody, chores, etc.). **(ii)** [Especially of children] To look annoyed (in response to something said).

face-man *noun* (Baha, Jmca). A well-dressed and attractive young man who is a criminal; a con man.

face.ty *adjective* (Jmca). **ECar** ***bold-face***. Bold and impudent. (Probably from a corruption or blend of obsolete English *facy* + influence of *hasty, nasty*.)

fair *adjective* (CarA). See CLEAR-SKIN(NED).

fair-skin(ned) *adjective* (CarA). See CLEAR-SKIN(NED).

false name *noun phrase* (Guyn). A nickname (usually something that is provocative).

fam.i.ly-land *noun* (Bdos, Jmca, Mrat). **Guyn** ***children-property*****; Baha** ***generation-property***. Land that cannot be sold because it is recognized as belonging to all succeeding generations of the identified members of a particular family.

fast (farse, fas', fass) *adjective* (CarA). **1.** (Bdos) ***gipsy***, (Nevs, StKt) ***jeps*****; Bdos** ***malicious***. Too inquisitive, meddlesome, interfering in other people's business. **2.** Impertinent, bold, rude.

fast.ness *noun* (CarA). **1.** Inquisitiveness, interference in other people's business. **2.** Impertinence; boldness; presumption.

fa.vour *verb* **1.** (CarA). **Bdos** ***feature***. [Especially of persons, but also of things] To resemble. **2.** (Jmca) To look like; to look as if. (From older English. See *Oxford English Dictionary favour* v 8. 'to resemble in features; (occasionally) 'to have the look of'.)

fe.de.ra.tion *noun* (Bdos). A noisy brawl or fight involving several people. (Distinguished from the proper noun which refers to the administrative grouping of 10 English-speaking Caribbean territories from 1958 to 1962, known as the Federation of the West Indies or the West Indies Federation.)

feg *noun* (Angu, BrVI, Guyn, USVI). **Bdos *fig*[2]; Gren, Jmca, StVn, Trin *peg*[1]; Baha, Belz *plug*; StLu *slice*; Antg *sprig*.** A section or segment of fruit, especially of a peeled orange, or of garlic, but also a section (especially in the British Virgin Islands of A SUGAR-APPLE or SOURSOP which contains a seed). (The word 'feg' is from Scottish and northern British English pronunciation of *fig*.)

fight.ing stick *noun* (ECar). **Dmca, Gren, Tbgo, Trin *bwa*; Tbgo, Trin *stick*[1].** A stick made of very tough wood, sometimes with a metal ring on each end, used by STICK-FIGHTERS.

fi.la.ri.a *noun* (Guyn). See BIG-FOOT.

fine *adjective* (CarA). **1.** Thin, extremely slender, unusually small. **2.** (Guyn) [Of a person's facial features] Delicate, particularly with straight nose, small nostrils, thin lips and a fairly small face. (In the Caribbean, this term often has the sense of 'nearer European than African in facial lines'.)

fin.ger-board *noun* (Bdos, Jmca). A narrow horizontal piece of board, pointing out a direction or indicating a street name, mounted on a signpost or lamp post.

fin.ny (fi.ni) *adjective* (Bdos, Gren, Guyn, Mrat, StVn). [Referring especially to the hand or foot] Sick; twisted; crippled. (Often found in compounds FINNY-HAND, FINNY-FOOT). (Probably of West African origin, from Fante *mfina* 'stunted'.)

fire-rage *noun* **1.** (Antg, Bdos, Guyn, Tbgo, Trin) Intense, uncontrolled, noisy anger. **2.** PHRASE **pick up/take up sombody's fire-rage** *verb phrase* (Antg, Bdos, Guyn) To take up somebody else's quarrel and pursue it as though it were your own. **3.** (Guyn) **Bdos *fire-tail*** An aggressive person, given to uncontrolled, undisciplined anger; a firebrand.

flask *noun* (Bdos). See HALF-BOTTLE.

flat.tie *noun* (Guyn). See HALF-BOTTLE.

fol.low-fash.ion *noun, adjective* (CarA). **Belz *follow-foot*; Bdos, Guyn *follow-pattern*.** A person ready to imitate what someone else is doing.

fond-name *noun* (Bdos, Guyn). Pet-name; a name used from childhood by family and other close associates.

food-car.ri.er *noun* (Guyn). **Jmca *shut-pan*.** A set of close-fitting enamel containers, held together in rows on a metal rack with a handle, and used for sending or carrying a hot lunch to somebody at work.

food.in *noun* (Guyn). A growing child with a hearty appetite.

food.ist *noun* (Bdos, Guyn). An adult glutton.

force-ripe (forced-ripe) *adjective* (CarA). **1.** [Of fruit] Picked when not quite fully mature and ripened under cloth or paper. **2.** [Of young persons] Precocious and somewhat offensive in behaviour; too advanced in dress or conduct for their age.

fore.day morn.ing *noun phrase (often functioning as an adverb phrase)* (CarA). Before dawn; the time between darkness and sunrise.

for.ty-e.le.ven *numeral adjective* (Bdos, Guyn). A great deal, so many, too many, an unnecessary number of (times, things, persons).

for.ward *adjective* (CarA). [Of a young person] Presumptious; saucy; not knowing your place as a child or youth.

for.ward.ness *noun* (ECar). Boldness; impertinence. (From FORWARD + Standard English suffix *-ness*.)

fraid.y *adjective* (Antg, CayI, Jmca, StVn, Tbgo, Trin). Timid; fearful; afraid or very unwilling to speak up for yourself.

free co.lour.ed *noun* (CarA). [Historical] A person of mixed race (black and white) who had been enslaved, or one of whose parents had been enslaved, whose freedom was paid for or granted before the abolition of slavery.

free.ness *noun* (CarA). **Antg, USVI** ***freebs***. **1.** Something for nothing, a free hand-out of money or other items (expected by the receiver). **2.** A party or picnic at which there is plenty of food and drink, to which you go uninvited, but expecting to share in everything.

free-pa.per *noun* (CarA). **1.** [Historical] A document signed by an enslaver confirming that the enslaved person has been freed.

French Cre.ole *noun phrase* **1.** (CarA). See PATWA. **2.** (Trin) A near-white person, usually with a French family name originating from the late 18th-century immigrants to Trinidad from Martinique and Guadeloupe.

fresh *adjective* **1.** (CarA). [Referring to young persons and old men] Sexually bold; making suggestive advances to members of the opposite sex. **2.** (Guyn, StVn) [Of meat, chicken] Raw-smelling; unseasoned (but not stale). **3.** (Bdos, Tbgo, Trin) [Of fish] Rank and unpleasant-smelling; stale-smelling. **4.** (Bdos) [Of music] The latest and most popular.

fresh.ness *noun* (CarA). Impertinence (especially the type that is sexually suggestive).

friend[1] *noun* (CarA). A lover; a sexual partner.

friend[2] *verb* (CarA) **1.** To form a sexual relationship. **2.** PHRASE **friend/friends with somebody** *verb phrase* (CarA). To have a sexual relationship with somebody without marriage.

frupse *noun* (Bdos, Guyn). A mean, worthless, little person; a person (or thing) of no account.

frup.sy *adjective* (Bdos, Guyn, Trin). Totally worthless-looking; cheap-looking (thing); bedraggled (person).

full *adjective* **1.** (CarA). [Of fruit] Completely mature; ready to be picked and allowed to ripen off the tree, or to be cooked. **2.** (CarA) [Of a person] Full-grown; able-bodied; mature. **3.** (CarA) Fully qualified. **4.** (Antg, Mrat, Tbgo, Trin) Pregnant. **5.** PHRASES **full of mouth; full of talk/tongue** (CarA) Emptily boastful; bragging but unable to carry out your boast.

funk.y *adjective* (CarA). **1.** Smelly, especially of the human body; sexually attractive [by extension]. **2.** [Of young people's dancing and music to go with that dancing] Exciting, passionate.

ga.bion(-bas.ket) *noun* (Bdos, Guyn). **TkCa** ***breaker***. A cage (about 2.5 ft × 1.5 ft × 1.5 ft) made of tarred wire mesh, packed tight with rocks, stacked closely together to prevent the erosion of soft, seaside land.

Gabion-basket

gal.va.nize (gal.va.nise) *noun* (CarA). **Guyn** ***zinc(-sheet)***. A corrugated metal sheet coated with zinc against rust, and usually used as roofing or fencing material.

Galvanize zinc sheeting

gang-gang *noun* (Guyn, Jmca, StVn, Tbgo, Trin). Familiar way of addressing an old woman; granny.

gap *noun* **1.** (ECar) The short space in the kerb or roadside providing entrance to a property; a short path leading to a house. **2.** (Bdos) A narrow roadway leading to a main road, usually a cul-de-sac.

Ga.ri.fu.na *noun* (Belz). **1.** A dark-skinned race of people descended from a warlike mixed race of escaped Africans and Caribs in St Vincent who were transported by force to an island of the coast of Honduras in 1797; they now live in southern Belize in the township of Dangriga and were formerly known as Black Caribs (a name no longer used). **2.** The Africanized Island-Carib language spoken by these people.

ga.yap *noun* (Trin). See LEND-HAND.

ga.yelle (ga.yal) *noun* (Trin). **1.** An arena for cock-fighting. **2.** A ring or square for stick-fighting. (French Creole from American Spanish *gallera* 'coop for game-cocks', *galleria* 'pit for cockfighting'. It seems that at one time ***gayal*** was reserved for sense 2, but now it has been replaced by ***gayelle***, which covers both senses.)

gear (down/up) for *verb phrase* (Bdos, Guyn, Trin). To prepare for, make yourself ready for (something), by dressing up, taking a position, etc. (Probably an older English survival. Compare *Oxford English Dictionary gear* v.1 (Obsolete) 'to adorn, array, dress'. The phrase *gear down* meaning to 'dress elaborately' is listed in Collymore's glossary for Barbados.)

ge.ne.ra.tion-pro.per.ty *noun* (Baha). See FAMILY-LAND.

George.town Ac.cord, The *noun phrase* (CarA). The agreement signed in Georgetown, Guyana, after the Eighth Conference of Commonwealth Caribbean Heads of Government in April 1973, by which the CARIBBEAN COMMUNITY or CARICOM was established.

geor.gie-bun.dle (geor.gy-bun.dle) *noun* (CarA). **1.** A small bundle of your scanty possessions packed up for you to leave a place. **2.** A collection of odds and ends belonging to somebody.

ghaut (ghut, gut) *noun* (Mrat, StKt, VIls). A valley in a mountain or hill-side; water running into the sea, particularly water coming down a hillside. (Probably a name still used by East Indians in Guyana). See also *Oxford English Dictionary ghaut* 2. 'a mountain pass', of Anglo-Indian origin.)

gin.al[1] **(jin.al)** *noun* (Jmca). A trickster (usually a man); a dangerously cunning person. (Creole pronunciation of Standard English *general*, referring mockingly to cunning and resourcefulness.)

gin.al[2] **(jin.al)** *adjective* (Belz, Jmca). Devious; able to get out of a difficulty by being clever.

girl-child *noun* (CarA). A daughter, young girl.

glass-bot.tle; grass bot.tle *noun* (ECar). One or more pieces of broken bottle (usually lying around where people walk).

goat-mouth *noun* (CarA). **Dmca *bouch-kabwit*** **1.** The ability possessed by some people to cause frustration or minor misfortune by predicting failure.

gob.let *noun* **1.** (Bdos, Guyn). **Bdos, Gren *monkey*.** A covered, brown clay pitcher in which water is kept cool by evaporation. **2.** (Antg, Dmca, Nevs) **Gren *monkey*.** A long-necked, open clay jar for storing and serving cool water. **3.** (Jmca) A large water jug used for toilet purposes.

god-bro.ther; god-sis.ter *noun* **1.** (CarA). The son/daughter of your godparents. **2.** Anyone who has the same godparents as yourself.

good hair *noun phrase* (CarA). [Of a black person] Soft, wavy hair; long hair, indicating evidence of European mixture.

good hand *noun phrase* (CarA). PHRASE **have a good hand** *verb phrase* (CarA). To be successful in planting and growing things. (Probably from West African languages, for example Krio *gud an* 'good hand'; natural expertise at cooking or doing work involving the fingers.)

good head *noun phrase* (CarA). Intelligence; good memory; special aptitude for something. PHRASE **have a good head for something** *verb phrase* (CarA). To be especially good at doing or remembering something. (Probably from African languages and also found in Caribbean French Creole *bon tèt* 'intelligence'.)

grand-charge[1] *noun* (StLu, Tbgo, Trin). A big bluff; loud, empty boast, promise or threat.

grand-charge[2] *intransitive verb* (Tbgo, Trin). To give a false, exaggerated image of yourself.

grand-stand *intransitive verb* (Bdos, Tbgo, Trin). To make a public show, or issue a threat, or take risky action simply to impress others during a dispute.

Gran.man; Grand-Man *noun* (Srnm). The head or chief of a Bush-Negro village or ethnic group in Suriname. (From Spanish *grande* 'great' + Dutch *man* 'man'). □ An official title in Suriname with certain rights attached to it.

grant *noun* (Guyn). A government concession of many hundred acres of forest-land to a person or a company, to carry out industrial logging.

grap *noun* (Dmca, Gren, StLu, Tbgo, Trin). A bunch or cluster (usually of fruit, coconuts, etc.). (French Creole from French *grappe* 'cluster, bunch'.)

grass-knife *noun* (CarA). A sickle.

Grass-knife

grass-piece *noun* (CarA). A pasture.

gra.va.li.cious (gra.bi.li.cious) *adjective* (Baha, Belz, Jmca). See BIG-EYE[1]. (Blend of *greedy* or *grab* + *avaricious* with change from 'r' to 'l'.)

G

Great House (Great.house) *noun phrase* (CarA). The residence of the plantation-owner, usually larger than the other buildings.

ground *intransitive verb* (CarA). To sit and talk with, or among poor, deprived people in gatherings in their own neighbourhood, in order to help them to develop a sense of social and political rights. (A reference to sitting on the ground where the noun becomes a verb.)

ground.ing(s) *noun (plural)* (CarA). **CarA *groundation(s)*; Bdos *groundsing*.** The act of talking together, sincerely and for an extended period of time if necessary, with socially deprived people in their own neighbourhood or homes, many sitting relaxed on the ground.

guard *noun* (CarA). **1.** An object put into a small packet, or a piece of washing blue or garlic put into a cloth, and worn around the neck to ward off evil. **2.** A charmed object, such as a bottle with white spots painted on it and turned upside down on a stick, or an animal's skull put in a vegetable garden to prevent harm from evil eyes.

gut.ta.perc (gut.ta.perch) *noun* (Bdos). A boy's catapult or slingshot made of a small forked stick with a piece of rubber or strong elastic attached to its two ends. (From *gutta percha*, a whitish rubber made from the gum of the gutta-percha tree and used commercially.)

gu.zu(m) (gu.zung) *noun* (Belz, Jmca). **1.** An act or wish by which some supernatural bad influence is believed to adversely affect somebody's effort. **2.** A charm prepared in order to protect somebody against evil. **3.** PHRASE **put/set guzu on (somebody)** *verb phrase* (Belz, Jmca) To try or intend to cause somebody harm by ill-wishing or by some act influenced by superstitious belief.

gwo boug (gros bourge, gros bouge) *noun phrase* (Dmca). A very well-off

G

Great house

upper-class property-owner or one from that type of family; a white, colonial, government top official or local resident VIP; a big shot. (French Creole from French *gros bougre* 'a big chap' with French Creole reduction of the */-re/*. The term *bougre* was derogatory in French and Creole speakers seem to have adopted it in order to refer to their white masters.)

gyp.sy *adjective* (Bdos). **CarA *fast* 1; Bdos *malicious* 2.** Irritatingly inquisitive and likely to gossip about what you have heard or found out. (Probably by shift from noun to adjective. See *Oxford English Dictionary gipsy* 2. 'A contemptuous term for a woman, as being cunning, deceitful, fickle or similar). Usually used to refer to a woman or child.

Ha.bra, Dab.ra and the crew *noun phrase* (Bdos). **Bdos *he, she and thingamerry*; Bdos *the duppy and the dog*; Bdos, StLu *tout moun bakaila*.** A large mixed up crowd, containing anybody you can think of, 'Tom, Dick and Harry'; every possible person imaginable.

ha.ckle *verb* **1.** *intransitive verb* (Jmca). To over exert yourself, to work too hard. **2.** *transitive verb* (Jmca). To harass or cause much trouble to somebody. **3.** PHRASE **3.1 hackle up** *verb phrase* (Baha) To beat up somebody in a fight; to maul.

hag[1] (heg, higue) *noun* **1.** (Baha, Belz, StVn). See SOUKOUYAN. **2.** (Baha, Belz, StVn). An extremely troublesome person. (An obsolete English word. See *Oxford English Dictionary hag* sb[1], 1, 2, 3.)

hag[2] (heg) *transitive verb* **1.** (Baha) To set a bewitching spirit on (a person or a house); to cast an evil spell on (somebody or something). **2.** (Bdos, Belz) To pester or to harass. (Obsolete English *hag* v[2] 'to torment, trouble as the nightmare', etc.)

hail 1. *transitive verb* (CarA). To greet somebody in passing. **2.** [Rastafarian] *formulaic greeting* Hello.

half-a-foot (half-foot) *adjective* (Bdos, Dmca, Guyn, Jmca, StVn, Tbgo). Having lost the whole or part of one leg whether walking on a crutch or a prosthesis.

half-a-hand *adjective* (Guyn, StVn). Having lost the whole or part of one arm. (In Caribbean English, 'hand' meaning the whole arm, so *half-a-hand*. (See HALF-A-FOOT.)

half-a-mad.man *noun* (Bdos) A total idiot.

half-bag *noun* (Guyn, Trin, VIls). A unit of measure, about 112 lb or a hundredweight of rice, peas, sugar, flour, etc.; a bag made to contain this amount.

half-bot.tle *noun* (CarA). **Bdos *flask*; Guyn *flattie, hippie*; Bdos *hip-flask*.** A small, round-shouldered, flat-sided bottle containing about 12 oz of rum; the body is slightly curved so that it can fit conveniently into a man's hip-pocket, hence some of the names. □ By itself, the term is generally known to mean 'of rum'.

half-scald *adjective* (Guyn). **1.** Someone with an unhealthy or unattractive light-coloured skin, obviously a European mixture, a mulatto with reddish skin. Often used to refer to Portuguese in Guyana. **2.** Cheap-looking; of low quality. (From Standard English *half-scalded* with the past tense ending, *-ed* deleted as is normal in Caribbean Creole English.)

hand-bas.ket *noun* (CarA). A small, usually round, sturdy wicker basket with a handle, used for shopping or for carrying a labourer's food into the fields. (So called because it is carried in the hand, in contrast to the large open basket carried on the head.)

hand.sel *noun* (Bdos). A shopowner's first sale for the day or the first taking (usually from the hand of a young person) in a fund-raising effort.

hard-back *adjective* (CarA). A person approaching middle-age or older; old enough to know or do better.

hard-ears[1] *noun* (CarA). Stubborn or persistent disobedience. (Noun made from a direct translation of West African languages, *ears are hard*, usually used in relation to children.)

H

hard-ears[2] *adjective* (CarA). **Belz *ears-hard*; ECar *harden[ed]*; Baha, Belz, Dmca, Gren, Guyn, Nevs, Trin *hard-head[ed]*.** Stubbornly disobedient. (Belz, Bdos, Guyn).

hard-head.ed.ness *noun* (CarA). Stupidity and stubbornness combined.

Hard.ing, Mr *noun phrase* (Guyn). **1.** A name used to refer to a very hard task-master, usually somebody not of the highest authority. **2.** (Bdos) [Historical] The figure of a man, stuffed with straw and wearing a hat, which was ceremonially burnt on the last night of the CROP-OVER festival, meant to symbolize the driving away of hard times that threatened in the future.

hard-seed *noun* (Bdos). **1.** A person who is admired for his skill and competence in what he does. **2.** A young man who is sought after by women.

hard-up *adjective* (CarA). Unable to attract a steady boy or girlfriend.

hawk.er *noun* (Bdos). **Jmca *higgler*.** A street vendor who sells fruits, vegetables or other types of food either by the roadside, or is licensed to sell in an open marketplace.

head *transitive verb* (Bdos, Dmca, Guyn). To carry a heavy load (especially of bananas, sugar-canes) on the head.

head-ker.chief *noun* (CarA). See HEADTIE.

head.tie *noun* (CarA). **CarA *head-kerchief*.** A cloth of either pure white or coloured cotton, worn by a woman, tied around the head, covering the forehead and knotted at the back or side, with two ends sticking out in different ways, which, in former times were meant to send messages to the opposite sex.

heat-cloud *noun* (Bdos, Guyn). A dark, low-hanging cloud accompanied by intense heat, sometimes followed by rain.

heats *plural noun* (Antg, Guyn, Tbgo). Tiny bumps on the skin, sometimes including facial acne, that may not cause any discomfort.

hig.gler *noun* (Jmca). See HUCKSTER.

high-brown *noun, adjective* (CarA). A person of light-brown complexion.

high-co.lour *noun, adjective* (CarA). **Baha, Bdos *high-yellow*.** (A person who is) extremely LIGHT-SKINNED, having a complexion and features that are more European than African.

hip-flask *noun* (Bdos). See HALF-BOTTLE.

hip.pie *noun* (Guyn). See HALF-BOTTLE.

hire-car *noun* **1.** (Guyn, StVn). A taxi. **2.** (Guyn) See ROUTE-TAXI. **3.** (Bdos) A rented car with a number-plate marked H.

hog up *transitive verb phrase* (ECar). **Tbgo *hog at*.** To speak insultingly and roughly to somebody in order to humiliate them.

huck.ster *noun* (CarA). **Bdos *hawker*; Jmca *higgler*; Guyn *trader*.** A person (usually a woman) who trades in fruits, vegetables and non-perishable food items and other domestic items, in some fixed open place, and often with many other similar persons.

hutch *(noun)* (Bdos). A tall, ornamental polished china-cabinet with glass doors and often with drawers in the lower section.

I

in-crop *adjective* (Bdos, Guyn). [Sugar industry] Employed specifically for the reaping of the sugar crop.

in.den.tured la.bour *noun phrase* (CarA). [Historical] The system by which labourers were imported, particularly from India, under special 'indenture' or agreement, to replace enslaved labour in the West Indies after Emancipation.

in.den.ture.ship *noun* (CarA). The hiring, especially of East Indians, under the system of INDENTURED LABOUR, for a fixed period of time.

In.do-Guy.an.ese; In.do-Tri.ni.da.dian, In.do-West In.di.an *noun* (CarA). An East Indian who is a citizen by birth of Guyana, Trinidad or any WEST INDIAN territory.

in.grease.ments *plural noun* (Bdos, Guyn). Savoury ingredients used in cooking or in preparing a meal.

i.tal[1] *adjective* (CarA). [Rastafarian] [Referring to food] Healthy, good to eat because it is produced naturally; vegetable.

i.tal[2] *noun* (CarA). [Rastafarian] Any vegetable, fruit or naturally produced food, as opposed to animal flesh; the food is cooked without salt.

Jack[1] *noun* **1.** Male name used loosely to refer to any person. **2.** PHRASE **give Jack his jacket** *idiomatic phrase* (Bdos, Guyn, Trin). To give credit where credit is due.

jack-i.ron *noun* (Gren, Guyn, StVn). See BUSH-RUM.

Jack Man.do.ra *noun phrase* (Jmca). Name used in the traditional ending of an ANANCY story.

Jah[1] *noun* (CarA). [Rastafarian] God. (From the Hebrew word *Yahveh*). □ A term widely used in the Rastafarian religion for God.

Jah[2] *adjective* (CarA). Belonging to the RASTAFARIAN sect, as a brother.

jip.pi-jap.pa *noun* **1.** (Belz, Jmca). The beige, fine-textured straw, coming from the palm-like leaf blades of a tropical American shrub which is used for delicate straw work. (From American Spanish *Jipijapa*, a town in Ecuador, probably named after the straw which is found in many parts of Central America). **2.** A panama hat.

jive[1] *noun* (CarA). Shallow talk, glib chat. (Probably from Black American English, an extended sense of *jive* 'dance characterized by individualistic expression, improvisation, etc.'.)

jive[2] *intransitive verb* (CarA). See OLD-TALK[2]. **2.** To talk nonsense, deceive by foolish talk.

Joe Heath's (Joe Heap mare) *noun phrase* (Bdos). **1.** A work horse. **2.** PHRASE **like Joe Heath's (Joe Heap) mare** *adjective phrase* Exerting yourself excessively; behaving in an excited, over-busy manner.

John Pub.lic *noun phrase* (CarA). (A collective term for) the ordinary citizen.

jook[1] (juck, juk[1]) *verb* (CarA). **ECar *chook*.** **1.** To poke, stab, or wound. **2.** To prick or pierce (the skin). **3.** [Of a doctor] To give an injection. (There are a number of words in West African languages which sound similar, Fulani *jukka* 'to poke', knock down (of fruit); Nembe *joku* 'to jut out, protrude'. Also in European languages like Dutch *deuken* 'to dent', Scottish dialect *jouk, jook, juck* 'to duck, dodge, cheat'. The spelling ***jook*** is the most frequent.)

jook[2] (juick, juk[2]) *noun* (CarA). **ECar *chook*.** **1.** A jab or a poke; a wound caused by something sharp. **2.** An injection.

K

jook.ing-board (juck.ing-board) *noun* (Bdos, Gren, Guyn, Tbgo, Trin). See SCRUBBING-BOARD.

jump.ing; jump.ing-up *noun* (ECar). Open-air dancing usually by a crowd, to CALYPSO misic.

junk (up) *transitive verb (phrase)* (Gren, Guyn, Jmca, StVn). To chop or cut roughly (especially meat); to cut large, clumsy pieces off (especially cooked meat.)

K

ka.ba-ka.ba (kab.ba-kab.ba) *adjective* (CarA). **1.** [Especially of a person or dress] Slovenly looking; ill-fitting, ill-matched, crude-looking. **2.** Cheap, worthless (especially referring to poultry or livestock); of poor quality. (In Yoruba *kaba-kaba* is widely used as an adjective or adverb 'below standard', 'of inferior quality'; Ewe *kaba-kaba* 'quick and shabby' (usually of work done).)

ka.bo.sé (kal.bo.sé) *adjective* **1.** (Dmca, Gren, StLu). **Dmca *kalbosé*.** Dented; battered; smashed. **2.** (Gren, StLu) Out of shape; unserviceable; [of bodily feelings] aching, limping. **3.** (Antg) [Of a person] Clumsy; crude-looking. (French Creole from French *cabosser* 'to dent, batter, bash in'.)

ka.gaj; ka.gaz *noun* (Guyn, Trin). [Indic] **1.** Any important paper or personal document such as a birth certificate, especially in Trinidad a certificate that would qualify its owner for a job. **2.** Paper money; money in general. **3.** A newspaper. (Bhojpuri from Hindi *kaagaj/ kaagaz* 'paper, document'.)

keep *transitive verb* (CarA). **1.** To organize and run (any group event, such as a wake, a dance, a wedding, etc.). **2.** To be principally responsible for collecting and keeping the money of a SUSU.

keep.er *noun* (ECar). A sexual companion (either man or woman), with whom one lives; a common-law spouse.

keep-miss *noun* (Bdos, Guyn, Tbgo). **Gren, Guyn *kep(t)-miss*; Bdos *kip-miss*; Antg, Tbgo *keep-woman*.** A mistress who is sheltered and maintained, together with any children from the relationship, usually by a married man.

kel.lick (kil.lick) *noun* (Belz, CayI, Tbgo). **1.** (Belz, Tbgo) [Fishing industry] A small anchor. **2.** (CayI) A heavy stone used as an anchor. (Scottish *kellick* 1. 'the mouth of a pickaxe'.)

kep(t)-miss *noun* (Gren, Guyn). See KEEP-MISS.

ker.nel *noun* (Bdos, Guyn). A swollen and somewhat painful gland in the groin, usually because of a wound in the leg or foot that has not been taken care of.

kha.ki-pants *noun* PHRASES **1. all (is)**

(the) same khaki-pants *idiomatic phrase* (Bdos, Gren, StLu, Trin). See ALL IS ONE. **2. the same old khaki-pants** *noun phrase* (Bdos, Trin, StLu). The same thing as before; a repetition of the same (undesirable, stupid, etc.) action(s).

kicks.ing *[verb]-ing participle* (Tbgo, Trin). Making fun; fooling around.

kip-miss *noun* (Bdos). See KEEP-MISS.

kiss-teeth *noun* (Jmca). See SUCK-TEETH.

kitch.en-bitch *noun* (Jmca). A home-made torch made of a condensed milk-tin with kerosene oil and a cloth wick struck through its top; it is fitted with a handle and used to light the way on dark roads in rural areas.

Kitchen-bitch

kitch.en-dress.er *noun* (Guyn). See DRESSER **2.**

kong.kong.sa[1] *adjective* (Jmca, Tbgo, Trin). **1.** Deceitful; hypocritical; likely to betray your trust. **2.** (Antg, Brbu) Biased to the point of being untrustworthy; usually ready to favour somebody of a better class.

kong.kong.sa[2]**; kon.go.seh** *verb* **1.** (Antg, Brbu). To take sides; to take a biased view. **2.** (Guyn) To gossip about somebody; encourage and share in gossip about somebody.

kon.mès (com.(m)ess) *noun* **1.** (Dmca, Gren, StLu, Tbgo, Trin, USVI). **Belz** ***ballahoo***. Noisy disorder; a disturbance; confusion or a confused situation. (French Creole from French *commerce* 'business', with a strong suggestion of it not being quite legal). **2.** (StVn) Scandal; gossip.

ko.té-si, ko.té-la (co.tay-ci co.tay-la, co.té-ci co.té-la) *noun phrase* (Dmca, Gren, StLu, Trin). **1.** Gossip that is usually amusing. **2.** And so on and so forth. (French Creole from French *coter* 'to quote', 17th-century French 'to repeat news', 'to gossip'.)

koud.men *noun* (Dmca, StLu). See LEND-HAND.

ku.nu-mu.nu (coo.noo-moo.noo. cu.nu-mu.nu) *noun* (CarA). A stupid man, especially one easily fooled and controlled by a woman; an idiot. (Probably from Yoruba *kumun* 'bashful, lacking in self-confidence' and Krio *munɔ* 'fool, stupid person'. The two forms could have been joined in Caribbean Creole as other redundant compounds were.)

la.gli (la.glee, la.gley, la.glie) *noun* (Dmca, StLu, Tbgo, Trin). A gum made from the sticky sap of trees like the breadfruit and the balata tree and used to trap birds. (French Creole from French *la glu* 'bird lime' by misplaced juncture.)

lan.yap (la.gniappe, la.yap) *noun* (Tbgo, Trin). See BRAATA.

lar.der *noun* (Bdos). See SAFE.

lard-oil *noun* (Bdos, Gren, Guyn). Oil made from melted and processed pig-fat and widely used for cooking in the past.

last-lick *noun* (CarA). A children's game in which each tries to be the last to hit or touch the other before they part.

la(t).ta *noun* (Bdos, Guyn, StVn, USVI). **Bdos, Trin *lota***. A skin disorder which manifests itself in unhealthy-looking, whitish blotches; a form of vitiligo.

law.less *adjective* (CarA). **1.** Unruly, irresponsible, troublesome. **2.** [Of a woman] Loose, shamelessly vulgar. **3.** [Of conversation] Loose, full of dirty jokes and chat about sex.

la.yap *noun* (Tbgo, Trin). See LANYAP.

leave-pas.sage *noun* (CarA). A paid return passage (usually from a Caribbean territory to Britain) given periodically to a senior civil servant or company official depending on the terms of the contract. □ This was the case before Caribbean English-speaking territories became independent, so it is no longer granted.

L

leg.go-beast *noun* (Gren, Jmca, StLu). A young woman who is morally loose; a prostitute.

lend-hand *noun* **Trin *gayap;* Dmca, StLu *koudmen*; Jmca *pardmer, partnership***. Labour done in a group by a person's neighbours and friends in a large private undertaking, like preparing land for farming or building a house, in return for which the person provides food and drink and commits his own labour to help others in the group.

li.ard[1] *noun* (CarA). A liar. (A survival from English dialect; *liard* is found in Somerset, Devon, Corwall, counties in England.)

li.ard[2] *adjective* (CarA). Untruthful.

lick.er.ish (li.cor.ish, lick.rish) *adjective* **1.** (Bdos, Guyn, StVn). See BIG-EYE[2]. **2. Bdos, Trin, USVI *cravicious*; Gren, Jmca, Nevs, StVn, Tbgo, Trin *craven*; StVn *cravenous*; Jmca *licky-licky*; Gren, StVn *raven*; Guyn *scraven***. Gluttonous, openly and aggressively greedy, particularly over food; ready to eat leftovers.

lick-mouth *noun, adjective* (Bdos). **1.** Cheap gossip; having a tendency to engage in or enjoy cheap gossip. **2. Angu. Bdos, StVn *busy-lick-um***. A person, especially a woman, who participates in cheap or wicked gossip.

lick.y-lick.y *adjective* (Jmca). See LICKERISH[2].

lic.o.rish *adjective* (Bdos, Guyn, StVn), See LICKERISH.

light-skin.(ned) *adjective* (CarA). See CLEAR-SKIN(NED).

lim.ber *adjective* (Gren, Guyn, Jmca, StVn). **1.** [Of a bush, pole, etc.] Slender; bending or too easily bent. **2.** (Bdos) [Of a person's body] Limp; supple.

limb.less *adjective* (Bdos). Astonished; limp with surprise. (*Oxford English Dictionary* gives the original meaning of *limbless* as 'having no limbs, or deprived of a limb'. However, The *English Dialect Dictionary*, citing the word in Dorset and Somerset, gives the meaning as 'all to pieces, utterly destroyed', which is closer to the Caribbean English meaning. The word is now obsolete in Standard English)

lime[1] *intransitive verb* (ECar). **1. Belz *base out*; Trin *buss a lime*; *make a lime*; ECar *pick a lime***. To sit, loaf or hang about with others, usually in some open spot, chatting casually, watching passers-by and sometimes making uncalled for remarks to them. **2.** (ECar) To idle either alone or with a work-group; to chat and relax on the job. **3.** (ECar) To pay a casual visit. **4.** *transitive verb* (ECar) To look on idly at something, often in the company of others, for example ***lime a funeral; lime a wedding***. (Probably originated in Trinidad during World War II, apparently applied to white American sailors from the naval base, who would hang around certain areas in groups. The verb '*to lime*' seems to have come from 'limey', a derogatory term for a white person of low class.)

lime[2] *noun* (Trin). **1.** A spontaneous social gathering, usually of young people, to spend time together chatting and joking. **2.** Any identifiable group of idlers. **3.** The place where such people agree to meet, or meet regularly.

lim.er *noun* (ECar). An idle person, a time-waster.

lime-skin *noun* (Bdos, Guyn). An old felt hat that is out of shape, having become too small for its wearer's head; the brim is usually pulled down to make it fit. (So called because it resembles a half-squeezed lime.)

lim.ing *noun* (ECar). The habit or action of idling in a public place or on a job.

line[1] *noun* (Bdos, Guyn). Any foot-path that runs through or along a cane-field, farm, or large expanse of commercially used land to enable haulage; a rugged track across fields. (Found in Irish dialectal English in the English Dialect Dictionary *line* 4. 'a road'). □ Found in some Guyanese place names, such as ***Skeldon Line-Path, the side-line trench*** etc.

line[2] *transitive verb* (Bdos, Trin). **1.** To lambaste; flog severely.

line-mark *noun* (Bdos). A surveyor's landmark either in the form of an 'X' cut into the coral, or a piece of iron driven into the ground and legally recognized as a boundary mark.

Lit.tle Eight, The *noun phrase* (CarA). The remaining eight island-states – Antigua & Barbuda, Barbados, Dominica, Grenada, Montserrat, St Kitts-Nevis-Anguilla, St Lucia, St Vincent & the Grenadines – after Jamaica and Trinidad & Tobago withdrew from the West Indies Federation in 1962. ('Little' in comparison with the population size and economic power of Jamaica and Trinidad & Tobago, which were the two largest of the ten federated states.)

Lit.tle Four, The *noun phrase* (CarA). The set of Windward Islands – Dominica, Grenada, St Lucia, and St Vincent & the Grenadines – considered as a possible political grouping after the breadown of the West Indies Federation in 1962. ('Little' with regard to the size of the population of each state.)

Lit.tle Sev.en, The *noun phrase* (CarA). The remaining seven island-states after Barbados withdrew in 1965 from the LITTLE EIGHT.

look for (somebody) *verb phrase* (Bdos, Guyn, Jmca). To visit somebody.

locks *plural noun* (CarA). See DREADLOCKS.

locks.man *noun* (CarA). A male Rastafarian.

long-bench *noun* (Belz). See LONG-METER.

long eye[1] *noun phrase* **1.** (CarA). Intense covetousness; overwhelming desire.

long eye[2] *adjective* **1.** (BrVI, Nevs, StVn). See BIG-EYE2. **2.** (Angu, Guyn, Nevs) Annoyingly covetous; illustrating a strong desire for something just seen. **3.** (Jmca) [Of a woman] Having a keen eye for men.

long-foot *adjective* (CarA) [Of a person] Long-legged.

long-me.ter *noun* (ECar). **Belz *long-bench*** A person who is tiresome in speech or conversation.

long-time[1] *adverb phrase* (CarA). **1.** A long time ago; some time ago. **2.** In the past; in days/years gone by. **3.** As promptly as ever.

long-time[2] *adjective* (CarA). Old fashioned.

Low Is.lands, the *noun phrase* (Bdos). A folk name for the other islands of the Eastern Caribbean, especially those where French Creole is spoken.

low-rate *transitive verb* (Bdos, CayI, Guyn, Trin). To belittle or make yourself or somebody else look inferior.

luck.y-seed *noun* (Guyn, Mrat). A smooth, hard, reddish-brown seed about 1½ in. long and somewhat triangular in shape; it is believed, by children especially, to bring good luck.

mac.co (mac.ko, ma.co) *noun, adjective, verb* (Dmca, Gren, StLu, Trin). See MAKO.

ma.ca.pal (me.ca.pal) *noun* (Belz). See WARISHI.

ma.co.cious *adjective* (Gren, Trin). Tending to carry news; spreading scandal.

ma.com.mè(re *noun* (CarA). See MAKOMÈ.

mad blood *noun phrase* (ECar). **1.** An itching of the skin. **2.** (Trin) Goose pimples. **3.** Having a tendency to mental illness.

ma.dwas (ma.dras) *noun* (Dmca, Guad, StLu). **1.** Brightly coloured, usually plaid material used to make scarves, handkerchiefs, or skirts for the national costume. **2.** The headtie or the skirt made from this material; the headtie is worn in different ways depending on the occasion. (From Madras province

Madwas

in India, where the material was manufactured and exported especially during the times of slavery.)

ma.guf.fy (McGuf.fy) *noun* (Bdos). **1.** A person as seen by others, or who sees himself as much more important or knowledgeable than he really is. **2.** Anything that is large and showy.

Main Guard *noun phrase* (Bdos). The Central Police Station in Barbados. (From Standard English *main-guard*, 'the building in which the main guard of a garrison is lodged'.) □ In Barbados, this is the term used instead of 'Central Police Station'.

Main Guard police station

ma.ko[1] **(ma.co, mac.co, mac.ko)** *noun* (Dmca, Gren, StLu, Tbgo, Trin). **1.** A person known to be intensely inquisitive, a gossip or busybody. **2.** A fool, an idiot.

ma.ko² (ma.co, mac.co, mac.ko) *adjective* (Dmca, Gren, StLu, Tbgo, Trin). Extremely inquisitive; meddlesome.

ma.ko³ (ma.co, mac.co, mac.ko) *adjeciive* (Dmca, Gren, StLu, Trin). Huge; too big; unreasonably large. (Probably from Haitian French Creole *makòn* 'many, a bundle of' which is probably from French *marquant* adj 'notable, considerable', becoming Trinidadian French Creole *makò*.)

ma.ko⁴ (ma.co, mac.co, mac.ko) *transitive verb* (Dmca, Gren, StLu, Tbgo, Trin). To mind other people's business; interfere in the affairs of others; gossip and spread scandal.

ma.ko.mè (ma.com.mè(re), ma.cu.meh) *noun* (CarA). **1**. A usually elderly female friend who is your child's godmother. (French Creole from French *macommère* 'fellow-sponsor at baptism; partner at a wedding' moving into 'gossip'). **2**. A woman's confidante, close friend or good neighbor. **3.** (Dmca, StLu). Especially in the form of MAKOUMÈ. A male homosexual.

mak.wèl (ma.cu.elle) *noun* (StLu). A female who is a malicious gossip; the female counterpart of MAKO¹. (French Creole from French *maquerelle* 'a madam'.)

mal.ka.di (mal.ca.di. mal.ca.dy) *noun* (Gren, StLu, Tbgo, Trin). An epileptic fit; epilepsy; convulsions. (French Creole from French *mal caduc* 'falling sickness, epilepsy'.)

ma.li.cious *transitive verb* (Bdos). To meddle in someone else's business; to be annoyingly inquisitive.

mal.pa.lan *adjective* (Dmca, StLu). See MOVÉ-LANG². (French Creole from French *mal parlant* 'evil-speaking' although this combination would not be found in French.)

mal pa.lé (mal par.ler) *transitive verb* (Dmca, StLu). See MOVE-LANG³.

ma.ma.guy¹ *transitive verb* (Gren, Tbgo, Trin). To fool, trick, deceive or mislead by using flattery or false promises. (From Trinidadian Spanish *mamar gallo* 'to suck (the) cock', a metaphor taken from cockfighting in Venezuela referring to a fighting cock that only pretends to, but doesn't really fight.)

ma.ma.guy² *noun* (Gren, Tbgo, Trin). Deceit using flattery; teasing.

ma.roon *noun* (CarA) [Historical]. Any of the descendants of those enslaved people who freed themselves by escaping or engaging in guerrilla fighting, and who established isolated communities in mountain or forest territory (especially in Jamaica).

mas.sa *noun* (CarA). **1.** [Historical] (During slavery, the form of address expected of an enslaved person to) a white planter or any white man belonging to the ruling class. **2.** [In modern times] Any man who shows off his authority. (From Standard English *master* through the loss of the final syllable and the addition of *–a*.)

mas.sa day *noun phrase* (CarA). The time of slavery; also the post-emancipation period, during which blacks were subservient to white rule up to the beginning of the independence of WEST INDIAN states in the 1960s.

mau.vais-langue *noun, adjective, verb* (StLu, Trin). See MOVÉ-LANG.

max.i-tax.i *noun* (Bdos, Trin). **Bdos** ***pick-up***. A small vehicle that can seat up to about 20 persons; it is usually privately owned and used like a bus operating on a fixed route for a fixed fare. (A blend of *maxi(mum) + taxi*.)

meet.ing *noun* (Bdos) See SUSU.

M

meet.ing-turn *noun* (Bdos). See SUSU-HAND.

mè.lé (mê.lée, me.lee) *noun* (Antg, Nevs, Trin, VIls). Gossip; scandal. (French Creole from French *mêlée* 'battle, fray'.)

mesh-wire *noun* (Bdos). See WIRE-MESH.

mill.wall *noun* (Bdos). The cone-shaped stone tower of the wind mill or water mill used to grind sugar cane in the past.

mi.ni.bus cul.ture *noun phrase* (Bdos). **Bdos *ZR culture***. The way in which secondary schoolchildren who use this form of transport behave, including their personal interaction with the drivers and conductors of minibuses serving routes to and from school.

mis.er.a.ble *adjective* (CarA). [Especially of children or sometimes adults or older people] Troublesome; tiresomely demanding, difficult to control; difficult to live or work with.

mo.ko-jum.bie (mo.co-jum.bie) *noun* (Gren, StKt, StLu, Trin, VIls). See STILT-MAN.

mon.key *noun* (CarA). One of two types of clay water-jug. See GOBLET 1. & 2.

moo.jin *noun* (Bdos). A foolish person.

moo.moo (moo-moo) (CarA). A person who is too timid or too shy to speak. (Compare Twi *e-munu* 'a person who is deaf and dumb'. (*The Dictionary of Jamaican English* also cites Ewe and Mende, etc. as sources of this word.)

morne *noun* (StLu). A small round hill. (The source of this word seems more likely to be Spanish *morro* 'hillock' rather than French. Although it is present in many French Creole place-names, there does not seem to be a French noun from which it originates.)

mor.tar *noun* (CarA). A heavy, wooden object, made by hollowing out a receptacle like a bowl in a solid block of cured wood; boiled plantains or root-vegetables are pounded with a MORTAR-PESTLE to make FUFU and other dishes.

mor.tar-pes.tle/stick *noun* (CarA). A heavy wooden pestle about 4 or 5 ft long, and about 3 in. in diameter, used to pound cooked food in a MORTAR.

mos.es(-boat) *noun* (Antg, Bdos, BtVi). **Grns, StVn *billy-boat***. An open wooden boat, about 20 ft long; it is either rowed or motorized and can carry goods and passengers from ship to shore; it is now used by fishermen. (Collymore cites from Gale: 'The Moses was a type of boat used on the Thames around the 17th century. The people of New England who traded quite heavily within the West Indies, saw the need for boats in the islands for carrying sugar to the ships, so they built Moses boats and sold them in the Caribbean. The Moses was usually about 18 ft long and could be easily shipped on top of the lumber that was taken to the West Indies.')

mouch.wê (mouch.oir) *noun* (Dmca). A coloured headtie worn by women, specially tied around the crown of the head with one end sticking up; this item has now become part of the national costume. (French Creole from French *mouchoir* 'handkerchief'.)

Mouchwê

mo.vé-lang[1] **(mau.vais-langue**[1]**)** *noun* (StLu, Tbgo, Trin). **CarA** ***bad-talk***[1]. Malicious gossip; scandalous rumours. (French Creole from French *mauvais* 'bad' + *langue* 'tongue', apparently a direct translation from West African languages comparable to the Creole English phrase BAD-TALK[1]. The grammatically correct French phrase ***mauvaise langue*** does not represent the French Creole expression.) Unlike BAD-TALK, which is usually done behind one's back, MOVE-LANG need not be.

mo.vé-lang[2] **(mau.vais-langue**[2]**)** *adjective* (StLu, Tbgo, Trin). **Tbgo, Trin** ***bad-tongue***[2]; **Dmca, StLu** ***malpalan***. Having a tendency to malicious gossiping; deceitful.

mo.vé-lang[3] **(mau.vais-langue**[3]**)** *transitive verb* (StLu, Tbgo, Trin). See BAD-TALK[2].

mus.tee *noun* (Bdos, Guyn). The child of a white and a mulatto parent. (A corrupt form of Spanish *mestizo*, Portuguese *mestiço* 'half-caste, half-breed', possibly borrowed from Elizabethan English and found in the speech of older and rural folk.)

nash *adjective* (Antg, CayI, Nevs, USVI). Lacking sturdiness of either body or mind; feeble; frail, weak. (Compare *English Dialect Dictionary nesh* adjective found in many English dialects 'delicate in health, weakly, sickly, effeminate'. Also written *nash* in Scottish.)

Neb.(r)u.a.ry morn.ing; nev.a.wa.ry, nev.u.a.ry *adverb phrase* (Bdos, Belz, Guyn). **Guyn** ***never-ready morning***. Never. (A blend of *never* + *February*.)

ne.gro.crat *noun* (Bdos). **1.** Someone who believes that black people of high social status have the right to lead a nation-state of the African diaspora; a member of a locally recognized black elite class, either in the Caribbean or in the United States. **2.** A person of African ancestry who feels that the community of the African diaspora in which they reside should pay homage to them because of social status. (A blend of *negro* + *(aristo) crat*.)

ne(n).nen (nen, nen.nie) *noun* (CarA). **1.** Godmother. **2.** (Affectionate address for) a woman, young or old, who may be the guardian to a young child. (Probably from Efik-Ibibio *mne* 1. 'mother, grandmother, old woman (*mne mne* 'grandmother') 2. 'a term of endearment for a young woman'.)

nev.er-see-come-fo [r]-see *noun* (Gren, Guyn, StVn, Tbgo, Trin). **Bdos** ***new nigger*** **1.** A person whose behaviour indicates that they are seeing the good things of life for the first time. **2.** A person who shows off new things just acquired or who makes an unnecessary and boastful show of new authority or status.

nig.ger-ten *noun* (Bdos). See X.

nut.ten-chops *plural noun* (ECar). Nothing to eat.

Ny.a.bin.ghi *noun* (CarA). [Rastafarian] **1.** A belief system arising out of spiritual resistence to foreign domination; it was introduced into Jamaica around the 1940s from East Central Africa and is becoming the fundamental religion of a large sect of RASTAFARIANS; the emperor Haile Selassie I of Ethiopia is proclaimed the direct descentant of the son of Solomon and the Queen of Sheba and as the promised Messiah. It seeks to liberate all black people from oppression.

2. A member of the Nyabinghi sect or the membership as a whole. (The name comes from East Africa.)

O

old-talk (ole-talk)[1] *noun* (Bdos, Dmca, Gren, StVn, Tbgo, Trin). **1.** Idle chatter; gossip; small talk. **2.** Empty chatter; fine promises that will not be kept. (Probably abbreviated from 'old people's talk' in Trinidad, and is most commonly used in that territory.)

old-talk (ole-talk)[2] *intransitive verb* (Bdos, Dmca, Gren, StVn, Tbgo, Trin). **CarA** ***jive***[2] **2.** To engage in idle chatter; to gossip; to make empty promises.

one-time[1] *adverb* (CarA). **1.** Once long ago. **2.** At one and the same time; in full and immediately.

one-time[2] *adjective* (CarA). **1.** Referring to some time in the past. **2.** Rare; unusual.

own-way[1] *noun* (CarA). [Referring to children] Stubborn disobedience; resistance to instruction or persuasion.

own-way[2]**; own-way.ish** *adjective* (CarA). [Referring to children] Stubborn; self-willed.

over-in-away *noun* (Bdos). Foreign countries.

o.vers *noun* (Guyn). See BRAATA(s).

P

pad.der-ten.nis (pad.dle ten.nis) *noun* (Bdos). See ROAD-TENNIS.

paip.sey *adjective* (Bdos). Pale; weak; ineffectual; unattractive. (Probably from English dialect *papes* 'A sort of thin porridge made of flour and water'. 'A foolish person'.)

pam-pa.lam[1] *noun* (Bdos, Guyn). **Jmca** ***pam-pam, palam-pam***. Fuss and confusion; a noisy row or disorderly behaviour. (Probably from Twi *pam* 'the report of a gun', *pam pam* 'to chase or drive away'.)

pam-pa.lam![2] *exclamation* (Bdos, Guyn). **Antg** ***Pampa-lele!*****; Jmca** ***Pam-pam!*****; StVn** ***pampi-luti!***. An echoic expression usually used by children showing some pleasure in another child's misfortune, such as a flogging, etc.; it is often accompanied by hand wringing.

pan-boil.er *noun* (Bdos, Guyn, StKt). [Sugar industry] **Bdos** ***sugar-boiler***. A professional supervisor of the process of boiling sugar.

pan-cart *noun* (Bdos). A wheelbarrow. (More commonly used among older folk.)

pan.ya-ma.chete *noun phrase* (Belz, Jmca). **TkCa** ***Spanish knife***. **1.** A cutlass or machete with both the edges sharp. **2.** A deceitful person; a hypocrite.

pa.pa.yo! *exclamation* (Dmca, Gren, Tbgo, Trin). Expression of happy surprise.

pap.py-show[1] **(pup.py-show)** *noun* (CarA). **1.** A ridiculous or embarrassing state of affairs. **2.** A person who deserves to be ridiculed; a complete fool.

pap.py-show[2] **(pup.py-show)** *adjective* (CarA). Ridiculous, absurd; disgraceful.

pap.py-show[3] **(pup.py-show)** *transitive verb* (Gren, StLu, Trin). To mock, make fun of, ridicule (somebody).

par.al.lel mar.ket *noun phrase* (Guyn). The recognized trading in household goods on sidewalks or in any other suitable place by unregistered retailers

Parallel market

who travel to other territories to obtain such items. (*Parallel* 'running side by side with' + *market* 'legitimate trade'.)

pard.ner (part.ner, pa(a)d.na) *noun* **1. (i)** (CarA). [Often a casual form of address] My friend, companion. (From Standard English *partner* with the *t* becoming *d*.) □ PARDNER is the form more commonly used by the folk. **(ii)** (Guyn) often in the plural PADNAS. See PORK-KNOCKER(s). **2.** (Jmca) **(i)** A participant in a PARTNER-WORK arrangement. **(ii)** Also see LEND-HAND. **3.** (Jmca) See SUSU. PHRASES **3.1 belong to/throw a partner** *verb phrase* (Jmca) To contribute to a savings scheme (called by that name). **3.2 draw your pardner/partner** *verb phrase* (Jmca). To receive your weekly or monthly lump sum in the savings scheme (called by that name).

pa.shu.ma; pa.shu.ba *adjective* (Guyn, USVI). [Referring to a child] Thin and sickly looking; undernourished; [of fruit] undeveloped; uninviting. (Probably from Arawak *pashima* 'stunted'. The alternative *pachima* also occurs in the USVI and the form *pansoema/passoema* 'slow to develop; wrinkled of fruit and metaphorically of people and children' is found in Suriname. The Surinamese word is said to be of Congo origin, so it may be a loanword in Guyanese Arawak.)

pass-o.ver *noun* **1.** (Bdos). A sudden loss of consciousness; a mild stroke. **2.** (Belz) A shower of rain that passes quickly, driven by a high wind.

peg *noun* (CarA). See FEG.

pe.tit-ca.reme *noun phrase* (Trin). A fairly long dry spell, lasting for a few weeks in the wet season of September and October. (French *petit carême* 'little Lent' meaning 'fasting, layoff', possibly.)

pla.tin(e) *noun* (Gren). See TACHE, BAKING-IRON.

plug *noun* (Baha, Belz). See FEG.

po.ca.te.ry (puc(k).a te.ry, pur.ka.tory) *noun* (Antg, CayI, Guyn). Trouble, mischief, worry. (By the religious influence of Standard English *purgatory* 'place of cleansing punishment' the meaning of which is extended to a state of trouble or confusion.)

po.li.tricks *noun* (CarA) The trickiness of politics. (From a blend of '*politics*' + '*tricks*'.)

poor-white *noun* (CarA). **Bdos *backra-johnny, ecky-becky, red-leg*; Dmca, Gren *béké*.** A descendant, in any Caribbean territory, of the earliest generations of 17th-century white plantation workers from Britain who have remained poor and despised, and usually socially isolated.

pop.pet (pop.pit) *noun* (Bdos). A fool; an idiot; a laughing-stock. (Probably originating from English dialect *poppet* (in Yorkshire, etc.). 1. 'a puppet; figuratively 'a silly, vapid female'.) □ In Standard English *poppet* is a term of endearment for a person who is well loved, particularly a woman.

pork-knock.er *noun* (Guyn). An individual prospecter for gold or diamonds in the rivers or damp soils found in the interior of Guyana, who uses home-made or domestic devices. (From (pickled) *pork* + *knocker* 'a hungry eater of pickled pork', *knock in* in Scottish, English and Irish dialects meaning to 'eat, consume, dispose of food'. Pickled pork was the regular diet eaten by such prospectors at the end of a day's work.)

pound an[d] a crown *noun phrase* (Gren, Guyn, Tbgo, Trin). A lot of money; too high a price. (From Standard English *pound* sterling + *crown* formerly one eighth of a pound). □ Used more by older folk.

press *noun* **1.** (Angu, Antg, Bdos, Jmca, Trin, UWVI). **Dmca, Guyn, StLu *dresser*.** A wardrobe.

pro.vi.sion-grounds/-land *noun* (CarA). [Historical] **1.** A piece of plantation land set aside for enslaved people to cultivate their own food. **2.** Rural farm land, usually far away from its owner's dwelling, cultivated for market gardening.

pup.py-show *noun* (Belz, TkCa). See PAPPYSHOW.

pwa.yen *noun* (Gren). See BRAATA(s).

qua(c).co (qua(c).koo) *noun* (Guyn, Jmca). A rough and gullible black man; any black person who accepts contemptuous treatment. (Probably influenced by a combination of Standard English *quack* + Twi *Kwaku*, day-name for a boy born on Wednesday. In Twi ɔ-*kwaku* also means 'a monkey'.)

quail *intransitive verb* (Bdos, Guyn, Tbgo.USVI). **1. (i)** [Of leaves] To shrivel up, wither, wilt or fade. **(ii)** (Guyn) [Of certain kinds of fruit] To grow soft when very ripe (like plantains) **(iii)** (Grns, StVn) [Of a tree] To dry up, lose its leaves and eventually die. (Evidently a dialectal English survival *quail* v[1] 1. (*obsolote or dialectal*) of persons, plants, etc., 'to fade, wither'.) **2.** *tramsiive verb* (Bdos, Guyn, Tbgo, USVI) **(i)** To cause leaves to wilt by heating. **(ii)** (Bdos) To braise meat. **(iii)** (BrVI) To put (wood) to dry before burning it.

quail.y *adjective* (Trin). Limp from age or loss of quality; dull. (See the historical note at QUAIL.)

quick time *adverb phrase* (Bdos, Guyn, Jmca). Immediately; very promptly; right away.

R

rag.gay (rag.get(te)) *noun* (StVn). See CHABEN.

ra.toon *noun* (CarA). [Sugar industry] **1.** The old stump of a sugar-cane plant that will grow again after the plant is cut. **2. CarA *ratoon-crop*.** The second crop that springs up from the new shoots. (Probably from Spanish *retoño* 'young shoot'.)

ra.ven *adjective* (StVn). **1.** See BIG-EYE². **2. Gren, StVn, USVI.** See LICKERISH.

re.con *noun* (Bdos). **Jmca *deportee*; Trin *roll-on roll-off*.** A used car imported usually from Japan to be resold in Barbados. (Reduced form of 'reconditioned car', meaning the mechanical renovation done to it before it is exported.)

red *adjective* (CarA). **CarA *red-skin(ned)*.** [Referring to a person's skin-colour] Being of any colour between brown to near white, showing different mixtures of black and white races.

Red House, The *noun phrase* (Trin). The House of Parliament in Port of Spain; other government administrative offices are also found in it.

red-leg (red.leg) *noun* (Bdos). See POOR-WHITE.

red nig.ger *noun phrase* (CarA). See BACKRA-JOHNNY.

red-skin(ned) *adjective* (CarA). See RED.

Re.pub.lic Day *noun phrase* (Guyn). 23 February, the date of the Berbice slave rebellion in 1763; now annually observed from 1970 as Guyana's official independence day.

ri.ver.ain *adjective* (Guyn). Of or on land bordering or near to a river.

ri.ver-bot.tom *noun* (Belz, Guyn). A river bed.

road-ten.nis *noun* (Bdos). **Bdos *padder-tennis, paddle tennis*.** A game like table-tennis, but played on a smooth road with a court 20 ft × 10 ft marked out, and an 8-in. wide piece of board used as a 'net' in the middle; the rackets are oval-shaped wooden bats.

roll-on roll-off *noun* (Trin). See RECON.

Red House, Port of Spain

roots *noun functioning as adjective* (CarA). [Rastafarian] **1.** Belonging to or displaying your own (and especially African) cultural origins or heritage; acknowledging or being conscious of common folk origins. (Originally used in Jamaica around the late 1960s as an abbreviation for 'African/Ethiopian roots', and spread through roots-reggae music to American English and the English of other Caribbean territories.) **2.** [Used as a familiar form of address to someone with whom one is on close terms] Good (friend)!

roots.y *adjective* (CarA). Displaying or promoting the display of (particularly African) folk cultural heritage in any type of social behaviour.

route-tax.i *noun* (Trin). **Guyn *hire-car*.** A privately owned car used as a bus, and having a fixed route; its fares are higher than regular bus fares.

rude-boy (rud.ie boy) *noun (phrase)* (Jmca). **1.** A young Black Jamaica male who acts like a social drop-out; he can be from the ghetto, a gang-member or one who has Rastafarian type habits. **2.** (***rudie, rudy***) Any young male or female who behaves like a social drop-out.

S

S

safe *noun* (CarA). **Bdos *larder*.** A moveable cupboard with a wooden frame, usually standing on legs, with fine-meshed doors and sides; it is used to store food items, keeping them safe from insects.

sa.ga (sag.ger) *adjective* **1**. (ECar). [Referring to dress, especially men's] Very fashionable, showy, over-stylish. (Probably from Standard English *swagger* noun and verb, by the reduction of consonant clusters and shift in grammatical function. Also note Krio *swag* 'to walk with shoulders moving from side to side' and Scottish *swag* 'sway from side to side'. The term may have spread through the use of colonial English.) **2**. [Referring to young people and by extension] Unworthy; smart; scampish.

Sa.ha.ra-dust *noun* (ECar). A greyish-brown haze caused by the spread of dust particles blown by the wind from the Sahara Desert across the Atlantic and covering the entire Eastern Caribbean.

salt-pork *noun* (Guyn). **1.** Pickled pieces of the domestic or wild pig usually used by PORK-KNOCKERS. **2.** Pieces of pickled pork on the bone, especially PIG-TAIL, used to flavour domestic cooking.

salt-soap *noun* (Guyn, Trin). Domestic washing-soap; kitchen soap.

sam.fie ((sam.fai, sam.fy)-man) *noun* (Jmca). A confidence trickster; a swindler. (Probably of West African origin from Twi *asama!fo* 'goblin, apparition', *asuma!fo* 'sorcerer, magician'. In Twi *-fo* is the suffix equivalent to the one in OBEAH-MAN.) □ The term ***samfie-man*** is also used in other Caribbean territories.

say *noun* (Bdos). A disagreement; a quarrel.

scat.ter.a.tion *noun* (CarA). The disorderly scattering of a crowd trying to get to safety. (From Standard English *scatter* + *-ation. Oxford English Dictionary* cites *scatteration* as the 'act of scattering').

schol.ar *noun* (CarA). In PHRASES **Barbados scholar, Guiana scholar, Island scholar, etc**. A young secondary school student named winner of the academic competition based on the British Advanced Level or Caribbean Advanced Proficiency Examinations, and given a scholarship to do a university degree.

scotch[1] *verb* (Bdos). **Jmca *cotch*[1]**. A tiny space at the edge of a seat or bench to give room to one or more persons to sit; any temporary accommodation provided to help somebody out. (A Standard English word meaning 'something wedged in'.)

scotch[2] *noun* (Bdos). **Jmca *cotch*[2] 1.** To squeeze, wedge in or be wedged in; to find or be given temporary accommodation. **2.** To make an opening (by wedging something in between). **3.** [Especially in relation to shoes] To limp painfully in discomfort; to tread cautiously or painfully.

scrav.en *adjective* (Guyn). See LICKERISH.

scrub.bing-board *noun* (CarA). **ECar *jooking-board***. A wooden washboard with two ends shaped like legs, so that it stands firmly in a tub of wet clothes when being used.

Scrubbing-boards

scrunt[1] *intransitive verb* (ECar). To experience very hard times; to have trouble making a living. (Found in dialectal English *scrunt* 'to scratch, scrub'. Compare also Standard English *scrounge*.)

Seawall

scrunt.er *noun* (ECar). A person who is down-and-out; a victim of hard times; somebody forced to beg.

sea-wall *noun* (Guyn). A wall, between 10 and 20 ft thick and 5 or 6 ft high, made of reinforced concrete, to keep the sea off a low-lying coast at high tides, [by extension] that part of it used as a promenade, especially in Georgetown.

sea-win.dow *noun* (Bdos). An area of seashore left free of construction or building of any kind in order to permit free, public views of the sea.

se.cond day *noun phrase* (Bdos). **Guyn *second Sunday***. The first (Bdos) or second (Guyn) Sunday after a wedding-day, when a special private celebration with friends is held for the newlyweds.

see-far man/wom.an *noun phrase* (Guyn). **BrVI, Gren, Trin *seer-man/woman* 1.** A person who is believed to be able to see into somebody's future or troubles and give helpful advice. **2.** See OBEAH-MAN/-WOMAN in the section on folklore.

S

set.tle.ment *noun* (Baha, Gren, TkCa). A small, isolated community provided with basic communication and medical facilities serviced by the government.

Set.tle.ment Day *noun phrase* (Belz). [Historical] A public holiday celebrated on 19 November to commemorate the arrival of the first Caribs in Belize.

sha(c)k. al *adjective* (Trin). Rough or unkempt in appearance and/or behaviour. (From French *chacal* 'jackal' because of this animal's association with meanness and carrion with shift in grammatical function from noun to adjective.)

shack.le *intransitive verb* (Bdos). To fall apart, come undone.

S

Shan.go *noun* (Gren, Guyn, Tbgo, Trin). **1.** [Historical] A Yoruba deity, god of thunder and thunderbolts, who punishes troublemakers and rewards those who worship him; ritual drumming, animal sacrifice, special foods and the colour red are associated with worship at his shrines; this deity was brought to the Caribbean by enslaved Africans. **2.** A folk religion in which Yoruba gods or 'powers' are worshipped but whose ritual is largely related to the deity SHANGO and which are sometimes linked to Chistian saints. (From Yoruba *Ṣọngo* 'the god of thunder and lightning'.)

Shango – god of thunder

side-board *noun* (Guyn). See WAGON.

side-line *noun* (Guyn). **1.** Either one of two DAMS around a plantation or an estate, that indicate its side boundaries; also ***sideline dam***. **2.** The trench dug to build the boundary dam, and used for estate drainage; also ***sideline trench***.

sin.door *noun* (Guyn, Trin). [Indic] **1.** A vermilion-coloured powder used to mark the face. **2.** The inch-long mark made with vermilion powder at the centre front of the part in the hair of a married Hindu woman. (From Hindi *sinduur* 'vermilion'.)

sing.ing an.gel *noun phrase* (Bdos). **Guyn *singing engine***. A kite made with flaps of thin paper called BULLS around its edges to produce a humming sound as they vibrate in the wind.

skip.per *noun* (Bdos, Guyn). [Respectful form of address to a man] Boss. (From Standard English *skipper* 'captain of a ship' transferred over time to general use.)

slack *adjective* (CarA). **1.** [Referring to persons] Sloppy, irresponsible. **2.** Indecent; vulgar; immoral. (From Standard English *slack* 1. 'negligent or lax in regard to one's duties'. This meaning is extended to moral looseness.)

slack.ness *noun* (CarA). **1.** Sloppiness; incompetence; irresponsible behaviour. **2.** Vulgarity; indecent behaviour.

slut-lamp *noun* (Bdos). See BOTTLE-FLAMBEAU.

small man, the *noun phrase* (ECar). Any small-scale entrepreneur or craftsman.

smut(-dis.ease) *noun* (CarA). [Sugar industry] A fungus which makes the stalks of the sugar-cane plant black and the cane unusable.

smut-lamp *noun* (Bdos). See BOTTLE-FLAMBEAU.

snack.ette *noun* (Bdos, Guyn, StKt, Trin). A snack-bar and lunch-counter.

Snackette

so.ca *noun* (ECar). A dance-tune with words included, combining the beat of Black American soul music with Trinidadian calypso; it became popular in the 1978 CARNIVAL. (A blend of *so(ul)* + *ca(lypso)*.)

so.ca.hol.ic *noun* (Bdos). A person who takes part in outdoor dancing to SOCA music. (Blend of soca + *-aholic* becoming popular from about 2002 in the CROP-OVER festival in Barbados).

so.ca.tol.o.gist *noun* (Bdos). A person who is fully acquainted with the nature of SOCA and is able to perform the variety of dance moves associated with the music. (A blend of soca + *-ologist* with 't' inserted for ease of pronunciation. Popular during the 2019 CROP-OVER season.)

soft-can.dle *noun* (Gren, StKt, StLu, Trin, USVI). **Guyn *soft-grease*; Bdos *candle-grease*.** Soft tallow shaped into a small thin rod like a candle and used as a poultice, etc.

some.ti.mish (some.time.ish) *adjective* (CarA). [Usually referring to persons] Moody; unpredictable; unreliable, especially in relation to personal relationships. (From *sometime(s)* + *ish*.)

soul *noun* (CarA). Friendly form of address or reference to an elderly woman. (Used in dialectal English in the plural as a form of address: 'friends, fellows'.)

soul-case *noun* (CarA). The body; the human frame. (Used in dialectal English in Scotland, Ireland and England. In Old English *ban-cofa (bone-case)* 'the body'.)

Span.ish knife *noun phrase* (TkCa). See PANYA MACHETE.

spite-work *noun* (Bdos, Guyn, Tbgo, Trin). A deliberately wicked act carried out effectively.

splif(f) *noun* (CarA). A hand-made ganja (cannabis) cigarette which is usually cone-shaped to facilitate 'drawing' or 'dragging' the smoke. (Probably a blend of Caribbean English *split*, referring to the ready-made wrap + Standard English *whiff* 'tobacco smoke or its smell, inhaled'. The word seems to have originated in Jamaica and has spread mostly through the RASTAFARIAN religion.)

sprig *noun* (Antg). See FEG.

squin.gy (squin.gee) *adjective* (ECar). [Usually referring to fruit or something edible] Shrivelled; wrinkled; of poor quality.

Stelling

stell.ing *noun* (Guyn). A long wooden pier going from the riverside mudflat to deep water in order to permit persons to board a steamer or ferry-boat; any wharf standing on wooden planks. (From Dutch *stelling* 'scaffolding' because of the cross-barred structure of the pier.)

stick *noun* (Tbgo, Trin). See BWA.

stick-fight; stick-fight.ing *noun* (ECar). **Dmca. Gren, StLu, Tbgo, Trin *bwa*; Bdos, Jmca *stick-licking*.** A (sometimes deadly) fight between two trained men, each using a specially treated STICK or BWA.

stick-fight.er *noun* (ECar). **Dmca, Gren, StLu, Tbgo, Trin *bwa-man*; Bdos, Jmca *stick-licker*; Bdos, Trin *stick-man*.** A man trained in the art of STICK-FIGHTING.

stilt-man *noun* (ECar). **Dmca *bwa-bwa*[1] 2. StVn *bwa-bwa-dancer*; Gren, StKt, StLu, Trin, ViIs *moko-jumbie*; Guyn *mother-sally*; Bdos *tilt-man*.** A traditional masquerade dancer mounted on high stilts, always a man in costume, which is usually a woman's dress in some territories.

Stilt-man

stone-feast (tomb.stone-feast) *noun* (CarA). A ritual feast, held during the day-time at the home of a deceased person, usually a year or two after the burial, to coincide with the construction of a tombstone at the person's grave, once the dirt has settled.

strong-eye[1] *adjective* (Gren, Guyn, Jmca). Sharp-eyed. covetous, and quite determined to get what you have seen. (Probably from West African languages.)

strong-eye[2] *noun* (Gren, Guyn, Jmca). Covetousness; ruthlessness.

strong-head.ed *adjective* (Bdos, StVn). Stubborn; headstrong. (Perhaps from a West African base. Compare STRONG-EYE. Standard English *strong* + *head* 'strong-willed'.)

stud.i.a.tion *noun* (CarA). **1.** Studying from books. **2.** Hard, troubled thinking. (From Standard English *study* 'consider carefully, investigate + suffix *-ation* which can be compared with 'botheration, vexation' etc., with slightly derogatory meaning.)

stu.pid.ness; chu.pit.ness *noun* (CarA). **1.** Nonsense; stupid thinking; absurdity. **2.** A stupid act; foolish or irritating behaviour; any of several annoying incidents. **3.** Nonsense!; Dammit!. (In Caribbean English this word has a stronger sense than Standard English *stupidity*.)

style(s) *noun (plural)* (ECar). Manner of behaviour, when either showy or unpleasant; display; affectation.

style (off) *intransitive verb* (CarA). To show off your dressy clothes; to walk in such a way as to attract attention.

suf.fer.a.tion *noun* (CarA). Prolonged, intense suffering. (From Standard English *suffer* + suffix *-ation* similar to STUDIATION.)

suck PHRASES **suck your teeth (at/on somebody)** *verb phrase* (CarA). **Tbgo, Trin *cheups*; Bdos, Dmca, Gren, Guyn, Jmca, Tbgo, Trin *chups(e)*, *chupes*; Bdos, Dmca, Guyn, Trin *stewpse*, *stupse*; Trin *stupe*.** To suck air in, through slightly parted lips and clenched teeth, producing a short or long unpleasant sound with the saliva, indicating disgust, contempt, frustration, irritation, or sometimes, self-pity.

suck-teeth *noun* (CarA). **Bdos, Guyn, Jmca, Tbgo, Trin *cheups*, *chups(e)*; Jmca *kiss-teeth*; Bdos, Dmca, Gren, Guyn, Trin *steups*, *stupse*; Nevs, Trin *stupe*. 1.** The action of SUCKING YOUR TEETH. (The sound is found throughout a number of West African cultures and other sub-Saharan cultures as well, in languages like Mende, Hausa, Yoruba, Efik, Ibibio, Wolof and Kikongo in which the sound also conveys disgust, contempt, impatience, and means 'to make a rude sound with the lips', and 'to make an insulting sound with the saliva'.) **2.** PHRASE **2.1 give a suck-teeth** *verb phrase* (CarA). See SUCK YOUR TEETH (AT/ON SOMEBODY).

su.gar-fac.to.ry *noun* (CarA). A plant where the entire process of making sugar from raw sugar-cane is carried out.

su.gar-mill *noun* (CarA). [Historical] A cone-shaped, stone windmill for grinding sugar-cane in the past; the juice was channelled off to the boiling-house to be processed into molasses and sugar.

Sugar-mill

su.su[1] **(sou.sou)** *noun* (ECar). **Baha** ***asu(e)*****; Guyn** ***box*****; Bdos** ***meeting*****; Jmca** ***pardner*****; Belz** ***syndicate*****.** A friendly cooperative savings scheme in which each of a small group of persons contributes either weekly or monthly an agreed equal sum of money to a trusted 'keeper', who pays the total amount, whether weekly or monthly to each participant in rotation. (From Yoruba *eesu, esusu* 'a fund where several persons pool their money, each paying a fixed sum weekly or monthly, and each participant drawing out the total in rotation'.)

su.su[2] **(soo.soo)** *verb* (Guyn, Jmca, StVn). To gossip, speak ill of, or whisper behind somebody's back. (Probably from Twi *o-susuw-kα̃* 'to utter a suspicion'. Compare Standard English *sussurate* 'to whisper'.)

T

su.su-hand *noun* (ECar). **Guyn** ***box-hand*** **Baha, Gren, Guyn, Jmca, Trin** ***hand***[1] **3. Bdos** ***meeting-turn*** **1.** The weekly or monthly contribution made by each participant to the savings scheme. **2.** The total sum received by a participant when it is their turn to 'draw'.

sweet-mouth[1] *noun* (CarA). **1. CarA** ***sweet-talk***[1]. Flattering, friendly, deceptive talk intended to persuade or pacify people. (From West African languages Twi *n'ano yɛ dɛ papa (he mouth be sweet too-much)* 'He is a flatterer'). **2.** [Especially of children] Excessive liking for tasty food; greediness.

sweet-mouth[2] *verb* (CarA). See SWEET-TALK[2].

sweet-soap *noun* (Bdos, CayI, Guyn, Trin). Toilet soap; bath soap. (So called because of its sweet smell.)

sweet-talk[1] *noun* (CarA). See SWEET-MOUTH[1].

sweet-talk[2] *transitive verb* (CarA). **CarA** ***give somebody a lot of sweet-talk*****; CarA** ***sweet-mouth***[2]. To persuade or pacify somebody by flattery or friendly, deceptive talk.

swib.bly *adjective* (Bdos) Having a wrinkled skin.

syn.di.cate *noun* (Belz). See SUSU.

T

tache (tayche) *noun* (Bdos, Dmca, Gren, Guyn). **Gren** ***platin(e)*** **2.** [Sugar industry] One of a set of copper pans formerly used to boil sugar-cane juice before it was transferred to a boiler to be crystallized into sugar. (Originally from French *tache, tèche* (now obsolete) 'plate of iron'.)

tag-day *noun* (Bdos, Guyn). A special day on which paper tags (usually from a non-profit organization) are sold to raise money; the tags are worn by people who buy them on that day.

ta.la.wa *adjective* (Jmca). [Referring to a person] Tough-minded; forceful; not to be interfered with. (From Scottish English *stalwart* 'resolute, determined'.)

tan.ta.ri.a *noun* (Guyn). A loud, physically aggressive, cantankerous woman, given to shouting abuse at others.

ta.ta *noun* (Antg, Belz, Jmca, USVI). Father; term of affection or respect for an older person. (Probably from a West African source.)

ta.wa *noun* (Guyn, Trin) [Indic]. See BAKING-IRON. (From Hindi *tavaa~tawaa* 'an iron plate for baking bread'.)

tea-meet.ing *noun* (CarA). A social function, usually held at night, especially in former times, and consisting of musical and other types of entertainment, including lofty speech competitions in which artificially made-up words and expressions were used; this entertainment was followed by eating and drinking, and was usually held during some festive season in order to raise money for a church or community organization.

tent *noun* (CarA). A venue where calypsos are performed every night during the period before CARNIVAL, CROP-OVER or similar cultural festival.

the.a.tre *noun* (Guyn, Jmca, Trin). A cinema.

thread-bag *noun* (Jmca). A small clothbag, tied with a string, in which a street vendor keeps money.

three-foot pot *noun phrase* (Bdos, Guyn, Jmca, Tbgo). **Belz** ***baking-pot*****; Baha, CayI** ***Dutch pot***. A large, old-fashioned iron pot without a lid, about 2 ft in diameter at the mouth but extending out in the middle and fitted with three handles and three legs; a cauldron.

ti.bi.si.ri *noun* (Guyn). A strong fibre made from strands of the young leaves of the ite palm which have been boiled, dried and twisted into strings; it is used by the Amerindians for making hammocks and other domestic items.

tin.nen *noun* **1.** (CarA). A piece of sheet of tinplate or galvanized iron; tin-sheet. **2.** (ECar). A tin-cup or tin of any size used for domestic purposes. (Originally from the older English *tinnen* 'made of tin'.)

tin.nin-ba.do/ba.doo *noun* (Bdos). A small, shabby dwelling, often one room, under a corrugated galvanized roof.

To.ba.go love *noun phrase* (Trin). An unrefined show of affection; timid love.

Tibisiri

to-do-ment *noun* (Bdos). See KADOOMENT.

top.side[1] (Top Side) *noun phrase* **1.** (Guyn). The upper parts of a river or of the interior of Guyana; the mining areas or other outposts far away from the coast.

top.side[2] *adverb* (Guyn, Jmca, Tbgo). Towards or in area indicated by TOPSIDE[1].

top.side[3] *preposition* (Jmca). Above; at the upper end or in the upper area of.

top.side[4] *noun* (Guyn). The head, especially the brain.

tou.blé *adjective* (Dmca, StLu). **Gren, Trin** ***tootoolbay***. Stupefied; flustered; confused. (French Creole from French *troublé* with los of 'r'.)

Tou.chau (To.shau, Tou.chou, Tu.chaw(s)) *noun* (Guyn). See AMERINDIAN CAPTAIN.

tout ba.gai (toute ba.gaille) *noun phrase* (Dmca, Gren, StLu, Trin). The whole; everything; everybody. (French Creole from French *toute (la) pagaille* 'the whole bundle'.)

T

tout moune (tout(e) monde, tout moon) *noun phrase* (Dmca, Gren, StLu, Trin). Everybody you can think of. (French Creole from French *tout le monde* 'everybody'.)

tou.toul.bé (too.tool.bay) *adjective* (Gren, Trin). **Dmca, StLu *toublé*.** Stupefied; dazed; madly in love (with the connotation of the state being brought on by witchcraft); bewitched. (French Creole from French *tout troublé* 'all upset with'.)

tra.der *noun* (Guyn). A TRAFFICKER who trades in domestic items; a person who does business in the PARALLEL MARKET.

traf.fick.er *noun* **1.** (Gren, StVn, Tbgo). **Guyn *trader*.** A person who trades in domestic items; a person who operates in the PARALLEL MARKET. **2.** (Tbgo) ***huckster*** A person who peddles goods in Tobago using a car or a small boat. (This item does not carry the sense of criminal activity.)

trans.port[1] *noun* (Guyn). [Property law] Legal title to the ownership of a piece of landed property. (Dutch *transport* 'conveyance'.)

trans.port[2] land/property to (somebody) *verb phrase* (Guyn). To transfer or convey ownership of property to (a buyer).

Trin.ba.go.ni.an *noun* (Tbgo, Trin). A citizen of the twin-island republic of Trinidad & Tobago. (Blend of *Trin(idadian)* + *(To)bagonian*.)

turn-out *noun* **1.** (CarA). Attendance at a funeral, lodge or organized function, especially when done in a procession. **2.** (Bdos) An undertaker's presentation of a body for burial. (Compare Standard English *turn-out* 7. 'get-up, equipment, outfit'.)

turn-tongue *adjective* (StVn). See TWO-MOUTH(ED).

two-by-two[1]/-three/-four *noun* (CarA). A very small dwelling, a one-room house.

two-by-two[2]/-four *adjective* (CarA). Petty; insignificant; extremely small.

two-mouth(-ed); two-tongue(d) *adjective* (CarA). **StVn *turn-tongue*** Deceitful; unreliable; unlikely to keep your word; lying.

u.nu (oo.noo, un.nu) *personal pronoun* (Bdos, Belz, CayI, Jmca). See WUNNA(H).

up.lift.ment *noun* (CarA). Improvement; enlightenment; increase in respect; uplift. (Standard English *uplift* + *-ment*. Compare *improvement*.)

up.per.side *adverb* (StKt, Tbgo). See ABOVE[1].

up.pish *adjective* (CarA). Rude in relation to your social status; offensively self-assertive.

van.i.ty *noun* (Guyn). See DRESSER[1].

vay-ki-vay (vaille-que-vaille, vi-ke-vie) *adverb, adjective* (Dmca, Gren, StLu, Tbgo, Trin). **1.** *adverb* In a disorderly way; haphazardly; carelessly; shabbily. (French Creole from French *vaille que vaille* 'at all costs, come what may', with a shift in meaning to 'any old how'.) **2.** Shoddy; haphazard; unplanned; unorganized.

Ves.try *noun* (Antg, Bdos, Jmca, StKt). [Historical] A group consisting of a small number of elected property owners in each parish, responsible for managing all aspects of local government.

Ves.try-man *noun* (Antg, Bdos, Jmca, StKt). An elected member of a VESTRY.

V

vex[1] *adjective* (CarA). **StLu *anwajé* 1.** Annoyed; very angry; vexed.

vex[2] *transitive verb* (CarA). To annoy; make somebody angry.

vex-mon.ey *noun* (Trin). Money carried by a girl on a date in case she has to return home on her own, having had a quarrel with her boyfriend.

vex-up *adjective* (CarA). Annoyed; furious; irritated.

vil.lage-ram *noun* (CarA). A man of low status, known to be involved in numerous sexual relationships; a confirmed philanderer.

Vin.ce.lo.ni.an *noun* (ECar) Vincentian.

Vin.cen.tian *noun, adjective* (CarA). **ECar *Vincelonian, Vincie*.** A person or thing belonging to the island of St Vincent.

Vir.gin Gor.di.an *adjective phrase, noun phrase* (CarA). A person or thing belonging to the island of Virgin Gorda, one of the British Virgin Islands.

voompse (vumpse) *verb* (Guyn). **1.** [Only used negatively] To pay attention to somebody. **2.** PHRASE **not even voompse [u]pon/at (somebody)** To ignore somebody entirely and rudely.

voop (vup) *verb* (CarA). [Cricket] To strike hard and wildly at a ball; to swipe.

voop.er *noun* (CarA). [Cricket] A reckless and unskilled batsman; a swiper. (From VOOP vb + Standard English suffix *-er*, referring to the person performing the action.)

wag.ga-wag.ga *adjective* (Jmca). Plentiful; abundant. (Possibly Twi *wakawaka* 'active, vibrant', Yoruba *waga-waga* 'bundled together'.)

wa.gon; wag.(g)on.ette *noun* (Bdos, Guyn). **Guyn *side-board*.** An old-fashioned piece of dining-room furniture, composed of a stand with two or three open ledges about 4 ft × 2 ft each (sometimes with a cupboard in the lower half), on which glassware was put.

Wagon

Wai.ka *noun* **1.** (Belz). A Miskito Indian or person of mixed Miskito and African blood. **2.** (Guyn) A small ethnic group of Amerindians in the Kamarang and Roraima areas of Guyana.

Wai-Wai *noun* (Guyn). A pale-skinned Amerindian ethnic group of Carib ancestry, usually distinguished by their bright body-paints; the males wear ceremonial nose-ornaments and their hair in a tube hanging down the nape of the neck and the back; they live in the Acarai Mountains on the southernmost border of Guyana with Brazil and are believed to be the most ancient of the aboriginal people of Guyana. (The name Wai-Wai is from the Wapishiana language and means 'tapioca'. The Brazilians look on them as the 'White Indians', but their name for themselves is 'Wewe' 'wood' and it means people who live in the forest.)

walk-about (walk-a-leg, walk-a-pick.y) *noun* (Angu, Antg, Guyn, Jmca, Nevs). A woman who gossips endlessly and walks around carrying news.

Wa.pi.sha.na (Wa.pi.si.a.na) *noun* (Guyn). **1.** An Arawakan ethnic group of people who inhabit the deep southwestern savannahs of Guyana. **2.** The language spoken by this people.

wa.ri.shi (wa.ra.shi, wa.re.shi, wa.ri.washee) *noun* (Guyn). **Belz *macapal*.** An Amerindian basket-type carrier, worn on the back like a rucksack and held in place by a broad strap suspended over the head. (Probably originating from Carib languages, like Akawaio *wariicha*.)

War.rau *noun* (Guyn). **1.** A coastal, Amerindian ethnic group which mainly inhabits the Orinoco Delta and the northwest region of Guyana; they are well known for the boat-building skills. **2.** The language spoken by this people (which is neither Arawakan nor Cariban).

Warishi

wash-down[2] *noun* (Mrat, StKt). See BUSH-BATH.

wash.ing-soap *noun* (CarA). Laundry soap; cake(s) of soap for washing clothes. Different from SALT-SOAP and SWEET-SOAP.

wash-pan *noun* (Bdos, Guyn, Tbgo). A large, oval-shaped, metal wash-tub with a big handle at each end.

wa.ter.ish *adjective* (Guyn, StVn, Tbgo, Ttin). [Referring to cooked root vegetables] Tasteless and not firm in texture; of poor quality.

wa.ter-wash[1] *transitive verb* (Bdos, Guyn, Tbgo, Trin). [Of clothes] To wash and soap clothes without starching or ironing them; to rough-dry them.

wa.ter-wash[2] *adjective* (Bdos, Guyn, Tbgo, Trin). Washed without being starched or ironed; rough dried, wrinkled.

West In.di.an; West.in.di.an *noun (phrase), adjective (phrase)* (CarA). (A person or thing) of or belonging to

W

any of the English-speaking islands including the mainland territories and the Bahamas archipelago that enclose the Caribbean Sea. (Derived from Columbus's mistake 'West India', hence West Indians, the name of the people and the adjective representing their nationality.)

West.in.di.an.ism; West-In.di.an.ism *noun* (CarA). A sense and recognition of a WEST INDIAN cultural and historical similarity, regardless of the geographical separation of the territories; an identification of the togetherness of WEST INDIAN peoples.

West.in.di.an.ness; West-In.di.an.ness *noun* (CarA). The state, condition, or quality that identifies a person, action or thing as being typically WEST INDIAN.

Win.dies *noun plural* (CarA). [Cricket] The West Indies cricket team.

Wind.ward Is.lands; Wind.wards, The *noun phrase plural* (CarA). **1.** [British group] The southeast group of Caribbean islands: Dominica, Grenada, the Grenadines, St Lucia, St Vincent. (Referred to originally by the Spanish as Islas de Barlovento, as being windward and closer to the Spanish Main). □ Barbados and Tobago were originally included in this group. **2.** [Dutch group] The northeast Caribbean group of islands: Saba, St Eustatius, St Maarten. (Referred to by the Dutch as being on the windward curve of the Caribbean archipelago.)

wire-bend.er *noun* (Tbgo, Trin). A person who is skilled in the art of creating in light wire, the supporting outline of an elaborate CARNIVAL costume.

wire-mesh *noun* (Bdos, Gren, Guyn). **BrVI** ***chicken-wire*****; Bdos** ***mesh-wire*****.** Wire netting, used for light fencing, making fish-traps, etc.

work.er *noun* (Bdos, Guyn). See NEEDLE-WORKER.

work-per.mit *noun* (CarA). A document issued to a non-national, giving legal permission to the person to do specified work in a particular Caribbean State.

work up (wuk/wuck up); wukkin(g) up *verb phrase* (Bdos, Guyn). To dance suggestively doing vigorous gyrations with the waist and hips. □ In Barbados, the most popularly used form is ***wuk up.***

wort(h).less (wot.less, wuf.liss, wus. less, wut.less) *adjective* (CarA). [Especially of persons] Unworthy; morally depraved; dishonest; loose and lazy; [of a young person] troublesome; unruly; mischievous. (Having a strongly condemnatory sense in Caribbean English from its origin in Elizabethan English.)

wort(h).less.ness (wuf.less.ness, wut.liss.ness) *noun* (CarA). Wickedness; moral depravity; vulgarity; irresponsibility.

wuk/wuck up; wukkin(g) up *verb phrase* (Bdos). See WORK UP.

wun.na(h) (wun.no, wun.nuh); un.nu *personal pronoun plural* (Bdos). **CarA** ***allyou*****;** ***you-all*****; Bdos, Belz, CayI, Jmca** ***unu*****; Baha** ***yinna*****. 1.** You (plural); all of you; you (singular) in particular. **2.** *Possessive* Your; belonging to all of you. (From Igbo *'you; all of you* with the 'w' being added for greater ease of pronunciation. The original form ***unu*** seems to have gone with settlers' enslaved people to Jamaica, and onward to Belize and the Cayman Islands. The form ***unno*** is now quite rare in Barbados and is said to be definitely derogatory).

X *noun* (Bdos). **Bdos** ***nigger-ten***. A land-surveyor's mark, cut into the coral as the letter X, and identifying a boundary.

x-ing *noun* (Bdos, Mrat, Nevs, StKt). [Building industry] The crossed wooden supports of the handrail of a staircase or verandah, looking like a succession of large Xs; they are commonly found in low-cost housing.

yab.ba (ya(b).ba-dish/-pot *noun* (Antg, Jmca, Mrat, Nevs, USVI). A round, open, earthenware pot used mostly for cooking; it can vary in size from a small shallow bowl to a large, heavy, deep one. (Probably a dialectal pronunciation of Twi *ayawa* 'earthen vessel, dish'.)

yard-fowl *noun* (Bdos). A political lackey; a person who makes himself availbale to do menial tasks for his party, in return for political favours off which he makes his livelihood. (From *yard* 1. + fowl 'chicken, hen'; these birds live in the enclosed yard and are fed kitchen and table scraps, hence the comparison).

yard-fowl.ism *noun* (Bdos). The political custom of giving or receiving favours in return for sycophantic behaviour in politics. (From *yard-fowl* + Standard English-*ism* 'system' as is found in *socialism*.)

yaws *plural noun* (CarA). **1.** An unsightly skin disease. **2.** A fatal disease, causing sores about the head, that attacks domestic hens.

yin.na *personal pronoun* (Baha). See WUNNA(H). (Most likely from Yoruba *yin, eyin* **1.** 'you people'; **2.** 'your'. The notable retentions of Yoruba in the Bahamas would account for the survival of this pronominal form (see UNU in Barbados) and note too Kikongo *yenu* 'you' 'your'.)

Z

za.fè (zaf.faire) *noun* (Dmca, Gren, StLu, Trin). Trouble; problem; concern. (French Creole from French *les affaires* 'business'.)

za.gai *noun* (Tbgo). A long-handled CUTLASS with a narrow, sometimes curved blade, used to cut grass and low-lying bush. (Probably from French *zagaie,* Standard English *assegai, assagai* 'a slender iron-tipped spear', originally from Arabic.)

Zou.ave u.ni.form *noun phrase* (Bdos). The original ceremonial uniform of the former West India Regiment, consisting of a turban, purple and white coat, blue velvet trousers, and white gaiters; it was retained in some territories and is currently the uniform of the Military Band of the Barbados Regiment. (From French *Zouave* originally from *Zwawa*, a Berber people under French colonial rule in the 19th century. Queen Victoria commanded an imperial imitation of their bright uniforms and the British West India Regiment was chosen to wear them.)

ZR cul.ture *noun phrase* (Bdos). See MINIBUS CULTURE.

Z(R)-van *noun* (Bdos) A longish, narrow, box-shaped vehicle about 10 ft long, used to transport passengers and having a flexible route. (Z/ZR because of the licence plate identification for registered route-taxis in Barbados.)

SELECTED IDIOMATIC PHRASES

be in goat heaven and kiddie kingdom (Bdos). To be in a state of great joy.

do dixie (Bdos). **1.** To behave in a completely uncontrolled manner (whether quarrelling or dancing). **2.** To do a very impressive and successful job of something; to make sure that things go exactly the way you want them to.

jook out somebody's eye(s) (CarA). To cheat someone in a business deal, take unfair advantage of somebody.

give (somebody) a basket to carry water (CarA). To give someone an extremely difficult or almost impossible task; to make life really difficult for someone; to pass on an excessively difficult responsibility to another person.

go through the eddoes (Bdos). [Referring to a plan, standards, etc.] To be ruined, finished, done for.

hard-ears you can't hear, own-way you will feel (Bdos). [Usually said to children] If you cannot be obedient, you will be beaten in order to make you obey.

lick loose (something) (CarA). To break up, detach something from a surface by a violent blow.

make like (doing something) (CarA). To appear to be, or give the impression of, pretend to be (doing something).

put your eye on (something) (Bdos, Guyn, StVn). To long for something as soon as you see it.

see your way to (do something) (Bdos, Gren, Guyn). To manage to (do something), to have or find the means to, or be able to (do something).

work out your soul-case (CarA). To overwork; to work excessively hard.

SELECTED CARIBBEAN PROVERBS

All skin-teet(h) na laugh (CarA). Not everyone who smiles with you is sincere, or is your friend.

Wah you yeye na see, haat na bu'n (Guyn). There is no need to feel upset about what you haven't seen.

One finger can('t) ketch louse (Jmca). **Wan finger kyaan ketch louse** (Guyn). In order to achieve anything, cooperation is essential, either between two fingers or maybe those of another person.

Night run till day catch him (Bdos). **Moon a run, but day ketch am** (Guyn). A person may continue to do wrong for as much, but not as long as they like, and eventually those misdeeds will catch up with that person and they will have to pay the price.

Grass a-grow, but haas a-starve (Guyn). You need to have some kind of immediate plan so that you can keep things going while you develop your long-term plan, if not your resources can be wasted.

Wen cockroach gi'e dance 'e nah ax fowl (Guyn). **Fowl-cock gi(ve) dance, cockroach na gat business deh** (Bdos). Never go where you know your enemies are going to be or you will surely suffer the consequences.

Han(d) wash han(d) mek han(d) come clean (Guyn). Your hands must work together in order to achieve your task, or you must sometimes work with another person in order to do so.

Wha(t) sweeten goat-mout(h) does bu(r)n (h)e tail (CarA). Found in slightly varying forms in several territories. What might be enjoyable to you might have painful consequences.

Two-smart dead a(t) one-smart door (Bdos, Guyn). You may consider yourself very smart but might be outwitted by another person's common sense or simple intelligence.

The higher de monkey climb the mo(re) (h)e show (h)e tail (CarA). A person who is unsuitable for a particular position will show his weaknesses the more he advances in his job.

Two smart-rat can(') live in one hole (Bdos). There can only be one head of a household. If two smart people are making an arrangement together, one will try to get the upper hand.

APPENDIX 1

A STEEL BAND PERFORMING

Steelpan instruments at Trinidad and Tobago Carnival

APPENDIX 2

NATIONAL SYMBOLS OF CARIBBEAN STATES

Territory	National Bird	National Flower/Tree
Anguilla	Turtle dove	White cedar
The Bahamas	Flamingo	Yellow elder (*national tree*: lignum vitae)
Barbados[1]		Barbados pride
Belize	Keel-billed toucan	Black orchid
Bermuda	Longtail	White cedar
British Virgin Islands	Mountain dove	Bermudiana
Dominica	Siserou parrot	Bwa Kwaib (Carib wood)
Grenada and Carriacou	Grenada dove	Bougainvillea
Guyana[2]	Canje pheasant	Victoria Regia lily
Jamaica	Doctor-bird (streamer-tail)	Lignum vitae flower (*national tree*: mahoe)
Montserrat	Montserrat oriole	Wild heliconia (lobster claw)
St Kitts and Nevis	Brown pelican	Poinciana
St Lucia	St Lucia parrot, 'Jacquot'	The Rose and the Marguerite
St Vincent and the Grenadines	St Vincent parrot	Flower of the Soufriere tree
Trinidad and Tobago	Scarlet ibis, Cocrico	Chaconia
US Virgin Islands	Bananaquit	Ginger Thomas

Note: Barbados and Guyana are the only two territories whose national flags are named.

[1]Barbados national flag: The Broken Trident

[2]Guyana national flag: The Golden Arrowhead

APPENDIX 3

DICTIONARY SKILLS

It must be noted that while a dictionary is traditionally regarded as a book in which people look up the meaning of words that they don't know, it is actually more than that. There are many different types of dictionaries, many of which are general dictionaries that seek to list all the words contained in any given language. *The Dictionary of Caribbean English Usage* is a general dictionary.

As has been explained in the introduction to this work, there are other types of dictionaries besides general dictionaries. This one is a thematic dictionary in which the items are listed under different topics or themes in order to assist students to better identify items and retain them as they are related to a particular topic.

A dictionary is necessary because it sets a standard for the language that it lists, in terms of form or spelling, pronunciation (this dictionary does not provide pronunciation), grammar, meaning, etymology or word history, and idioms. It is a chronicle not only of the language of a particular people but also of their culture and their general way of life. It therefore teaches people about themselves and their language.

In order to assist teachers and students to benefit as fully as possible from this dictionary, a list of activities is suggested in these appendices which will enable both teachers and students to see that a dictionary is more than a list of words and their meanings: it is an active and valuable teaching and learning tool. The following are some of the skills that can be acquired by the creative use of a dictionary in the language arts classroom.

DICTIONARY SKILLS

What are dictionary skills? Dictionary skills are ways of using a dictionary to develop a number of competencies in language. They include spelling, pronunciation, vocabulary building, recognition of synonyms and antonyms, being able to match words, crosswords, puzzles, quizzes, using brief definitions of items to identify various people, objects, shapes, and so on. There are a number of competencies that can be acquired by using a dictionary and students can be helped to acquire these competencies and have fun while they are doing so.

In the introductory material, there is a diagrammatic representation of the features of this edition. This will help teachers to understand what goes to make up each dictionary item and to realize that not every item in the dictionary will have all the fifteen features outlined, but will at least have some of them which are absolutely necessary. First, every entry will have a headword, a part of speech, and a territorial label or labels, as well as a definition, except if it is a 'See' entry. Second, depending on the type of entry, there will also be cross-references preceded by a territorial label or labels, then the definition(s) if the word has one or more meanings, and, if available, the etymology or source of the item. In some cases, there will be a usage note after the etymology right at the end of the entry.

APPENDIX 4

HOW TO APPLY DICTIONARY SKILLS IN THE CLASSROOM

The dictionary skills that have been outlined for you can help to make the teaching of language arts in your classroom much more interesting and enjoyable. The idea here is to use a variety of strategies to assist your students in learning how to use a dictionary creatively.

The skills that you wish to pass on to your students include a variety of activities that involve spelling, word formation, word building, word recognition, and the development and broadening of the students' vocabulary.

The first skill that you will have to pass on to your students is how to look up words in a dictionary, something that you most likely have already done, but there are a few more easier ways that you can use to help them find the task less laborious.

On teaching your students how to look up words in the dictionary, you can work by identifying page numbers where a word or words that you want your students to find will occur.

WORKING WITH THEMES

By working with the themes treated in the dictionary, you can help build your students' vocabulary in Caribbean English. This approach helps the students to build vocabulary in a more structured and systematic way.

For example, you may wish to pick out the following themes or topics:

1. Architecture
2. Festivals
3. Foods
4. Articles of clothing
5. Fauna
6. Music, musical instruments and dance

You may choose whatever theme especially interests you, and ask the students to think about the names of various items under each heading or theme and then you have them look up the meanings of these items in the dictionary that they use.

An interesting point arises here, and it is that instead of using the standard British English dictionary that is usually used in schools, you are using a dictionary of Caribbean English, geared specifically to labelling items that are a part of the Caribbean environment and culture.

EXERCISES

You can create a variety of exercises to show how to use the dictionary.

Riddles

If you think you know the answers to these riddles, look up the word that you think answers the question in the dictionary:

- What is the name of the fruit that has as part of its name an item that can be used as a dessert?
- This fishing boat has a unique name in Barbados.
- What is the name of the Hindu festival that celebrates light?
- What is the term used to describe men who went to seek gold in the interior of Guyana?

Matching Exercise

You will find a word on the left-hand side of your page and a group of words on the other side. Circle the word in the group on the right which would fit into the group described by the word on the left.

Insects	calalu, shrimps, god-horse, chicken, dove
Game	soda, bread, cheese, milk, pick-ups
Fruits	lemonade, dessert, custard, mammee-apple, cake
Buildings	train, shed-roof, bird, elephant, hammer
Folklore	wheel, rolling-calf, bulb, chair, snail

Foreign Language Loanwords

Find five foreign language loanwords which occur in the *Dictionary of Caribbean English Usage: School Edition*. Look up their meanings and see whether you can make up five sentences in which each one of these words occurs.

Finding Synonyms to Caribbean English Words in Standard English

The following five words are all Caribbean English words. See if you can find Standard English words that are similar in meaning.

1. bazo(u)di
2. obsocky
3. limber
4. paipsey
5. gypsy

Finding Antonyms to Caribbean English Words in Standard English

The following five words are all Caribbean English words. See if you can find Standard English words that are opposite in meaning.

1. hard-ears
2. hungry-belly
3. sometimish
4. bad-talk
5. mauger

Identifying People or Things by Filling in the Missing Letters

Read the meanings of the following words which have letters missing. See if you know the word(s) and then look them up in the dictionary to make sure that you have spelled them correctly. Look at the following example.
The name of a well-known Caribbean flower: b_li_ier

The name of the national bird of Dominica: s_s_e_ou (p_r_ot)

Very inquisitive: m_l__i_us

A well-known insect: _on_f_y

Odd or clumsy-looking: o_s_c_ky

A popular carnival character: m_ko_j_mb__

Name: ______________________________

Animals

Find the following words in the puzzle.
Words are hidden → ↓ and ↘ .

CENTIPEDE
COW
CRAB
DONKEY
DOVE
EAGLE
EEL

ELEPHANT
GRASSHOPPER
HORSE
LION
LIZARD
MILLIPEDE
MONKEY

SHARK
SNAIL
SPARROW
TIGER
WORM

Created by J. Allsopp using Word Search Generator on
Super Teacher Worksheets (www.superteacherworksheets.com)

These are just a sample of exercises that teachers can create to make the use of this dictionary an exciting adventure with Caribbean words. It is hoped that teachers will also be able to create their own activities and games that can be used very effectively in the language arts classroom, as well as in social studies and science.

Many cultural traditions and activities can also be explored using this dictionary so that both students and teachers will become aware of Caribbean culture and the Caribbean environment in general.

BIBLIOGRAPHICAL REFERENCES

Allsopp, Richard. *Dictionary of Caribbean English Usage*. Oxford: Oxford University Press, 1996. Reprint, Kingston: University of the West Indies Press 2005.

Cassidy, Frederic G., and Robert B. LePage. *Dictionary of Jamaican English*. Cambridge: Cambridge University Press, 1967, 1980. Reprint, Kingston: University of the West Indies Press 2005.

Collymore, Frank A. *Notes for a Glossary of Barbadian Dialect*. First published 1955. Bridgetown: Barbados National Trust, 1970 [4th ed.], 1976 [5th ed.].

Simpson, John, and Edmund Weiner, eds. *Oxford English Dictionary*. 2nd edition. Oxford: Oxford University Press, 1989.

Santeria Diccionario general de americanismos.

A TRIBUTE TO WENDY GRIFFITH-WATSON

JEANNETTE ALLSOPP

I first met Wendy Griffith-Watson (1947–2020) over thirty-five years ago through my husband, Richard Allsopp, when she was a graduate student and part-time lecturer at The University of the West Indies, Cave Hill campus, Barbados. From the time we met, we realized that we were kindred spirits. Both linguists, passionate about language and language education, highly appreciative of English and Caribbean literature, and good-humoured. She was many things, starting out as a nurse in England and ending up as an educator, having become an English teacher, senior teacher, then deputy principal and principal of The St Michael School, and finally chief education officer of Barbados.

We grew closer when I went on to teach English and Spanish at The St Michael School from September 1985 to March 1987, and we were of course both in the Department of English, which she headed. I was impressed by her grasp of English and Caribbean literature, as before going fully into linguistics, I taught Spanish and Latin-American literature at the University of Guyana, some of it in translation. We were also extremely interested in the English language, as taught in Barbadian and Caribbean schools, and we were both members of the Barbados Association of Teachers of English, BATE, as it was more familiarly called, and participated in panel discussions organized by the association.

At the time that I met Wendy, Richard and I were fully taken up with trying to complete the *Dictionary of Caribbean English Usage*, which he had begun in Guyana by collecting Guyanese words, phrases and expressions, and continued in 1963, making it a fully Caribbean English dictionary, when he was appointed as vice-dean of the College of Arts and Sciences (later became The University of the West Indies, Cave Hill campus).

Later in the 1980s, as I got deeper into the work of the French-Spanish Supplement to the *Dictionary of Caribbean English Usage* that Richard invited me to do, I was also fully involved in item-writing to help him with the compilation of the dictionary. Our then university dean, Helen Pyne-Timothy, suggested that he be assigned a full part-time team of research assistants, including item-writers. As head of that team, I immediately invited Wendy to join us. Her experience in both English language and literature made her an ideal member of the team and I enjoyed introducing her to the duties of an item-writer, which she quickly learned and her work proved most valuable. I was at the time tutor in modern languages and history at the Erdiston Teachers College, and she had been transferred to the Ministry of Education and Culture as deputy chief education officer first, then as chief education officer. Together, Wendy and I organized teacher workshops, and she also invited me to head a team to produce an alternative curriculum to the Caribbean Examinations Council curriculum in modern languages for the Ministry of Education and Culture, as it was then.

It is not surprising that when she retired as chief education officer in 2011, having done a really outstanding job in that post, and I told her of my plan to produce a school edition of the *Dictionary of Caribbean English Usage*, as my late husband had made me promise to do, she was excited at the chance to work with me as the co-editor. Our long collaboration continued and we started work in 2013 after I retired from The University of the West Indies at Cave Hill. We completed our work in late 2019, and went over it carefully together, then I proceeded to obtain pictures to illustrate the dictionary, and early in the new year I began to seek a publisher. We were happy to have completed the work, so when she left on one of her periodic visits to her son in the United States, I could hardly have thought that she would not be there to see the dictionary published.

Indeed, before Wendy passed away, I had already secured a publisher, but when I told her and tried to get her CV, I sadly realized that my dear friend had really taken a turn for the worse and I tried to come to terms with the fact, but could hardly get my head around it. I fearfully inquired of her condition, but nothing I heard was positive. She died on the night of Friday, May 22, 2020.

We had a wonderfully profitable and meaningful personal and professional relationship over the many years that I knew her. She is, and will continue to be, sorely missed, especially as she will not be here to see the *Dictionary of Caribbean English Usage: School Edition* published and launched. Nevertheless, may she continue to rest in peace eternal.

Ave atque vale, Wendy.

ADDITIONAL PHOTO CREDITS

Ackee: Ralf Steinberger from Northern Italy and Berlin, CC BY 2.0 <https://creativecommons.org/licenses/by/2.0>, via Wikimedia Commons

Ajoupa: Photo by Infrogmation of New Orleans or one of his parents, CC BY-SA 3.0 <https://creativecommons.org/licenses/by-sa/3.0>, via Wikimedia Commons

Alligator: Unknown author, CC BY-SA 3.0 <http://creativecommons.org/licenses/by-sa/3.0/>, via Wikimedia Commons

Balata: Nicholas Laughlin, https://www.flickr.com/photos/nicholaslaughlin/409126021/in/album-72057594077186225/

Bananaquit: Charles J. Sharp, CC BY-SA 4.0 <https://creativecommons.org/licenses/by-sa/4.0>, via Wikimedia Commons

Banga mary: Clara Costa D'Elia, CC BY 4.0 <https://creativecommons.org/licenses/by/4.0>, via Wikimedia Commons

Barracuda: Laban712, https://commons.wikimedia.org/wiki/File:Barracuda_laban.jpg

Bat: Damion Whyte, https://twitter.com/Roosters_World/status/1444374808234504195/photo/1

Black-belly sheep: Bradley Bishop, CC BY-SA 4.0 <https://creativecommons.org/licenses/by-sa/4.0>, via Wikimedia Commons

Blue land crab: Damion Whyte, https://twitter.com/Roosters_World/status/1412585298668789762/photo/1

Boa constrictor: Heinrich Rudolf Schinz (1777–1861), lithographer Karl Brodtmann, Public domain, via Wikimedia Commons

Bottlenose dolphin: safaritravelplus, CC0, via Wikimedia Commons

Breadfruit: Ashay vb, CC BY-SA 4.0 <https://creativecommons.org/licenses/by-sa/4.0>, via Wikimedia Commons

Butterfly: Charles J. Sharp, CC BY-SA 4.0 <https://creativecommons.org/licenses/by-sa/4.0>, via Wikimedia Commons

Camoodi: Cristóbal Alvarado Minic, https://www.flickr.com/photos/ctam/2659904418

Canje pheasant: barloventomagico, https://www.flickr.com/photos/barloventomagico/2801075713

Cannonball tree: Mokkie, CC BY-SA 3.0 <https://creativecommons.org/licenses/by-sa/3.0>, via Wikimedia Commons

Cattle-egret: Corey Seeman, https://www.flickr.com/photos/cseeman/26233670387

Chattel house: Shardalow, CC BY 2.0 <https://creativecommons.org/licenses/by/2.0>, via Wikimedia Commons

Cocoa house: Larry Syverson, https://www.flickr.com/photos/124651729@N04/50969610907

Cocoa: gailhampshire from Cradley, Malvern, U.K, CC BY 2.0 <https://creativecommons.org/licenses/by/2.0>, via Wikimedia Commons

Cocrico: Fernando Flores, CC BY-SA 2.0 <https://creativecommons.org/licenses/by-sa/2.0>, via Wikimedia Commons

Conch: Damion Whyte, https://twitter.com/Roosters_World/status/1438974964657491969/photo/2

Cow-fish: Pauline Walsh Jacobson, https://www.flickr.com/photos/coralreefdreams/28212384369/

Doctor-bird: Charles J. Sharp, CC BY-SA 4.0 <https://creativecommons.org/licenses/by-sa/4.0>, via Wikimedia Commons

Dolphin-fish: Klaus Rassinger (Museum Wiesbaden), CC BY-SA 4.0 <https://creativecommons.org/licenses/by-sa/4.0>, via Wikimedia Commons

Flying fish: Gervais et Boulart, Public domain, via Wikimedia Commons

Frigate-bird: David Stanley from Nanaimo, Canada, CC BY 2.0 <https://creativecommons.org/licenses/by/2.0>, via Wikimedia Commons

Gibnut: Dick Culbert from Gibsons, B.C., Canada, CC BY 2.0 <https://creativecommons.org/licenses/by/2.0>, via Wikimedia Commons

Goat-fish: Ian Skipworth

Grass knife: Sickle_hanging_from_a_rusty_nail_at_Ardeshir's_farm.jpg: Christopher Walker from Bielsko-Biala, Polandderivative work: Amada44 talk to me, CC BY 2.0 <https://creativecommons.org/licenses/by/2.0>, via Wikimedia Commons

Grasshopper: Damion Whyte, https://twitter.com/Roosters_World/status/1401898282369142792/photo/1

Great House: Urban Walnut, CC BY-SA 3.0 <https://creativecommons.org/licenses/by-sa/3.0>, via Wikimedia Commons

Green heron: USFWSmidwest, Public domain, via Wikimedia Commons

Green monkey: Postdlf, CC BY-SA 3.0 <http://creativecommons.org/licenses/by-sa/3.0/>, via Wikimedia Commons

Grenada dove: https://grenadanationalarchives.wordpress.com/1995/01/10/grenada-heritage-the-grenada-dove/

Grey snapper: Brian Gratwicke, https://www.flickr.com/photos/briangratwicke/4785268312

Ground lizard: Will George, https://www.flickr.com/photos/runnerwill/4675231531/

Guinep: Filo gèn', CC BY-SA 4.0 <https://creativecommons.org/licenses/by-sa/4.0>, via Wikimedia Commons

Harpy eagle: Mark Morgan, https://www.flickr.com/photos/mmorgan8186/34948661073/

Hawksbill turtle: NOAA, Public domain, via Wikimedia Commons

Hog-fish: Rein Ketelaars, https://www.flickr.com/photos/reinketelaars/6343231005/

Holi: Nicholas Laughlin, https://www.flickr.com/photos/nicholaslaughlin/3360325934/in/album-72157615346069278/

Hosay: Nicholas Laughlin, https://www.flickr.com/photos/nicholaslaughlin/5271820234

Hummingbird: Mark Yokoyama, https://www.flickr.com/photos/theactionitems/10174432466/

Iguana: Nicholas Laughlin, https://www.flickr.com/photos/nicholaslaughlin/3466854748/in/album-72157617010308391/

Jack Spaniard: Mark Morgan, https://www.flickr.com/photos/mmorgan8186/4099835929

Jerk pit: Daimon Eklund, https://www.flickr.com/photos/slack13/3526632637/

Jew-fish: Gary Rinaldi, https://www.flickr.com/photos/54556732@N00/179364262/

John Canoe dancers: Photo by WikiPedant at Wikimedia Commons, CC BY-SA 4.0 <https://creativecommons.org/licenses/by-sa/4.0>, via Wikimedia Commons

Kitchen-bitch: Institute of Jamaica, https://www.facebook.com/instituteofjamaica.ioj/photos/pcb.10159420183458713/10159420183388713/

Kumina: Unknown, https://www.flickr.com/photos/32357038@N08/3135887249

Lacatan banana: Obsidian Soul, CC0, via Wikimedia Commons

Leatherback turtle: US Fish and Wildlife Service Southeast Region, https://www.flickr.com/photos/usfwssoutheast/5839996429/

Additional Photo Credits

Locust: Mark Yokoyama, https://www.flickr.com/photos/theactionitems/26198032065/

Love vine: Damion Whyte, https://twitter.com/roosters_world/status/1331781713949827072

Macaw: Kevin Charpentier, CC BY-SA 4.0 <https://creativecommons.org/licenses/by-sa/4.0>, via Wikimedia Commons

Madras: https://repeatingislands.com/2020/03/10/caribbean-museum-center-for-the-arts-to-exhibit-art-made-from-madras/

Main Guard: David Stanley, https://www.flickr.com/photos/davidstanleytravel/46875941734

Malacca apple: PaulaTorrecillas, https://pixabay.com/de/photos/obst-costa-rica-markt-exotische-4748768/

Mangrove: Gauthier Geoffroy, CC BY-SA 4.0 <https://creativecommons.org/licenses/by-sa/4.0>, via Wikimedia Commons

Manicou: Mark Morgan, https://www.flickr.com/photos/mmorgan8186/17919487490/

Margate: Williams, J. T.; Carpenter, K. E.; Van Tassell, J. L.; Hoetjes, P.; Toller, W.; Etnoyer, P.; Smith, M., CC BY 2.5 <https://creativecommons.org/licenses/by/2.5>, via Wikimedia Commons

Morocoy: Flints, CC BY-SA 3.0 <https://creativecommons.org/licenses/by-sa/3.0>, via Wikimedia Commons

Mouchwe: https://dominicanewsonline.com/news/homepage/news/culture/cultural-division-releases-video-on-creole-head-tying/

Mountain-chicken: TimVickers, Public domain, via Wikimedia Commons, https://commons.wikimedia.org/wiki/File:Leptodactylus_fallax_(1).jpg

Nurse shark: Matt Kieffer, https://www.flickr.com/photos/mattkieffer/16234958007/

Ocelot: Ana_Cotta, CC BY 2.0 <https://creativecommons.org/licenses/by/2.0>, via Wikimedia Commons

Parallel market: JR Harris, https://unsplash.com/photos/afVzV0gvnpY

Parrot: Damion Whyte, https://twitter.com/Roosters_World/status/1382312093794365440/photo/1

Phagwah: Nicholas Laughlin, https://www.flickr.com/photos/nicholaslaughlin/3361111384/in/album-72157615346069278/

Piranha: gorartser, https://pixabay.com/de/photos/amazonas-der-amerikaner-tier-wasser-2691048/

Portuguese man-of-war: Image courtesy of Islands in the Sea 2002, NOAA/OER., Public domain, via Wikimedia Commons

Rambutan: Nicholas Laughlin, https://www.flickr.com/photos/nicholaslaughlin/3463708190/in/album-72157617010308391/

Rastafarian: Mattstone911, CC BY-SA 3.0 <https://creativecommons.org/licenses/by-sa/3.0>, via Wikimedia Commons

Red cedar: Photo by David J. Stang, CC BY-SA 4.0 <https://creativecommons.org/licenses/by-sa/4.0>, via Wikimedia Commons

Red House: Random 00021 at English Wikipedia, CC BY-SA 3.0 <http://creativecommons.org/licenses/by-sa/3.0/>, via Wikimedia Commons

Rose apple: barloventomagico, https://www.flickr.com/photos/barloventomagico/2452373151

Royal palm: James St. John, CC BY 2.0 <https://creativecommons.org/licenses/by/2.0>, via Wikimedia Commons

St Lucia parrot: Joseph Smit, Public domain, via Wikimedia Commons

Saman: Mokkie, CC BY-SA 4.0 <https://creativecommons.org/licenses/by-sa/4.0>, via Wikimedia Commons

Sansevieria: JOAN, CC BY-SA 4.0 <https://creativecommons.org/licenses/by-sa/4.0>, via Wikimedia Commons

Sari: Sajedulislam25, CC BY-SA 4.0 <https://creativecommons.org/licenses/by-sa/4.0>, via Wikimedia Commons

Scotch bonnet pepper: Zinnmann, CC BY-SA 3.0 <https://creativecommons.org/licenses/by-sa/3.0>, via Wikimedia Commons

Sea wall: David Stanley, https://www.flickr.com/photos/davidstanleytravel/13930073174

Snackette: Ken Bosma, CC BY 2.0 <https://creativecommons.org/licenses/by/2.0>, via Wikimedia Commons

Steelband performing at Carnival: https://commons.wikimedia.org/wiki/File:Steelpan_Instruments_at_Trinidad_and_Tobago_Carnival.jpg

Stelling: KennardP, https://www.flickr.com/photos/kpillay/4855612215

Stilt-man: Gruepig, CC BY-SA 4.0 <https://creativecommons.org/licenses/by-sa/4.0>, via Wikimedia Commons

Sugar mill: Pat Hawks, CC BY 3.0-2.5-2.0 1.0 <https://creativecommons.org/licenses/by/3.0-2.5-2.0-1.0>, via Wikimedia Commons

Sugar-apple: Damion Whyte, https://twitter.com/Roosters_World/status/1458454941207605254/photo/1

Tapia house: StayTnT, https://m.facebook.com/StayTnT/

Tibisiri: https://dpi.gov.gy/quality-crafts-done-the-santa-mission-way/#jp-carousel-50408

Warishi: https://www.thingsguyana.com/chenapou-village-things-you-did-not-know/

Warri: Jimmy Henks, CC BY-SA 4.0 <https://creativecommons.org/licenses/by-sa/4.0>, via Wikimedia Commons

Zouave uniform: https://commons.wikimedia.org/w/index.php?curid=26967836

ZR van: https://m.facebook.com/pg/Minibuses-in-Barbados-1475188976112875/photos/?tab=album&album_id=2301940743437690